MIRACLE MEN

How Rassie's Springboks won the World Cup

LLOYD BURNARD

Jonathan Ball Publishers
Johannesburg • Cape Town • London

All rights reserved.

No part of this publication may be reproduced or transmitted,
in any form or by any means, without prior permission
from the publisher or copyright holder.

© Text Lloyd Burnard 2020
© Photographs as credited individually
© Published edition 2020 Jonathan Ball Publishers

Published in South Africa in 2020 by
JONATHAN BALL PUBLISHERS
A division of Media24 (Pty) Ltd
PO Box 33977, Jeppestown, 2043

This edition published in 2021 by Jonathan Ball Publishers
An imprint of Icon Books Ltd,
Omnibus Business Centre,
39-41 North Road, London N7 9DP
Email: info@iconbooks.com
For details of all international distributors, visit iconbooks.com/trade

ISBN 978-1-77619-115-4
ebook ISBN 978-1-77619-043-0

*Every effort has been made to trace the copyright holders and to obtain their
permission for the use of copyright material. The publishers apologise for
any errors or omissions and would be grateful to be notified of any
corrections that should be incorporated in future editions of this book.*

Cover photo: Siya Kolisi (centre) lifts the trophy as South Africa win
the 2019 Rugby World Cup final match at Yokohama Stadium.
(Photo by David Davies/PA Images via Getty Images)

Printed and bound in Great Britain
by Clays Ltd, Elcograf S.p.A.

Contents

Preface vii
1 Celebrating unity 1
2 Darkest before the dawn 15
3 The Afrikaner from Despatch 38
4 Rolling up the sleeves 55
5 Kolisi 69
6 Tears of joy in Wellington 82
7 Never stop learning 96
8 Reconnaissance 110
9 The final cut 121
10 Body and mind 137
11 A losing start 148
12 The Bomb Squad 162
13 Japan's pride 175
14 The soul of Wales 188
15 World champions 203
16 Legacy 223

Appendix 233
Acknowledgements 241

Preface

On the night before the 2019 Rugby World Cup final, Rassie Erasmus sat in his Yokohama hotel room surrounded by family and friends, enjoying a few drinks and listening to South African music.

He did not stay up until all hours ironing out last-minute details, nor did he obsess over how the Springboks were going to overcome their underdog tag to knock over Eddie Jones' England in front of 70 000 people and win a third Webb Ellis Cup.

Instead, he enjoyed a 'kuier' (visit) with the people he loves most.

His wife, Nikki, was there. His right-hand man and friend of nearly two decades, Jacques Nienaber, and his wife, Elmarie, were there. His brother-in-law, his cousin and friends Jaco Peyper and Marius Jonker were all there too.

'There were 12 South Africans in my room, and we went to bed at around 3 am just having drinks and chatting,' Erasmus remembers.

The next day's game was one of the most important, maybe the most important, in the history of South African rugby, but there was nothing more that could be done. Erasmus, Nienaber and the rest of the coaching staff had, over the previous 18 months, guided the team this far. The rest would be up to the players.

A calm washed over Erasmus despite the obvious nerves.

'We wondered what the weather would be like, so we Googled

that. We chatted rugby, but it was just a lot of banter with some good people,' Erasmus says. 'You know what you want to say to the boys in the morning and you can't really change anything. You know the World Cup is finishing tomorrow and you're in the final.'

The Springboks of 2019 – some at the beginning of their journeys and others at the end – were about to etch their names into their country's sporting history, and by the time the game ended, they would be immortal.

On 2 November 2019, Erasmus's Springboks brought an entire nation together. Sixty million people were captivated for 80 minutes, and when it was all over, one of rugby's most magical stories had been completed.

If it had been a movie, the genre would have been 'fantasy' and Johan Erasmus, an Afrikaner from Despatch, the director.

Every single member of the Springbok squad – the 33 players, the coaching staff, the medical team, the logistics team – played their part, and this was their date with destiny. Every player had his own unique script that led to this point, but there was a unity in achieving something that, for a moment in time, made South Africa and its rainbow nation the centre of the universe.

Erasmus had arrived when South African rugby was at its lowest point. When he was done, these Boks had the world at their feet. For Erasmus, it was a journey that had started more than 20 years earlier.

In 1998, just three years into his professional playing career at the Free State Cheetahs, he purchased a computer from the Israeli government with the help of the Council for Scientific and Industrial Research (CSIR). Whereas most in his position were focused solely on their playing careers, Erasmus had begun to manifest a fascination with all things analytical. He was one hell of a player, but his true vocation lay in coaching.

'It could do these stats where you could actually log a tackle, or whatever happened, with video and you could print it out. You had to sit and code it yourself,' Erasmus says.

He had only just become a Springbok the year before, but Erasmus was already ahead of his time. He would use the computer to help coach Peet Kleynhans at the Cheetahs and then the highly rated New Zealander Laurie Mains during his time at the Cats.

Erasmus was developing into a student of the game, and it was obvious to all who knew him that he would move into the world of coaching.

When that happened in 2004, when Erasmus was given the Free State Cheetahs side for that year's Vodacom Cup while sidelined with injury, he could not have known the journey that awaited him.

Erasmus had freakishly injured his foot in training. After a trip to Germany to consult a specialist, it was revealed that he had sustained a fracture that could not be seen on the X-rays. The injury would ultimately cut short his career, but it also opened the door to coaching earlier than anticipated.

'The Cheetahs were paying me a salary, so they suggested I coach the Vodacom Cup side and I said "sure". I remember we lost in the semi-finals against the Blue Bulls and Heyneke Meyer, who had been fired from the Super Rugby side.'

Erasmus was coaching with a player's contract.

He returned to the playing field for the 2004 Currie Cup in what would be his final season, and in 2005 eyebrows were raised when he was given the full-time head coach position at the Cheetahs, replacing Kleynhans. He won the Currie Cup that year – Free State's first in 29 years – and shared the title with the Blue Bulls the following year.

In those formative coaching years, Erasmus began to hold up colour-coded signs during matches, offering instructions to his players on the field. The story of how that trademark routine was born is another indication of exactly how much those around Erasmus valued his technical acumen.

'We had a warm-up game and at training we used to use colours to run our plays. Different colours would be different plays,' Erasmus says.

'I hadn't appointed a captain. I'd been the captain the previous year of Os [du Randt], Naka [Drotske], Ollie [le Roux] ... it was a great time. I didn't appoint a captain because we didn't operate like that when I was the captain. The captain just tossed, otherwise we made all the decisions together.

'When the referee wanted to toss in that warm-up match, I told Os to be the captain and he said he didn't want to be. Then I went to Ollie and told him to be the captain and he didn't want to be either. Neither did Naka. Eventually I said, "Fuck, boys, somebody has to do the toss!" Ollie said, "You go!" so I went as the coach.

'When I came back, I said, "Right, who is going to call the calls?" The flyhalf was Willem de Waal and when I asked him, he said the guys hadn't studied very well, but they knew the plays. Ollie suggested that I sit next to the field with Helgard Muller, my assistant coach, and we use the colour cones that we warm up with to tell the players what plays to run.

'As we got to the first scrum, I forgot, and held up a yellow sign, which was to go to a maul. The whole team looked at me and shook their heads wondering how to do a maul from a scrum.

'When we got it right, we started scoring and the team felt it had worked. They made signs out of Perspex of different colours. I've still got them in my bar. Later, the players even made a box with lights and switches. It was their idea and whatever we decided during the week, we would work out and call it our menu or play sheet.'

Back then, Erasmus had even thought about using the big screen or stadium scoreboard as a vehicle to convey the colour-coded instructions to the players. 'The problem was that Free State didn't have one,' he laughs.

The story of how Erasmus transformed the Boks from a side that was walloped 57–0 against the All Blacks in 2017 to the best in the world is one worth telling, but it started a long time ago when a spritely, self-motivated Springbok loose forward from Despatch began looking at rugby differently.

It is also not a story about rugby alone. It is a story of how a team, and a leader in Siyamthanda Kolisi, grew from a collection of individuals into a band of brothers that provided hope to a nation.

We will, almost certainly, never see anything like it again.

Chapter 1

Celebrating unity

The Springboks, once banished to the dark, lonely halls of international isolation, had won their third Rugby World Cup. If it wasn't clear before the final at International Stadium Yokohama, on 2 November 2019, that this was the win South Africans so desperately needed, it was revealed in abundance in the days and weeks that followed as millions came together to celebrate a rugby team that had conquered the world.

Given how far the Boks had fallen towards the end of the Allister Coetzee era in 2017, their commanding 32–12 win over Eddie Jones' England was a sporting miracle.

The win meant the Boks had drawn level with New Zealand as the most decorated side in the tournament's 32-year history, but this had become about so much more than rugby. The Boks had won the contest long before referee Jérôme Garcès blew the final whistle. They had been dominant in all facets, and while their defences had been tested, they had rocked England for most of the contest. When flyhalf Handre Pollard kicked the ball deep into the Yokohama night sky to bring the final to an end, the feeling of release and relief was tangible.

Some, like Cheslin Kolbe, could only collapse in disbelief. Others danced around the Yokohama turf, unable to contain the thrill of a lifetime. Pollard embraced his childhood hero, Frans Steyn. Up in the stands, President Cyril Ramaphosa hugged England's Prince Harry. Captain Siya Kolisi was gracious in victory, shaking the hands of the distraught Englishmen first. It was a killer blow for the favourites, who a week earlier had provided one of the great World Cup performances with their 19–7 semi-final win against the defending champion All Blacks.

None of that mattered to South Africans. Back at home, the earth shook.

At Gqalane Tavern in Zwide, where a 16-year-old Kolisi had watched the Springboks win the World Cup in 2007, there was delirium.

'There was so much emotion in that tiny, cramped little tavern,' recalls *Sunday Times* journalist Jeff Wicks, who was there that day. 'It was something I will never forget. Guys were on tables, there was beer spraying everywhere, people were hitting the ceiling with their fists. They didn't stop singing.'

'You asked me to do it. You asked us to do it. We did it,' Kolisi told journalist Elma Smit, who fell into the skipper's arms on the pitch in Yokohama, sobbing, in a captured moment that was as raw and beautiful as any in the immediate aftermath.

Politically, racially and socially, a divided South Africa was united.

'I could not think of a nation that needs it more than you guys right now,' Prince Harry relayed to the victorious Boks in their change room in the aftermath.

The party was under way, but those words provided a dose of perspective. This win was different to the others, and the scenes that unfolded in South Africa over the course of the next week confirmed exactly that.

It was not the first time the Springboks had won the Rugby World Cup, but it was the first time they had done so with a side that demographically represented their country. For the first time, the Boks had black African heroes in their World Cup-winning side, and one of them was the leader.

'People in the taverns, people in the shebeens, people on the farms, homeless people, people in rural areas ... thank you so much,' Kolisi said at his pitch-side interview.

With his final words, the soft-spoken South African captain summed up exactly what this moment meant to South Africans.

'We can achieve anything if we work together as one.'

It was a message that hit home in a country that, 25 years after the advent of democracy, had not reached its potential. State capture, corruption, poverty, racial division, dysfunctional leadership, gender-based violence, crime, unemployment ... South Africa's troubles painted a picture of a country nowhere near realising Nelson Mandela's dream of a thriving 'rainbow nation'.

In the 1995 final, the Boks had stunned New Zealand and the world with a Joel Stransky drop goal that instantly became one of rugby's most iconic moments. That 15–12, extra-time win at Ellis Park, in South Africa's first World Cup appearance, injected hope into a newborn democratic society. As Mandela and Francois Pienaar stood side by side in lifting the Webb Ellis Cup, they symbolised a nation that was ready to heal.

Then, in 2007, Jake White's Boks waltzed through the competition undefeated, dominant from start to finish. That they avoided meeting the All Blacks and Australia on the way to the title was a talking point that some believe watered down the success, but it could not detract from the achievement of a side that was as clinical as any Bok outfit that came before or after.

Both of those victories helped the Boks carve out a reputation for themselves as a global giant of the game. While the social significance of 1995 was naturally immense, it was fundamentally different to 2019. The win in 1995 told a new nation that the future together was bright, but the win in 2019 came at a time when, for many, the fairy tale had lost its wonder. Japan 2019 showed, both on the field and off, what South Africa could achieve through inclusion, but it also provided a crushing reminder that the country had not come as far as it should have.

On 24 June 1995 – the day of the Johannesburg final against the All Blacks – Chester Williams was the only player of colour in the squad of 21. On 20 October 2007, Bryan Habana and JP Pietersen were the only players of colour to line up against England in Paris. Before 2019, a total of 42 South Africans had been included in World Cup final squads. Thirty-nine of them were white.

In Yokohama on 2 November, the Boks fielded Kolisi, Lukhanyo Am, Makazole Mapimpi, Tendai Mtawarira, Bongi Mbonambi, Damian de Allende and Cheslin Kolbe in their starting line-up – a total of seven players of colour in the starting XV.

For years, transformation in sport and quotas at international level had caused more division than unity in South Africa. In 2019, there was no space for such conversation because every single member of this victorious squad – black or white – proved that he belonged on this stage. It was South Africa's first real sporting example of how things can be, where the country's best play together in a racially representative side where nobody is picked on the basis of anything other than merit.

Never before had a South African sporting success so clearly illustrated what the country was capable of in its unity, and because of that the story of the Rugby World Cup 2019 triumph transcended sport.

When the Boks arrived back in South Africa on 5 November as champions of the world, they could not have known the eruption that awaited them.

At OR Tambo International Airport, all three tiers surrounding the arrivals hall were packed for hours before the Boks touched down. Young and old, black and white, male and female ... this celebration was for everybody. Some had arrived as early as 9 am, meaning the wait for Kolisi and the trophy had lasted for around 11 hours by the time the skipper emerged, to a rapturous reception.

The Gautrain offered free trips to and from the airport for anyone wearing a Springbok jersey – not that fans needed any added incentive.

Kolisi and Erasmus, along with Pollard, were due to arrive in the first batch but their flight was delayed. It didn't dampen the energy one bit. There was singing, dancing, a South African Police Service brass band and media from every corner of the country waiting to catch a glimpse of the men who had done the unthinkable.

Deafening waves of 'Shosholoza' echoed throughout the terminal building and flowed out into the parking areas.

Then, finally, security and police began to scurry. The Boks had arrived and the waiting was over.

Damian de Allende was the first player through the sliding glass doors, pumping up the crowd with two raised fists. Scrumhalf Faf de Klerk was greeted with high-pitched screaming. This would be the case throughout the country on the five-day trophy tour that followed. Images of him in the change room on the night of the final, sporting briefs adorned with the South African flag, had gone viral, and De Klerk's long, blond locks made him easy to spot on the celebration tour that started on that magical evening in Johannesburg.

Frans Steyn high-fived his way through a mob that was pushing security to its limits, while a special cheer was reserved for final heroes Am, Mapimpi and Kolbe.

But the moment Johannesburg was waiting for was when Kolisi and the Webb Ellis Cup came home.

As he looked upward to the two overflowing tiers of support above him, a smile of bewilderment washed over Kolisi's face. When he lifted the trophy over his head and pumped his fists in celebration, the crowd roared on behalf of a nation.

It was only the beginning.

On Thursday 7 November, just two days after arriving home from a near two-month stay in Japan, the Boks embarked on a trophy tour that will be remembered forever by everyone who witnessed it.

Over five days, aboard open-topped buses, the Boks visited Johannesburg, Durban, East London, Port Elizabeth and Cape Town. They made their way through city centres and surrounding communities as the country showed off its finest qualities of national pride and unity.

It was this celebration that revealed the significance of what the Boks had achieved in all its glory. This win was for everyone, and nowhere was this seen more vividly than in the townships of the Eastern Cape as the Boks who had starred on the grandest stage of them all came home: Mapimpi returned to Mdantsane, where thousands screamed his name; Am went home to King William's Town as royalty; and Kolisi brought people to their knees in Zwide.

Images of grown men in tears were commonplace throughout the tour. There was even a brief homecoming for coach Rassie Erasmus, who was born in the quiet town of Despatch, while assistant coach Mzwandile Stick went back to New Brighton.

The Boks shared a chartered plane with their management team and a few select stakeholders and members of the media as they took the Webb Ellis Cup to as many South Africans as possible. It was a responsibility that Kolisi took seriously, repeating again and again that this win belonged to everyone. On numerous occasions flights were delayed by hours, but it was a sacrifice that the skipper and his Boks were willing to make.

Even at the private and exclusive Fireblade Aviation facility, on the edge of OR Tambo, where there were no adoring fans, Kolisi and the Boks could not escape the spotlight as airport staff on the runway waited patiently for them to arrive. After a draining day that had seen the Bok bus travel through Pretoria, Johannesburg and Soweto, Kolisi stopped for photographs with the men and women directly responsible for the departure of their flight.

The hype was relentless, with the only rest coming when the Boks closed their bedroom doors each night. Hundreds of supporters would camp outside the team hotel for the start of the next day's bus tour. After a full day of celebrating with their people, the Boks would find hordes more waiting for them at whatever airport awaited them next that evening. It was the same wherever they landed, at whatever time, and no matter where they stayed. With each new group of supporters came another burst of explosive energy.

Not once did Kolisi turn down a request for a photograph or autograph.

For the Boks, it was the final stretch on the most incredible journey of their lives, and they found a way to get up for each leg despite fatigue becoming a factor. 'I don't know how we're still going ... it's like the adrenaline takes over,' fullback Willie le Roux said to me on the way to pick up his luggage shortly after landing at King Shaka International in Durban.

Tendai 'Beast' Mtawarira was the hometown hero in Durban, and chants of 'Beaaaaast' followed his every movement. A city that is so often criticised for its failure to show up for major events, Durban obliterated that reputation on the day. Thousands gathered outside the City Hall and lined the streets of the CBD with Mtawarira, Kolisi, Am and Mapimpi the centres of attention.

At a function at Moses Mabhida Stadium, where the Boks were put through their obligatory daily schmooze with local officials,

MIRACLE MEN

Mtawarira spoke about his retirement and ending an 11-year, 117-Test career on the ultimate high. Never a man of many words, Mtawarira thanked the people of Durban for accepting him as one their own since he first joined the Sharks back in 2006.

Former Sharks and Springbok coach Ian McIntosh was one of the high-profile names in attendance at that function. Revered in Sharks country, McIntosh's reaction when Mtawarira completed his duties and was escorted back to the Bok bus told its own story of exactly how great this moment was.

'Sorry, I've got to get Beast quickly,' McIntosh yelped at me in mid-conversation, scampering off towards the huddle that had formed around the third-most-capped Bok of all time. 'I've got to get this signed for my grandson,' he added, holding up a Springbok jersey.

Even a former Bok coach was not immune to the ecstasy that was in the air that week.

That afternoon, the Bok plane flew to East London, landing just before 5 pm. East London Airport is modest in size, and at one stage the glass doors separating baggage reclaim from domestic arrivals looked set to buckle under the weight of the hundreds of supporters pressed up against them in anticipation. Eventually the doors slid open and the Boks, led by hometown hero Lukhanyo Am, trophy in hand, made their way out.

The flimsy security tape that had been erected to create a pathway for the Boks was swept aside, and the arrivals hall, like almost everywhere else on the trophy tour, turned into an uncontrollable throng. The reactions were almost spiritual, but Am took them in his stride, wearing a slight smile and showing the same composure and panache he had displayed in setting up Makazole Mapimpi for that historic try during the World Cup final.

The scenes outside the East London City Hall the next day were even more staggering. Thousands had crammed into the main square in what must have been an excruciating wait. Signs celebrating Mapimpi and Am's homecoming were everywhere. The sheer number of people was intimidating, and Springbok media manager Rayaan Adriaanse had to pull an overly enthusiastic Herschel Jantjies away from the crowd as the Bok scrumhalf looked set to hop over the railings and celebrate with the masses.

Kolisi and his men eventually left the bus to make their way towards a stage where the skipper would deliver yet another speech. There was an uneasy moment on the way back when the crowd broke through one of the barriers keeping a safe distance between them and the bus. Security got most of the Boks back on board in time, but a lagging Francois Louw was swallowed up in the pandemonium. He eventually extricated himself, but by then the green-and-gold vehicle was surrounded by a rapidly growing and overexcited swarm of people. It could have turned into a serious security issue, with traffic and metro police unable to move the fans back.

In a moment as electric as any on the trophy tour, a fearless Kolisi then climbed onto the roof of the bus, launched the Webb Ellis Cup over his head, and celebrated as if he'd just won the final all over again. In that moment, the bus could have toppled over, but it wouldn't have mattered. This was South Africa coming together to celebrate, and nothing was more important to the captain. The mob never subsided, but somehow the bus driver was able to guide the vehicle on its way out of the city centre.

For many of the players, this was the first time they had been to communities like Pefferville, Buffalo Flats, Gompo, Scenery Park, Mdantsane and Zwide. The Eastern Cape has long been considered a nursery of black South African rugby talent, yet its parent unions – Border and Eastern Province – have consistently underdelivered on the professional stage. The lack of black players at Springbok level over the years, combined with the fact that private schools in South Africa have historically been the breeding ground for professional players, painted a picture of rugby as not being for everyone. The Eastern Cape leg of the trophy tour suggested otherwise.

The Boks were celebrated by poorer communities, and though their difficult living conditions were obvious, these people rejoiced. This time, the Bok heroes they were celebrating belonged to them, and it was unlike anything they had seen before. 'Rugby here means so much to so many people, and we saw that today,' Am offered at the end of the East London leg.

On the next day, in Port Elizabeth, one dedicated fan kept up with the Bok bus on foot for over ten kilometres from the city centre to Mzwandile Stick's home township of New Brighton before he eventually ran out of steam.

In Zwide, the attention shifted to Kolisi. The bus drove past Dan Qeqe Stadium, the home of the African Bombers Rugby Club, where Kolisi honed his skills as a youngster.

Springbok captains are not meant to start here.

'That's the road where Siya watched the 2007 final in a tavern,' offered one local who had booked a ticket on the sponsors' bus that was following the Boks. Throughout Zwide, the feeling of pride was clearly evident. A community living on the breadline had produced a World Cup-winning Springbok captain, and that would be celebrated.

On dusty streets of poverty and desperation, Kolisi and the Boks had given a voice to a black community in need of inspiration. On that leg of the tour, rugby was not the only story but rather a vehicle for achieving something far greater.

In his press conference after the final, Erasmus was asked to talk about how his side had dealt with the pressure of the occasion. 'We talked about what pressure is,' he said. 'In South Africa pressure is not having a job. Pressure is one of your close relatives being murdered.

'There are a lot of problems in South Africa which are real pressure. Rugby shouldn't be something that creates pressure; rugby should be something that creates hope.'

This group, led by Erasmus and Kolisi, performed a rugby miracle in Japan. When Erasmus took over from Allister Coetzee, the Boks had slipped to number seven in the world, and they suffered some of the most embarrassing losses in their history in 2016 and 2017. At that stage, a World Cup win looked a million miles away.

Yet, on the eve of the 2019 World Cup final, having done the unthinkable, the conversations in the dressing room were about what a win would mean for the people back home. This was the driving force behind their success, and it would become an integral part of what made this journey so special.

As the Bok plane approached Cape Town International for the final leg of the trophy tour, spirits remained high. Francois Louw, nursing a bottle of Klipdrift under his seat, was the squad barman. One by one, starting with Faf de Klerk, several Boks made their way over to Louw, armed only with a cup of ice and an unopened tin of Coke. They returned with smiles on their faces and drinks full. Somehow, these Boks were still going. Mumblings of a lavish party in Stellenbosch that night did the rounds and a few of the players seemed up for it.

Herschel Jantjies was visibly excited. He confessed that this was the longest he had ever been away from home. When asked if he would be joining the Boks at their function that evening, he answered quietly but firmly. 'I'm going home,' he said, longing for a return to his mother, father and brother in the town of Kylemore, outside Stellenbosch.

It had been an incredible year for the young scrumhalf. His two tries against Australia at Ellis Park on 20 July, exactly two months before the start of the World Cup, will go down as one of the most memorable Springbok debuts of all time.

The Cape Town leg of the tour was the last the Boks had to get through before they could go their separate ways. As Kolisi stood in a function room inside the City Hall, where he was due to meet Desmond Tutu, he could hardly keep his eyes open. Visibly and emotionally drained, the Springbok leader had emptied the tank both on the field in Japan and off it during the trophy tour. The end was in sight, but a trip through the CBD and surrounding communities had to be completed first.

Kolisi, his wife, Rachel, and the entire Bok team met Tutu in a moment that cemented this triumph as genuinely historic. The expression on Tutu's face when he looked up at the towering Eben Etzebeth was priceless, and the diminutive cleric started jumping on the spot in a vain and excited effort to reach the lock's eye level.

Kolisi then led the Boks outside to a stage that had been set up on the Grand Parade. Thousands of Capetonians were waiting. The players walked out to the sound of Leon Schuster's 'Hie' Kommie Bokke', which threatened to burst the speakers.

There, on that stage, Kolisi brought tears to the eyes of South African men and women, showing in the process that he had completed his development from an uncertain youngster into a man who could silence a crowd with his mere presence.

Most politicians will advance through their entire careers without ever saying anything as remotely powerful as Kolisi did that day, but for him this was not about winning votes or approval. For Siyamthanda Kolisi, this was one more opportunity to deliver a message that this country still hadn't internalised 25 years into the democratic era.

'Aweh, ma se kind!' he said, finding energy from somewhere as Cape Town exploded in unison. 'It's really been a tough journey. We have been together for 20 weeks. I think this week has been the most amazing one.

'Look at us,' he continued, gesturing towards the Bok squad that had gathered behind him on the stage. 'We are all different races, from different backgrounds.'

Then, Kolisi pointed out the diversity in the crowd.

'And take a look around at you guys,' he said. 'There are different races, different people of different backgrounds, but look how you have made this special for us.

'It's time for us South Africans to stop fighting and stop arguing. Let's put South Africa first. We appreciate you.'

The exhausted Boks and their leader pushed forward for one last meaningful ride on their chariot.

The short trip through the Cape Town city centre took hours. The bus could barely move. From Darling Street to Long Street and then along Strand Street, the city came to a stop. People were hanging over balconies, leaning dangerously out of windows and balancing in trees and on top of traffic lights. It was as if a victorious army was returning from war – and in many ways it was.

In comical fashion, the Bok bus broke down on the N2 highway on the way out of town. It would have been the perfect excuse for the players to hop off and be whisked away to their families, considering how many of them are based in Cape Town, but that was never an option. Before long, they were on their way again and Kolisi and the Boks danced with the people of the Western Cape as the sun began to set.

The party may have ended, eventually, but the legacy of what the Springboks achieved in 2019 will live forever.

It is made even more incredible by the fact that, less than 18 months before the start of the tournament in Japan, the Boks had found ways to reach new lows.

While Siya Kolisi was rightly the face of the celebrations, it was the tactical nous, technical genius and meticulous planning of coach Johan 'Rassie' Erasmus that facilitated one of the greatest turnarounds world rugby has ever seen.

What happened in Japan will be remembered and replayed for generations to come, but the road to World Cup glory was littered with potholes and speed bumps.

It would take an engineer to pave a new way forward.

Chapter 2
Darkest before the dawn
||||||||||||||||||||||||||||||||||||||||||||||

The honour of being the seventh head coach to lead the Boks into battle at a Rugby World Cup was never meant to belong to Rassie Erasmus. It was instead reserved for Allister Coetzee, who was unveiled as the replacement for Heyneke Meyer on 12 April 2016 with the aim of guiding the Boks through the next four-year cycle. That, at least, was the plan.

Erasmus was involved in the conversations surrounding Coetzee's appointment given his position as GM: High Performance at SA Rugby, the commercial arm of the South African Rugby Union (SARU). He, like most, believed that Coetzee was the right man for the job at the time and he relayed as much to chief executive officer (CEO) Jurie Roux.

Coetzee's 22-month tenure would go down as one of the darkest periods in South African rugby history. It was characterised by uncertainty and desperately poor results, and led to a national outcry from an expectant and passionate public. The Coetzee era coincided with SA Rugby coming under severe pressure administratively. President Oregan Hoskins, who had proudly unveiled Coetzee as coach, stepped down from his role just over four months later. He left under a cloud of controversy surrounding his relationship with Roux, who was at the centre of a reported R37-million lawsuit involving an alleged misuse of funds during his time as senior director in the finance department at Stellenbosch University. Roux had served in a management capacity at the university's rugby club for ten years before becoming SA Rugby CEO in 2013.

Hoskins had also received criticism for his handling of the financially troubled Southern Kings franchise, which gave up administrative control to SA Rugby in late 2015 before being officially liquidated in August 2016.

The Boks, meanwhile, lost two key sponsors at the end of 2015, with Absa and BMW both opting not to renew their deals with the national side. It was a massive financial blow; the Absa deal alone was worth a reported R100 million per year.

In addition, SA Rugby and the Springboks had come under significant governmental pressure over a perceived unwillingness to prioritise transformation. Much of this had to do with Meyer's selections before and during the 2015 Rugby World Cup, but things became critical when the Department of Sport and Recreation, under minister Fikile Mbalula, temporarily banned SA Rugby from bidding for, or hosting, major tournaments. This came less than two weeks after Coetzee's unveiling as coach, and as a result of findings from a government-funded Eminent Persons Group report. While three other sports federations were banned – cricket, athletics and netball – the decision hit SA Rugby particularly hard given its ambition to bid to host the 2023 Rugby World Cup.

This was the climate into which Coetzee stepped, but his stellar reputation still gave reason for optimism. While he had never gone the distance in Super Rugby with the Stormers, Coetzee had guided the Cape-based franchise to three South African Conference wins out of five. Coetzee had also led Western Province (WP) to four successive Currie Cup finals between 2012 and 2015, winning two of them. He was easily the most experienced South African Super

Rugby coach at the time, and his appointment was widely accepted as the right one. Coetzee had also been a part of Jake White's backroom coaching staff during the 2007 World Cup in France where the Boks cantered to their second Webb Ellis Cup. He was heavily linked to the head coach role after that tournament, before losing out to Peter de Villiers. But by 2016 he had built the pedigree to take the step up.

Coetzee set to work immediately and made some bold statements early on in preparation for a three-Test visit from Ireland in June. Team culture and instilling a passion to play for the green and gold were part of his early comments, suggesting that the Boks would look to evolve their style of rugby while staying true to their traditional strengths. 'There is nothing wrong with the way we have played ... I will maintain that and make sure we keep what we're good at,' Coetzee said at his unveiling. 'I won't be stupid. I'll make sure we tick all the boxes.'

The question at the time was how the Boks would close the gap on the All Blacks, who had knocked them out of the 2015 World Cup with a 20–18 win in the semi-finals and were still the undeniable benchmark in international rugby.

While Meyer's side had achieved a respectable third-place finish at the 2015 World Cup, the tournament will forever be remembered as the year the Boks were defeated by Japan in Brighton. The dramatic, last-gasp 34–32 loss to the Brave Blossoms, in South Africa's opening game of the World Cup, was as shocking as anything seen on a rugby field before, and the Boks would sink even lower in the months to come. Despite their improvement over the rest of the competition, the result was widely seen as the first warning sign of more challenging times ahead.

SA Rugby had given Coetzee the freedom to pick overseas-based players in 2016, but it was announced that the policy would soon be revisited. The organisation clearly wanted to back local players and Coetzee knew that when he joined.

It was also confirmed around this time that Erasmus had accepted a job with Irish club Munster, as their new director of rugby, and would be leaving after the Ireland series. Jacques Nienaber, who had been operating as the Junior High Performance manager, would accompany Erasmus to Munster but Coetzee would make use of his defensive expertise for the Ireland series.

Just three overseas-based players were selected in Coetzee's first 31-man squad for that series – Duane Vermeulen, Francois Louw and Steven Kitshoff. With nine uncapped players, it was a squad that, on the surface, signified a promising new dawn for South African rugby.

Coetzee, somewhat surprisingly, then appointed veteran hooker Adriaan Strauss as his captain. He said it was an easy decision, adding that Strauss would have a strong core of leaders around him in Patrick Lambie, Warren Whiteley, Frans Malherbe, Tendai Mtawarira, Louw and Vermeulen.

Stormers flank Siya Kolisi was not even on the radar at this stage.

Ireland, meanwhile, arrived in South Africa with a somewhat watered-down squad following injuries to key players such as Jonathan Sexton, Rob Kearney, Luke Fitzgerald and Dave Kearney. The Boks entered the series as overwhelming favourites, and with the speculation over, Coetzee got his tenure under way in the first Test at Newlands on 11 June in front of a hometown crowd. It turned out to be a horrible day for South African rugby, and not just because the Boks lost.

In the 22nd minute of the match, South African-born Irish flank CJ Stander went crashing into Bok flyhalf Lambie's head while attempting a charge-down. It was a sickening blow, and as Lambie lay motionless on the Newlands turf, a deathly hush fell over the stadium. It was clear that it was a serious head injury – and one that the Sharks playmaker would never fully recover from. Stander was shown a straight red card and Elton Jantjies replaced Lambie at number 10 to give the Boks a numerical advantage for the rest of the game. However, tries from Lwazi Mvovo and Pieter-Steph du Toit were not enough as the hosts fell to a disappointing 26–20 loss. The Coetzee era was off to the worst possible start.

Coetzee kept faith with his players for the second Test in Johannesburg on 18 June, though he was forced into changes through injury. Seasoned veteran Morne Steyn came in as flyhalf cover for Jantjies, while the uncapped Franco Mostert was included among the substitutes following an injury to Lood de Jager in Cape Town. It looked as if the Boks were slipping to a shocking series defeat when they went into the break 19–3 down, but four tries in the second half launched a stunning comeback that saw the hosts emerge 32–26 winners, with second-half replacement Ruan Combrinck named man of the match on his debut. Following a wave of criticism after the woeful Newlands defeat, Coetzee lauded the Bok attitude and fight in getting the job done.

The Boks were more clinical in the third Test, a week later, digging deep to grind out a 19–13 win at Nelson Mandela Bay Stadium in Port Elizabeth. Ireland, a score away from securing a famous series win, threatened the Bok line relentlessly in the closing stages of the contest, but Coetzee's men held on. While it was far from perfect, the Boks had ticked their first box under his tutelage.

Scrumhalf Faf de Klerk was superb throughout the series, particularly in the second and third Test matches, but the Boks would have to improve markedly if they were to mount a challenge in that year's Rugby Championship.

The defence coach position would prove to be problematic for Coetzee, and after Nienaber and Erasmus left for Munster, he brought in Chean Roux to fill the role. It was an appointment that took many in Springbok circles by surprise given Roux's lack of experience as a defensive specialist.

Kolisi, who started all three Tests against Ireland, was then injured on Super Rugby duty in the Stormers' 60–21 quarter-final loss to the Chiefs at Newlands and was ruled out of the Championship.

The Boks, never dominant and very much second best at the set piece, scraped an uncomfortable 30–23 win over Argentina in Nelspruit in their opener. Combrinck, on the wing, was a try scorer again that day, as was former Cheetahs man Johan Goosen at fullback. It was another come-from-behind win, with the Boks 23–13 down with less than a quarter of an hour to play. Whiteley scored the winner as Coetzee again praised the character of his side in coming out on top from a position of seemingly certain defeat. De Klerk was a standout once again for the Boks and was named man of the match.

In what would be a missed opportunity in the search for momentum and consistency, the Boks headed to Salta for the return leg against the Pumas on 27 August and fell to a 26–24 defeat that was not received well back home.

Almost immediately, Coetzee was under pressure, with critics quick to point out that he had notched up two unwanted firsts on his résumé after just five matches in charge. Before Coetzee took charge, the Boks had never lost to Ireland on home soil or to Argentina away.

After the side returned home from Argentina, Adriaan Strauss announced that he would be retiring from international rugby at the end of 2016. The announcement was even more surprising than his initial appointment. Strauss had come in for criticism for his performances throughout the Ireland series and in those first two Rugby Championship matches, while Malcom Marx of the Lions was knocking hard on the door as hooker, but it was still a shocking revelation just five Tests into his Bok captaincy. Even more bizarrely, Coetzee confirmed that he had known of Strauss's intention to retire at the end of the year when he first appointed him captain. While that raised its own questions over Coetzee's identifying a leader to take the side to the 2019 World Cup, the coach continued to pick Strauss as his skipper for the remainder of 2016.

A 23–17 loss to a struggling Australian outfit in Brisbane, at a time when Coetzee desperately needed something to go his way, saw under-fire Wallabies boss Michael Cheika end a six-match losing streak for his side, but more importantly it further exposed the Boks as devoid of ideas on attack. Elton Jantjies was taking heat over a perceived inability to control Test matches, while De Klerk's form was dipping too. Coetzee, though, remained optimistic in the press and bemoaned his side's struggles to convert opportunities into points.

Next up was the All Blacks in Christchurch on 17 September. While the Boks took an early 7–3 lead, thanks to a try from Bryan Habana, they were comfortably outplayed in every department thereafter and fell to a heavy 41–13 defeat. It was surely the final straw for Jantjies, who had received Coetzee's backing ever since Lambie went down in the first Ireland Test. While consistently impressive in a Lions jersey at Super Rugby level, Jantjies had not delivered for Coetzee. That result saw the Boks slip to three Rugby Championship losses in a row. Coetzee needed a quick fix.

It came in the form of Morne Steyn, who was picked to start a Test match for the first time in over two years when the Boks hosted the Wallabies at Loftus on 1 October. It was a selection and performance that showed just how desperate Coetzee was to secure a result. At a time when the Boks looked toothless with ball in hand, Coetzee reverted to the very style of rugby that South Africa's Super Rugby coaches were trying to move away from, as Steyn kicked all the points – including two drop goals – in an 18–10 win. The Boks were dominated in both the territory and possession statistics and, as SuperSport pundit and former national coach Nick Mallett pointed out afterwards, never looked like scoring a try. Steyn, though, was unrelenting with his kicks both at goal and out of hand. It was an awful game for the neutral to watch, but the Boks were back to winning ways.

That performance earned Steyn another start the following weekend – it would also prove to be his last – against the mighty All Blacks at Kings Park. Given what South Africans had witnessed in round four of the competition in Christchurch, there was hardly reason to believe the Boks could turn their fortunes around, but nobody could have predicted how badly things would go in Durban. Steyn kicked three first-half penalties to see his side go into the break 12–9 down, but the signs were there, with the All Blacks owning 72 per cent of first-half possession. The wheels came off spectacularly for the hosts in the second period as New Zealand ran in nine unanswered tries to secure a 57–15 victory – their biggest win over the Boks in 95 years of competition.

The backlash, understandably, was brutal. The Boks were a million miles behind the world champions in every aspect and they finished that year's Rugby Championship in third place and on 10 log points – a staggering 20 behind the All Blacks, who rumbled to a clean sweep of 30 points.

Question marks hovered over Coetzee, and, equally, over SA Rugby's role in the downfall of the national side. The popular thinking was that a style of South African rugby needed to be settled on and then implemented at franchise level, with all Super Rugby coaches on the same page and buying into a Bok 'blueprint' at training and in matches.

Coetzee heard the cries from the rugby community and called for a 'coaching indaba' to be held in Cape Town in October, where the country's top coaches and rugby minds could come together to identify the way forward. The idea was to implement a national blueprint with everybody on board, from top to bottom. While the ambitions were noble, and Coetzee left the two-day indaba encouraged about the future, he needed instant improvement in the form of results on the Boks' 2016 end-of-year northern-hemisphere tour, where Tests against England, Italy and Wales awaited.

Chean Roux's brief tenure came to an end when he was sacked before the tour, with Lions defence coach JP Ferreira joining the fray. Cheetahs boss Franco Smith was also added to the backroom staff as an attacking consultant, increasing speculation that Coetzee was unhappy with what he was getting out of former Southern Kings backline coach Mzwandile Stick.

A 31–31 draw against the Barbarians at Wembley Stadium, which also marked Patrick Lambie's return to the national side following his recovery from concussion, kickstarted the tour in light-hearted fashion. The real test, though, would come in the form of Eddie Jones' England at Twickenham a week later. At that stage, England were already being identified as potential challengers to the All Blacks at the 2019 World Cup, and the consensus was that the Boks would start as underdogs. That proved to be the case, and then some, as the English secured their first win over South Africa in ten years with a 37–21 scoreline that, if anything, flattered the visitors. It was arguably England's worst performance of the ten matches they had played under Jones, but it was still more than enough to floor the Boks.

The clash with Italy in Florence, though, provided the Boks with a fixture that would surely give their under-fire coach a much-needed victory. Instead, 19 November 2016 would go down as one of the darkest days in South African rugby history. As if the run of poor results wasn't enough, this match was the beginning of the end for Coetzee.

Ten of the 23 players in the match-day squad that day would be World Cup winners less than three years later, but they didn't play like it. The Boks were awful on attack from start to finish, despite running in two tries through Bryan Habana and Damian de Allende inside the opening quarter. Once again, they were nowhere with ball in hand and could not find any dominance at set piece or through their rolling maul. As the game grew older, and as the Boks continued to stumble around the Florence turf, the possibility of a stunning Italian win grew. When the final whistle blew, the number-13-ranked side in the world, who had been battered 68–10 by the All Blacks in Rome just a week before, had pulled off a 20–18 win and the greatest in their rugby history against the two-time world champions.

'It was a feeling of cluelessness in not knowing where we were going and why there were so many different things being raised at a point when we needed clarity from the top level down,' Bryan Habana recalls from the moments in the change room following the Italy match, which would prove to be his 124th and final Test for the Boks before retirement.

'We sat there not knowing how to get out of that rut.'

In the SuperSport studios after the match, former Springbok captain Jean de Villiers summed up the situation, calling it an 'all-time low', while Afrikaans newspaper *Rapport* awarded all 15 starting Boks a player rating of zero out of ten for their efforts. Calls for Coetzee's head rang louder than ever, and SA Rugby released a statement that evening saying they would conduct a full season review following the next weekend's year-ending Test against Wales. For Coetzee, the end of the year couldn't come soon enough, but he had one last shot in Cardiff to restore some much-needed credibility to what was fast becoming a nightmare for him.

With Elton Jantjies back at number 10, and with Coetzee handing debuts to Uzair Cassiem, Jean-Luc du Preez and Rohan Janse van Rensburg, the Boks slumped to a 27–13 defeat. It left Coetzee winless on the end-of-year tour and with just four wins from 12 in his first year in charge. With a win percentage of just 33.3 per cent – the worst of any Bok coach ever – it began to look unlikely that Coetzee would have a job at the start of 2017.

After months of speculation, a decision was eventually taken in February 2017 to back Coetzee. It did not go down well with the majority of South African rugby lovers, who had lost faith in the green and gold.

There were further changes to the backroom staff, with Stick demoted to the Junior Springboks while Franco Smith stayed on as an attacking consultant. It was also announced that the Boks had secured a high-profile defensive guru, later unveiled as the highly rated Brendan Venter, also in a consultancy capacity. It was an appointment not without complication given that Venter was still contracted to the Italian national side and had helped orchestrate the upset in Florence.

With renewed backing and an opportunity to put things right, Coetzee's first port of call was to assemble a squad – and appoint a new captain after Strauss's retirement – for a three-match inbound series against France.

Few were surprised when Coetzee turned to likeable Lions number 8 Warren Whiteley to lead the new-look Boks. The Lions were easily the form South African side in Super Rugby, having lost in the tournament final in 2016 under Whiteley's leadership. A respected workhorse with natural man-management qualities, Whiteley was a popular appointment, even if it did pose a possible selection dilemma down the line, with Duane Vermeulen an obvious option at the back of the scrum.

The France series would also represent Coetzee's last opportunity to pick whoever he wanted, with SA Rugby announcing that its policy on overseas-based players would change at the end of the series. From July 2017, only overseas-based players with 30 Test caps or more could be selected for the national side. It didn't matter in the case of Frans Steyn, though, whom Coetzee named on the bench for the first Test against France at Loftus on 10 June.

Faf de Klerk, who would make a move to English club Sale Sharks after struggling in Bok colours towards the end of 2016, was binned as Coetzee handed Lions number 9 Ross Cronje a Test debut. Fullback Andries Coetzee and left wing Courtnall Skosan were also given debuts in the starting lineup. With Jantjies continuing at fly-half – Handre Pollard was still out injured – there was a strong Lions flavour to Coetzee's new-look Boks, particularly in the backline.

On the surface, it was the obvious thing to do given the franchise's local dominance on attack under coach Johan Ackermann, and Coetzee's first Test of 2017 provided some relief as the Boks secured a comfortable 37–14 win.

Siya Kolisi played all 80 minutes that day in the number 6 jersey, but the star performer was Lions hooker Marx, who was a menace on the ground and a physical force on defence and attack.

Kolisi was at his best in the second Test at Kings Park, though, with a man-of-the-match performance that included a now-famous intercept try, a series of attacking runs and a ferocious defensive display as the Boks won 37–15. There were still issues – the Boks were dominated in the possession and territorial statistics and continued to struggle at scrum time – but with the series won, Coetzee and his Lion-heavy Boks had made a near-perfect start to 2017.

The day of the third Test, played on 24 June at Ellis Park, will be remembered for the news that emerged in the morning. Whiteley, after a flawless introduction to the captaincy, had been ruled out with a groin injury. Whiteley's struggles with injury were well known, but nobody could have predicted that this would be the beginning of the end of his Bok career and ultimately cost him a shot at leading his country in Japan. With the series won, Whiteley's exclusion seemed more precautionary than anything else, but it would prove to be far more significant, as his troubles with injury only escalated in the months ahead.

Eben Etzebeth was named as the stand-in captain for the day, and even then there were many voices on social media who felt that Coetzee had missed a trick by not giving the captaincy to the in-form Kolisi. The final score was 35–12 – another comfortable win – and meant that the Boks had won the series 3–0. Coetzee was naturally pleased with the turnaround, saying his side had 'set the record straight'. While the upcoming Rugby Championship would be the obvious test of exactly how much the Boks had evolved, the mood surrounding the state of the Springboks had improved significantly.

It was around this time, though, that reports first surfaced that former Springbok flank and Munster coach Rassie Erasmus was being lined up for a potential return to South Africa and a position as director of rugby. It was a role he had performed previously at the Stormers while Coetzee was there, and the simple plan was for Erasmus to help get the Boks back onto the same level as the world-champion All Blacks. He was still contracted to Munster, though, so any move back home would not materialise overnight and Coetzee would still have to negotiate the rest of 2017 and look to build on what had been achieved in the France series.

Etzebeth, meanwhile, was given the captaincy for the 2017 Rugby Championship, with Whiteley still sidelined. Kolisi was confirmed as vice-captain.

'He enjoys the respect of his team-mates and also commands respect on and off the field,' Coetzee said of Etzebeth. Few could argue with those sentiments, but given that Kolisi captained Etzebeth at the Stormers, it was a decision that got people talking.

In a column for the *Sunday Times* in August 2017, Gary Gold, former Springbok assistant coach and then director of rugby at Worcester Warriors, wrote: 'Siya Kolisi encapsulates the new-found attitude in the Springbok camp and wears his heart on his sleeve. Eben Etzebeth has done a wonderful job as captain in Warren Whiteley's injury-enforced absence but there are many reasons why I feel Kolisi should comfortably be the next Springbok captain. He is a world-class player, a natural leader and, as the incumbent Stormers skipper, has already proven his leadership ability. I'm not for a second taking anything away from Etzebeth but Kolisi leading the Springboks makes sense for South Africa.'

The Boks, with their new skipper, hosted Argentina in Port Elizabeth for their first match of that year's Rugby Championship. Coetzee again backed his Lions spine of Cronje, Jantjies and Coetzee, and there was also a debut off the bench for exciting Sharks youngster Curwin Bosch. By then, though, the Boks had the job done, as they landed an encouraging 37–15 win – their fourth in a row in 2017. Etzebeth, comically, praised the Boks after the match for securing a four-try bonus point, momentarily forgetting that the bonus-point system now required a side to score three more tries than their opposition, which the Boks had not done. That aside, the Boks were off to a winning start in the tournament and, for the first time in the Coetzee era, they looked to be on the right track.

As part of an initiative from new sponsors MTN, the Boks wore red when they travelled to Salta for the away leg against the Pumas the next weekend. Kolisi, again, was outstanding as he bagged two tries on his way to another man-of-the-match performance and a 41–23 win that saw the Boks move to the top of the Rugby Championship log. Having won just four from 12 in his first year, Coetzee had improved his overall record to nine out of 17 (52.9 per cent) thanks to the clean sweeps over France and Argentina. The Australasian leg of the Championship, though, was where the Boks needed to show that they were ready to tough it out against the world's best. Instead, it was a tour that went a long way towards burying Allister Coetzee.

A 23–23 draw in Perth saw the Boks overturn a 20–10 deficit in the second half, with Kolisi and Pieter-Steph du Toit immense. Du Toit, remarkably, had been used as a substitute throughout the year and this was his first start in a Bok jersey in 2017 as he replaced Franco Mostert at number 5. It was a gritty performance from South Africa given how poor they had been for the first 50 minutes of the contest, and what they displayed in the final 30 minutes was a reminder of how much they had improved.

Against the All Blacks in Albany, though, they would have to be at their best for 80 minutes to stand any chance. New Zealand presented an opportunity for Coetzee to show that he had closed the gap on the world champions since 2016. What followed was a sporting massacre and a day that, ultimately, Coetzee could not recover from.

After a bright start, the Boks fell apart as the All Blacks ran in eight unanswered tries to win 57–0. It was South Africa's biggest defeat in Test rugby, surpassing the infamous 53–3 hammering they had suffered against England at Twickenham in 2002. It was a devastating blow to Coetzee, and rendered meaningless all the strides the Boks had made in 2017. South Africans were unlikely to accept a result like this against their fiercest rivals, and Coetzee was squarely back in the firing line. It was another unwanted 'first' for 'Toetie', who was defiant in his reaction.

'One loss doesn't define this team,' Coetzee said on his side's return to Johannesburg. 'There is still a lot of belief in this team and there is a lot of belief in myself and the plan going forward … There is a process that we're following, and I couldn't care what Twitter is saying. I'm working for SA Rugby, not for Twitter, and we really are moving in the right direction.' He continued: 'This doesn't push us back at all. It's still a massive progression … this is the only Test we've lost so far [this year]. The bounce of the ball and everything just favoured them [New Zealand] on Saturday.' Coetzee added that there were 'positives' to take from the match, despite the scoreline.

'That's just the type of person Allister is,' Bryan Habana remarks. 'He was like that when I started my career in 2004 and at the Stormers. He was always trying to be positive.'

Pollard had made his return from injury in that match, entering the fray in the 57th minute for his first taste of international action since the third/fourth-place playoff against Argentina at the 2015 World Cup, but it went by unnoticed in the understandably heated aftermath.

With the Rugby Championship on a two-week break, the Boks were exposed to a trying period of public condemnation. Some fans, Etzebeth said, were so infuriated that they launched attacks on the players and their families.

The 30 September clash against the Wallabies in Bloemfontein was a must-win. The nightmarish defensive performance in Albany saw wing Raymond Rhule lose his place to Dillyn Leyds, while Coetzee also picked the returning Francois Louw at number 7.

In another result that helped neither coach – Cheika was still under pressure in Australia – the match ended in a 27–27 draw. Jantjies, continuing at pivot, had a chance to secure the win with a late penalty from close to the touchline, but it sailed wide. Coetzee, in his post-match press conference, started to crack.

Asked a question about the possibility of assistant coach Johann van Graan moving to Munster to take up the role of director of rugby, replacing Erasmus, Coetzee was visibly irritated. 'Have you seen his contract?' he barked angrily at the journalist. 'He is a contracted assistant coach to SA Rugby and those are the facts. What Munster says is hearsay. There is nothing official.'

Perhaps it was missing out on a win that would have eased the pressure on him that caused the outburst, or perhaps it was the fact that the wheels were already in motion to bring in Erasmus to rescue

South African rugby. More than likely it was both of those factors, but Coetzee made himself look vulnerable and the pressure he was under was telling.

The match in Bloemfontein will also be remembered for Israel Folau's pulling Leyds down by his ponytail, with Cheika famously arguing afterwards: 'Mate, he gripped him by the collar!'

Because of what had transpired in Albany, the Boks were given no chance in their clash against the All Blacks at Newlands the following weekend. As a curtain-raiser to the sold-out fixture, a celebrity tag rugby match was held to hype up the 48 000 supporters in attendance. It would prove to be a career-threatening day for South African 2016 Olympic hero Wayde van Niekerk – Cheslin Kolbe's cousin – who sustained a freak knee injury during the friendly runaround. It was the most unnecessary of injuries, and a marketing nightmare, as one of the country's most celebrated athletes limped off the Newlands turf. The extent of Van Niekerk's injury was not known at the time, though, with the focus firmly on the Springboks.

The Boks lost 25–24 in what was an undoubtedly improved display, but it was another loss and on home soil. Marx was superb for the hosts, who put in a heroic defensive effort during a 50-minute first half, but there were more problems at number 9 and number 10, where Ross Cronje and Elton Jantjies, in particular, struggled. Handre Pollard was introduced before the hour mark, but was on the field for just 17 minutes before he went off for a concussion test.

Forwards coach Matt Proudfoot would later pinpoint this as the day the Springboks identified the blueprint for playing against the All Blacks, with Coetzee backing the physicality of his forwards.

The Boks finished third in the Rugby Championship with two wins over Argentina, two draws against the Wallabies and two losses to the All Blacks. It was a far better showing than that dished up in 2016, but the jury was still out on Coetzee, and the Boks went into their end-of-year tour with much to prove. Fixtures against Ireland, France, Italy and Wales awaited as talk grew of Erasmus's imminent arrival in South Africa.

Coetzee named the uncapped Lukhanyo Am in a 34-man squad for the tour. Etzebeth was named captain once again, while Kolisi was only available for the first two matches and would return home after the France Test to be with his wife, Rachel, who was due to give birth.

The clash against Ireland on 11 November was up first. On paper this was arguably the toughest of the four Tests for the Boks given how highly rated Ireland were under coach Joe Schmidt. Pollard, fully fit, was benched as Coetzee sought continuity and backed Jantjies yet again, while there were returns to the starting lineup for Damian de Allende and Coenie Oosthuizen. Before the match, Coetzee explained that Duane Vermeulen and Frans Steyn were still part of his broader plans despite the pair not having been included in the squad for the tour.

When Oosthuizen dropped to the Dublin turf in agony in just the second minute with a devastating knee injury, it was a sign of things to come for the Boks as they were hammered 38–3. It was a disastrous result for Coetzee. The Boks, once more, were erratic and error-prone and were bossed all over the park, particularly in the aerial battle. Jantjies and Cronje, encouraged to play such an enterprising, fearless brand of rugby together at the Lions, were not clicking under Coetzee. It was yet another unwanted first for the coach and Ireland's highest-ever winning margin over South Africa, surpassing a 32–15 victory in Dublin in 2006.

Vermeulen was immediately called into the squad as the pressure on Coetzee grew. Ahead of the France game, the Boks had it confirmed that they would lose Van Graan to Munster. Defensive consultant Brendan Venter also returned to South Africa due to a conflict of interest arising from his role with Italy. Coetzee made a total of ten changes for the Test against France in Paris, including handing Pollard his first Test start in two years since the bronze play-off at the 2015 World Cup.

The major news that week, though, was that South Africa lost out to France on the right to host the 2023 World Cup. The sports minister had lifted the bidding ban and South Africa had entered the voting as overwhelming favourites to host their first World Cup since 1995. Continental governing body Rugby Africa's two votes went to France, as did those of Japan, and the decision left SA Rugby president Mark Alexander and CEO Jurie Roux red-faced. Alexander acknowledged afterwards, and again in 2019, that SA Rugby should consider not bidding for further World Cups given their history of disappointments.

As much as that story dominated headlines that week, with South African rugby lovers furious, it added an element of spice to the affair in Paris. Unfortunately, the match that unfolded was anything but tasty and showed two sides who were far from their best. France had lost 38–18 to the All Blacks the week before and were clearly low on confidence, and this was reflected in their performance against the Boks. South Africa, through tries from Dillyn Leyds and Jesse Kriel, eked out an 18–17 win. Vermeulen, Louw and Kolisi played together in a forward pack that ultimately ground out the win for the Boks, while Pollard missed four kicks from seven to complete the rustiest of returns.

Afterwards, Coetzee hailed the character of his Boks in overturning the Ireland result as 'unbelievable', but few were convinced given how poorly France had played, having lost 13 of their last 20 Tests.

There would be no repeat of Florence 2016 when the Boks travelled to Padua for their next Italy Test. Coetzee took no chances in experimenting with fringe players and was rewarded with a dominant forward performance as the South African maul steamrollered the Italians. The Boks emerged comfortable 35–6 winners with five converted tries, but the manner of the win told its own story of a South African side that had not evolved into an enterprising attacking unit under Coetzee. It was the win South Africans had expected in 2016, and few were moved by the result a year later.

As the last Test of the year approached, against Wales in Cardiff on 2 December, rumours of Coetzee's sacking were flying. With the match falling outside the international window, both sides lost a host of players. For the Boks, Francois Louw, Duane Vermeulen and Franco Mostert were unavailable. South African media reports suggested that regardless of the result, Coetzee's fate was sealed and he would be sacked at a general council meeting on 13 December.

Coetzee looked on as his side fell to a 24–22 defeat thanks to a brace of tries from New Zealand-born centre Hadleigh Parkes on debut. The Boks had held a 22–21 lead going into the last quarter, but a Leigh Halfpenny penalty on 67 minutes buried the visitors, who had limped to two wins from four on their tour.

South Africa had seen enough, the SA Rugby bosses had seen enough, and so Allister Coetzee's time was up. 'I'm signed on until 2019,' Coetzee said following the loss to Wales. 'That's what my contract says. The team has really grown. It's a really healthy team environment. They are hurting at the moment. They feel that they let themselves down and the country down. You can only feel like that if you have a good team environment ... That wasn't the case last year. Last year was a fiasco. Definitely a fiasco.'

While there were improvements in results in 2017, Coetzee's 'fiasco' in 2016 was ultimately what cost him. By the time he was sacked, his record read: played 25, won 11, lost 12, drawn 2, for a win percentage of a mere 44 per cent. It didn't stack up well against his predecessors: Heyneke Meyer had finished with 71 per cent, while Peter de Villiers and Jake White finished on 68 per cent each. Coetzee simply hadn't been good enough to inspire confidence that this side could challenge for the World Cup in 2019. Change was on the horizon.

As an official review into Coetzee's tenure drew closer, there was perhaps the subtlest indication of things to come as Siya Kolisi was handed the Players' Player of the Year award at the 2017 BrightRock Players' Choice Awards. Even when the Boks were at their worst, Kolisi still commanded the respect of his peers.

The process of getting rid of Coetzee ended up being a long and tedious one, with SA Rugby taking their time to ensure they did not cross any legal boundaries. The official review only took place in the new year, by which time Erasmus had been officially appointed as the new director of rugby. The uncertainty surrounding who would coach the Boks in 2018 grew as the year began.

Things turned nasty towards the end of January, when Coetzee wrote an explosive letter to SA Rugby that was leaked to the public. With the parties unable to come to an agreement, Coetzee attacked the SA Rugby administration, accusing them of pushing him to become a 'ceremonial coach' under Erasmus should he not agree to go quietly.

'Should I be reduced to the position of a ceremonial coach I would have to face the indignity of reporting to Rassie. The fact that a decision has been made that I will be reduced to a ceremonial coach should I resist any attempt by SARU to terminate my services does not only constitute an unfair labour practice but again infringes my right to dignity and equality,' Coetzee wrote. 'I will not allow elements in SARU to wilfully destroy me and render me unemployable.'

Less than a week later, Coetzee was officially sacked as coach of the Springboks.

In many ways, everyone involved with South African rugby gave a collective sigh of relief. Coetzee's intentions were pure, and he wanted desperately to succeed, but his tenure had reduced the Boks from a powerhouse in world rugby to a side that no longer possessed any fear factor, even against the likes of Italy.

There were things that were out of his control. The administrative uncertainty at SA Rugby, governmental pressures, the policies on overseas-based players, not being able to appoint a backroom staff of his choosing and the fact that the best flyhalf in South Africa was injured for most of his tenure ... all these factors had played a role. Coetzee, though, did himself no favours through puzzling selections and an inability to identify and nurture a clear playing philosophy.

'It was initially a very difficult one,' Bryan Habana observes. 'He got appointed very late in 2016 and then didn't get the support he deserved. He got logistics plans that he wasn't privy to before his appointment and only had two weeks before that first Ireland series ... I did feel sorry for him. It was a difficult situation. I don't want to say he was set up to fail, but I think he tried his best in an environment where he didn't get to choose his entire management staff or his own logistics man when SA Rugby was maybe not that fond of international players.'

SA Rugby said they would announce the new coaching staff by the end of February 2018. The Boks, sixth in the world rankings and without a head coach, were directionless. Erasmus was now the man in charge, in his capacity as director of rugby, but how could one man fix something that was this far gone?

In the build-up to the Italy Test – Coetzee's penultimate Test in charge – Jake White penned a column for the All Out Rugby website. 'The rugby romantic will say it can be done, because it has been done in the past, but I don't think there's enough time between now and the 2019 Rugby World Cup for the Springboks to turn it around,' White wrote. 'I'm not saying it's impossible for South Africa to be a force in Japan in 22 months' time, but I'd say that line of thinking is more for the dreamer than for the guy who understands the quality of the competition you're up against at a World Cup.'

Thankfully for South Africa, Jake White was mistaken, though few would have disagreed with him at the time.

The Springboks would go on to achieve the unthinkable in Japan – ironically, where Coetzee ended up, as coach of the Canon Eagles. A man who had given so much value to South African rugby over the years certainly didn't deserve such a rough ride, but at the very top level there is seldom room for sentiment and Coetzee knew that before he took the job.

'It's water under the bridge,' Habana says. 'We are world champions and Allister is not going to get given any credit for that, because Rassie took over when we were in the doldrums. It was a disappointing way to end.'

Chapter 3
The Afrikaner from Despatch

With a little more than 18 months to go until the 2019 World Cup, and lacking a clear game style and far from knowing what their best XV was, the Boks were already being written off. Rassie Erasmus arrived with an undeniable pedigree, but the task at hand was surely too immense for anyone to salvage.

The aftermath of Allister Coetzee's sacking was an emotional period for South African rugby. Coetzee had failed, but the blame could not rest with him alone, and the SA Rugby leadership was understandably taking flak. While there was no clarity on exactly what would happen from a coaching point of view, it began to look likely that Erasmus, in his role as director of rugby, would double up as head coach until the World Cup. This arrangement was confirmed on 1 March 2018.

A loose forward with natural skill and an X factor with ball in hand, Erasmus's 36 Test caps would almost certainly have been more were it not for injury. He played in the 1999 World Cup and wore the number 6 jersey when the Boks were devastated by a Stephen Larkham extra-time drop goal in their semi-final against the Wallabies at Twickenham. But Erasmus would only feature in another eight Tests before a foot injury forced him to retire. His last Test match came in 2001, and his final season with the Free State

Cheetahs in 2004, but coaching had been on the cards for him long before his career as a player came to an end.

Those who played with Erasmus will tell you of a tactical acumen and a near-obsession with analysis that consumed him, even at the height of his playing career.

'He always showed a very keen interest in the finer intricacies of the game,' former Springbok captain Corné Krige said in an interview with *Sport24* in 2019 after the Boks kicked off their campaign in Japan, adding that Erasmus would take his analysis into his hotel room long after training or after a match had ended. 'He had this computer that could rewind, and he would slow it down and go through all the frames.'

Born in the Eastern Cape town of Despatch, nestled between Port Elizabeth and Uitenhage, Johan Erasmus grew up in love with rugby. This revealed itself in every aspect of his school life at Despatch High, where he was a prefect before matriculating in 1990. Locals describe Despatch as a rugby-mad community, and that much was seen on the 2019 trophy tour when the usually quiet streets burst into life to welcome their Rassie back home. Erasmus spent almost all of the trophy tour on the bottom level of the bus and out of public sight, allowing his players to soak up the limelight. He made an exception in Despatch, climbing to the roof and waving to the people he had known since he was a boy.

Because the bus took so long to make its way through the streets of Port Elizabeth, Erasmus was unable to attend a function at the local rugby club, where family and friends had gathered to meet him. Instead, he and Siya Kolisi were whisked away to the airport to leave for Durban, where they were due to attend the South African Sports Awards that night.

'Some of my family drove three or four hours to be there, so it was a pity,' Erasmus remembers of that return to Despatch. 'I did go back there afterwards, though, with the trophy, and I went to the school to speak to the kids and the teachers just to say thank you.'

Born on 5 November 1972 to Abel and Marie Erasmus, Rassie was raised in a traditional Afrikaans household with strong religious beliefs. He was the oldest of three children – he has two younger sisters – and grew up to be a likeable character who earned the respect of his peers and teachers.

Elsje Ferreira taught Erasmus English at Despatch High School and she remembers him as exuding a quiet confidence. It was a very different attitude, Ferreira says, from former Springbok centre Danie Gerber, whom she also taught at the school and remembers as being outwardly more confident. Popular by virtue of his rugby conquests, Erasmus was always polite and respectful in Mrs Ferreira's class. She remembers him well, even where he sat, which is not something she can say about all of her students.

'He was one of those boys who would say something when he wanted to say it and people would listen to him. He was very quiet, but he would just have this little smile when he knew he was right about something and I knew he was amused,' Ferreira says. 'I never knew he was going to become so famous, but he was just one of those boys that without saying anything would make an impression with his whole attitude.'

Erasmus was 'not the best' when it came to English class, Ferreira says, but then few from Despatch were at that time. 'A lot of kids who were good at something would have an attitude, but he was never like that,' Ferreira recalls. 'On TV, when I see him now, I see him as he was in class. It makes one proud because we've had just a little hand in his upbringing.'

Ferreira would eventually retire from teaching in 2011, having spent the better part of 35 years at Despatch High. In that time,

THE AFRIKANER FROM DESPATCH

she helped mould the futures of thousands of children, including Erasmus's sister Martlie. None, however, would have the global impact Erasmus had.

From the very beginning, Erasmus was a player that coaches and players noticed, even if he played for a school that was not considered a Springbok breeding ground. In his early years of high school, Erasmus operated as a flyhalf and was always good enough to command a place in the first sides, earning provincial representation from as early as Under-13 level. The decision to move Erasmus into the loose forwards was largely down to his coach, Coenie Strumpher.

By Grade 11, Erasmus had made the first team and he had started that year at number 10 when Strumpher made a call that would change the course of his career.

'I always called him Hannie,' Strumpher recalls. 'He was quite tall, and he had the heart of a lion and I knew that if you wanted to be a good forward, you needed that. That's one of the reasons I brought him to flank and number 8 ... and he was very fast as well.'

Erasmus, Strumpher adds, knew at school that he wanted to play for Free State. Strumpher had to explain to him that if he went to the University of the Free State, he would have to compete with the highly rated loose forwards coming out of Grey College, Bloemfontein. It was a challenge that Erasmus was up for, and he later managed to shift his compulsory military training from Oudtshoorn to Bloemfontein to accommodate such a move.

Erasmus, the newly discovered loose forward, captained Despatch High in Grade 12 and was an obvious selection in the Eastern Province (EP) Craven Week side that year.

Off the field, Strumpher remembers Erasmus being a leader in the school's Student Christian Association. Faith was a significant part of Erasmus's home life, and it was something that would feature prominently in his school life too.

Rugby, though, was always the priority. It didn't matter what position he was playing, or what team he was playing for. If Johan Erasmus was on the field, he commanded attention. Strumpher tells the story of a day at Despatch when the school was hosting zonal trials for the EP Craven Week side. 'One of the selectors came to me and said: "Listen here, who is this Johan Erasmus?" I told him to just watch the trials and that he would immediately see who Johan Erasmus was.'

Strumpher recalls, as clear as day, how an opposition wing was gliding towards scoring what looked a certain a try in the corner when Erasmus scampered across the Despatch turf with pace to tackle him into touch.

'When he made the tackle, this coach asked me: "Who is that player?"'

'I said to him: 'Just wait for him to stand up ... then you will know it's Johan Erasmus.'

Erasmus, at that young age, had developed the trademark of wiping his hands on his shorts after making a big tackle and Strumpher knew it was coming. As Erasmus did exactly that, every selector at the Despatch field that day was introduced to a youngster who would go on to be one of the central figures in South African rugby history. He made the EP Craven Week side in 1990 – a no-brainer for anyone who saw him.

Strumpher was involved in coaching the first team at Despatch High for 19 years and he always made a point of facilitating a strong relationship with his captains. In Erasmus's matric year, when he skippered Despatch, the signs of a different level of leadership were already beginning to emerge. Strumpher remembers involving Erasmus in a selection conundrum he had over two scrumhalves for one match.

'I would always ask the captains for their input because they are the ones on the field,' Strumpher recalls. 'I remember he said to me: "Sir, these are the one scrumhalf's strong points and these are the other scrumhalf's strong points."

'He did not tell me which one I should choose, but we spoke about it and I can still remember the way he looked at the game was sometimes a way I hadn't seen it. It wasn't only on the rugby field, sometimes it was at school as well. He came forward with certain ideas and he knew that the kids would listen to him, but he did not force anything on anyone. If he was wrong, he would admit it. I won't forget that about him. He was an extraordinary boy at school.'

It was during his two years of military service that Erasmus met Jacques Nienaber, a young sports nut from Bloemfontein. The two immediately clicked. Erasmus and Nienaber were not in the same military unit during that first year, but one of Erasmus's room-mates, Hennie Fourie, was a close friend of Nienaber's and ultimately the person responsible for introducing them.

'From there we just became friends and then later he moved closer to us,' Erasmus recalls. 'He became a corporal and I became a lieutenant, but then we saw each other regularly because he moved to our base.'

Springbok legend Os du Randt was also stationed in Erasmus's unit during that time, but Erasmus actually spent his first year out of school focused almost entirely on his military obligations. It was only in his second year, when he was a lieutenant in 1992, that he started playing more regularly and seriously. He made his way through the military playing ranks – from Military Under-21s to SA Military and then all the way to the SA Forces side. It was also in that year that Erasmus broke through into the Free State Under-21s as he began to eye a move into academics.

Erasmus enrolled at the University of the Free State and studied for a BCom degree from 1993 to 1995. He continued with Free

State's senior sides during that time and grew closer to Nienaber, who was studying physiotherapy at the university.

'He loved rugby and all sports,' Erasmus says of Nienaber. 'He was a massive runner and I think one of the top 1 500-metre runners in the country. He was a long-distance guy. I don't know how many marathons he has completed already. He always went to the games when we were at varsity when he was still studying as a physio. He would sit and watch a whole cricket game. He was very into rugby, but he played it socially.

One of Erasmus's team-mates at Shimlas – the Free State University side – and then later at Free State was former Springbok hooker Naka Drotske, who is almost two years older. The two were room-mates at university and Drotske remembers their time together well, particularly a 1994 trip to the United Kingdom with Shimlas, when their friendship began. Drotske was already a Springbok by then and would go on to be an unused substitute in the 1995 World Cup final.

Erasmus joined the senior setup at the Cheetahs in 1994, when he was just 21, but playing time was extremely limited. He considers 1995 his real breakthrough year in professional rugby. The game had entered the professional era by then, and Erasmus arrived at a time when competition for places was increasing. The Springboks were now world champions and money was becoming more of a factor in the game. Though not the strongest individual in the side, Erasmus's lanky build and unique way of running with the ball made him stand out.

'He was still a youngster but a really clever player and very creative,' Drotske says, recalling those early days in Bloemfontein. 'He had a lot of skill and could always put the player next to him in a gap.'

Erasmus began making waves through consistent improvement, and another breakthrough came when the Cheetahs joined Super Rugby (then known as Super 12) for the first time in 1997, replacing

THE AFRIKANER FROM DESPATCH

Western Province, who had slipped outside the top four in the previous season's Currie Cup. It was a major moment in the history of Free State rugby, and the men from Bloem were more than credible as they finished in seventh position on the 12-team log.

The main course for that year from a South African rugby point of view was the mid-year British & Irish Lions tour, and thanks largely to his form in Super Rugby, Erasmus earned a maiden call-up to the national side. He did not feature in the first two Tests, but was handed a Springbok debut in the third, at Ellis Park, where the Boks won 35–16, though they went down 2–1 in the series. His Springbok story was under way.

For Drotske and many others who played alongside him in those early years, Erasmus's interest in all things tactical had already become clear. 'The first time I really saw him take control was in 1996 with [Free State coach] Peet Kleynhans when he joined a players' committee with myself, Brendan Venter and Helgard Muller,' Drotske says. 'You could see there that he and Brendan were both very good rugby brains and thinking ahead of their time. You could see that in the things they wanted to change and the way we started playing. Whenever you saw him away from the field, he was on a laptop working out moves and analysing.'

Throughout his four years with the Cats – Super Rugby's combined Cheetahs and Golden Lions franchise – Erasmus solidified his position as one of the most skilful and dynamic loose forwards in the country and he began to own a place in the Springbok side as a result. One of his crowning moments as a player came in 1999 when he captained the Boks against Australia in Brisbane, even if they went on to lose 32–6. It was the one and only time Erasmus skippered his country – an unforgettable moment for any player – though he would later reveal that he was offered the captaincy twice under former Bok coach Nick Mallett and turned it down on both occasions.

There would be more leadership success the following year when he captained the Cats to a semi-final appearance in Super Rugby 2000.

Erasmus's final Test match was in 2001, bringing an end to a five-year international career that saw him go through highs and lows and learn a lot about himself and the type of player and man he wanted to be. The lessons Erasmus learnt as a player would help to shape his move into the coaching world.

After the 2019 World Cup, Erasmus would reveal that he struggled mentally with becoming a Springbok and dealing with the sideshows that accompanied that success. Looking back, he acknowledges a level of arrogance and an entitled outlook that annoyed some of his coaches and peers. He calls it being 'windgat' (Afrikaans slang for boastful). He used himself as an example when addressing his 2019 Boks before the World Cup, explaining that a sense of entitlement was unavoidable when you became a Springbok. The trick, he stressed, was breaking out of that phase as soon as possible.

Erasmus was the captain and an undeniable leader at the union but his playing career ended fully in 2004 when Free State lost the Currie Cup final to the Blue Bulls 42–33 at Loftus. The Cheetahs, somewhat controversially, immediately moved to hand Erasmus the reins as head coach.

It was a development that ruffled feathers, says Drotske, who had returned to Bloemfontein after a three-year stint abroad with London Irish. Peet Kleynhans had been the Cheetahs' coach since 1996, and now that he was planning his exit from the franchise, there were a number of university and club coaches from Bloemfontein who thought they should be given a look-in at the Free State job. Kleynhans and Free State president Harold Verster had already identified Erasmus's coaching potential and decided to gamble on him, with Verster adding that there had been interest from French and English clubs in securing Erasmus's services as a player/coach.

'There was definitely a lot of criticism with him going from captain to coach. There wasn't an application process followed, but coach Kleynhans knew, and we knew, that he was the best candidate. The detractors were soon proved wrong because we had an awesome season,' Drotske says.

Erasmus already had experience as a coach. He had undergone foot surgery in 2004, and, with his leg in a cast and already on the Cheetahs payroll, he coached the Vodacom Cup side to second place on the log before they lost to the Blue Bulls in the semi-finals.

'I remember when I couldn't make the Cheetahs team in 1993 and 1994, Joe Beukes was the guy who played ahead of me, and in 2004 he was still playing and I was coaching him in the Vodacom Cup team,' Erasmus recalls.

He returned for one last playing stint before retirement at the end of 2004. But had he done enough to be entrusted with the full-time job for the 2005 Currie Cup?

It was also in 2004 that Jacques Nienaber and Erasmus first started working together in a coaching capacity. Nienaber had served as the physiotherapist to the Free State Cheetahs and the Cats throughout Erasmus's years at the union but then made the move into coaching, and began operating as the Cheetahs' strength and conditioning guru. It was the beginning of one of rugby's great coaching partnerships, and the two would work closely together for the next 15 years.

In 2005, Erasmus's first season as head coach of the Cheetahs, expectations were measured. Free State had not won the Currie Cup in 28 years. The new man in charge, while an undeniably gifted Springbok, was just 32 years old and untested at this level of high-performance coaching. In Kleynhans's final season as coach, in 2004, the Cheetahs had finished agonisingly close but had fallen short at the final hurdle.

However, 2005 would be their year, as Erasmus hit the ground running in stunning fashion. It wasn't long before he became known for his 'sign-coaching' method, and those who follow rugby closely will remember him perched at the top of the grandstand at the Free State Stadium, using colour-coded signs to get instructions to his players on the field.

'The benefit of Bloemfontein is that it's a city, but it's small,' says Erasmus. 'You know what every single player is doing every night, because there are not ten nightclubs and there is only one golf course and one shopping mall. Players couldn't go off the rails there.

'When you selected a squad there, you could very quickly work out the guys who weren't there for the team. You would sign a great player and within a month you would see that this guy is just not productive and into it. The whole team's mission was to win the Currie Cup and we signed guys for that.'

It was a stellar year for Free State rugby, with the Cheetahs winning all six of their qualifying matches to finish top of their section and enter the Premier Division. Things got tougher after that, with Erasmus's men losing four times during the regular season, but they comfortably secured a place in the semi-finals and a trip away to Western Province.

It would become one of the golden weeks in Free State rugby history as a tactical masterclass from Erasmus saw the Cheetahs edge WP 16–11 in the Newlands rain, and then, a week later, beat the Springbok-laden Blue Bulls 29–25 at Loftus to give Free State their first Currie Cup title in 29 years. Erasmus, in just his first year of coaching, and younger than some of the players on the field, had taken a significant step towards proving that the hype surrounding his perceived tactical intellect was justified.

'The 2005 final at Loftus was really amazing. We were the underdogs playing against a squad with 13 or 14 Springboks,' remembers Drotske, who captained the Cheetahs that year. The Bulls boasted the likes of Morne Steyn, Bryan Habana, Fourie du Preez, Pedrie Wannenburg, Victor Matfield, Bakkies Botha, Gary Botha and skipper Anton Leonard in their starting lineup that day.

'In the week before the final we watched that clip from the movie *Any Given Sunday* about a thousand times,' continues Drotske. In that 1999 sports flick, Al Pacino plays the role of Tony D'Amato, coach of the fictional NFL team the Miami Sharks. In the minutes leading up to their 'Currie Cup final', Pacino delivers a motivational speech that amplifies the importance of fighting for every inch in the pursuit of victory. Erasmus's pre-game talk ahead of the 2019 World Cup final, in which he put pressure into perspective, would be much more memorable, but even in his earliest days as a coach he was finding ways to motivate his players.

'On days off, instead of playing golf, he would enjoy it more to sit and analyse rugby games. It's his passion and that's what he enjoys,' Drotske adds.

In 2006, having finished top of the Currie Cup standings but level on points with the Blue Bulls, Erasmus's Cheetahs would go the distance once more, this time sharing the trophy with the Pretoria union after an epic 28–28 draw after extra time in Bloemfontein in what is still remembered as one of the great Currie Cup finals. It would be Erasmus's last year coaching the Cheetahs in the world's oldest domestic rugby tournament, though he did stay on as the franchise's Super Rugby coach until the end of the 2007 season. Two Currie Cup titles in two years was how Erasmus started his full-time coaching career.

Erasmus then jumped into a fresh challenge, moving on from his beloved Cheetahs to join Western Province and the Stormers, replacing outgoing director of rugby Nick Mallett while also taking on a role with SA Rugby as a technical advisor. Erasmus's hand in the Springboks' 2007 World Cup victory in France will always be underrated given that he was no longer part of the setup by the time the tournament actually took place, but with a blank canvas at Newlands, he had a new challenge following his instant success in Bloemfontein.

Harold Verster acknowledges that while he was sad to see Erasmus go, they could not stand in his way. There was an understanding that this was the next chapter in his coaching career. 'It was difficult, but the offer that he received was so far out of our reach,' Verster recalls.

Erasmus had given Drotske his blessing as his replacement, and the Cheetahs gave their head coach job to the former Bok hooker, who would also find success at the union.

The expectation in Cape Town was different given WP's status as one of the country's powerhouse unions. So Erasmus set about his work, helped by Nienaber, who had joined him in the move. Erasmus's track record at the Cheetahs, as both player and coach, had been all the evidence WP needed to approach him. Rob Wagner, CEO of the union at the time, remembers how impressed the board was with Erasmus. They had identified their man and made their move.

'The appointment was based very much on him as a player who punched above his weight, and one of the reasons why he could do that was his analysis of the opposition,' Wagner says. 'At the Cheetahs he proved to be extremely innovative and his understanding of the rules of the game was second to none. He found ways and means of interpreting rules, not where he would cheat, but where he would do things that the rules had not covered.'

At the time, Wagner and the WP top brass did not know much about Nienaber, but they quickly understood that his accompanying Erasmus was non-negotiable: 'Rassie's assessment of people in rugby playing positions was so accurate and it was just automatically accepted that Jacques Nienaber would come with him. The Stormers defence became watertight.'

Nienaber was developing all the time, and under Erasmus he went from being a physiotherapist to a strength and conditioning coach at the Cheetahs to a defensive specialist at the Stormers. He is still considered key to laying the foundations for the Stormers' success during his time there.

Erasmus's contracting of players at the Cheetahs was another attribute that Wagner and the WP leadership noticed. 'He contracted a lot of good players who hadn't been signed by any of the big four – the Sharks, Stormers, Lions or Bulls. There he really proved himself to be a good coach because he took these "second string" players and made them an incredible, unified team that started to believe in themselves,' says Wagner. 'He proved himself to be a master tactician because they were always playing against a more fancied team in semi-finals and finals, but they were winning those matches.'

Erasmus joined the Stormers in a dual role as director of rugby and head coach, and he provided immediate stability in 2008 by guiding the franchise to a fifth-place Super Rugby finish, narrowly missing out on a semi-final place on points difference to the Hurricanes. It was still a marked improvement for the Cape franchise after finishing tenth the year before.

In 2009, Erasmus then sparked a structural change that saw Allister Coetzee given the Super Rugby head coach position at the Stormers from 2010. Coetzee and Erasmus, somewhat ironically given what would transpire between 2016 and 2019, proved a formidable team, and together they gave the Stormers their most successful period in Super Rugby. Coetzee had been involved at WP since 2008 in various coaching capacities, and this was another way Erasmus empowered those around him.

2010 was an important year for the franchise as the Stormers lost the Super Rugby final to the Bulls in Soweto on one of the iconic days in South Africa's history in the tournament. The next year, the

Stormers were losing semi-finalists in Super Rugby. Coetzee also guided WP to five Currie Cup finals between 2010 and 2015, winning the title in 2012 and 2014 after Erasmus had left the union.

'Allister gets a tough time,' says Rob Wagner, 'but if you look at his record as Super Rugby coach, it is probably one of the best records of all the Super Rugby coaches over the years. He was a very good coach, backed by a very good director of rugby.'

While Erasmus gave Coetzee the freedom to operate in his coaching role, he was busy behind the scenes and particularly in the contracting of players like Duane Vermeulen, Bryan Habana and Jaque Fourie. Every player signed, Wagner recalls, formed a crucial part of Erasmus's desired game plan.

When Erasmus moved on from the Stormers in 2012 to take on the role of GM: High Performance Teams at SA Rugby, Wagner, like Verster before him, knew that there was little he could do. It was the next step in the evolution of a coach who was enriching his rugby knowledge by gaining the necessary experience. Erasmus had served as a technical analyst for Peter de Villiers at the 2011 World Cup in New Zealand, during which the Boks were knocked out in controversial fashion after Bryce Lawrence's poor refereeing helped Australia to an 11–9 quarter-final win.

Looking back, Wagner is convinced that Erasmus is one of the most academic rugby brains he has ever worked with. 'He's a lad who went to Despatch, not a big rugby-playing school, and yet his rugby intelligence came to the surface and allowed him to walk on the stage at the highest level and leave with a World Cup medal. It's a remarkable story,' Wagner says. 'He has an ability to identify people, bring them through and allow them to blossom.

'He is meticulous in his planning, and if he gets four hours' sleep a night, it must be a lot. He's like a guy driving a motorcar who sees a bicycle coming out of a side street 200 metres ahead and he works it all out. He's a remarkable rugby academic. It doesn't just fall into his lap; it is hard work.'

While Erasmus's new role saw him actively involved in SA Rugby structures, working closely with head coach Heyneke Meyer until the 2015 World Cup, Nienaber stayed behind at the Stormers as Coetzee's defence coach until 2014. The pair remained close throughout that period, with Erasmus regularly roping Nienaber in to assist with the national sides.

Their next major move came after the 2015 World Cup when, in 2016, Erasmus accepted the director of rugby role at Irish PRO12 (now PRO14) side Munster and took Nienaber with him. An overseas stint was always on the cards for Erasmus in his never-ending efforts to expand his rugby mind, and this next chapter would expose him to a different rugby culture and a new style of play.

Less than four months into his role as director at Munster, the franchise's 42-year-old head coach Anthony Foley died tragically in his sleep at the team hotel ahead of their opening 2016–2017 Champions Cup clash against Racing 92 in Paris. Everyone at the club was stunned, and in the immediate aftermath Erasmus was asked to take on the head coach responsibilities for the remainder of the season. Under Erasmus, Munster finished as PRO12 runners-up, losing the final 46–22 to Welsh side Scarlets. In the semi-final of the Champions Cup, they went down 26–10 to Saracens. There may not have been silverware, but Erasmus's efforts that season were enough to see him named PRO12 2016–2017 Coach of the Season as his star continued to rise.

Erasmus had signed a three-year deal with Munster, but the Springbok job was one he could not turn down. As 2017 wore on, the noise surrounding his appointment grew louder until it was deafening. Erasmus stayed with Munster until the end of 2017, handing over to Coetzee's assistant coach, Johann van Graan. And then, just like that, he and Nienaber were on their way home to take on a job more daunting than any that had come before.

By the time Erasmus returned to South Africa, he had carved out a reputation for himself as one of the best tacticians in world rugby, at the age of just 45. His ability was never once in question and it was accepted that, with time, he could turn the fortunes of the Springboks around. He had done it at Free State and the Stormers, and at Munster he was well on his way.

Time, however, was not something that Erasmus had when he put pen to paper with the Springboks. The World Cup was just 18 months away.

Chapter 4
Rolling up the sleeves

There was little time to spare when Rassie Erasmus returned home looking to turn the fortunes of the Springboks around. As a result of their poor world ranking, the Boks were not among the top seeds at the 2019 World Cup draw, held in Kyoto on 23 May 2017. As a result, they were pooled alongside defending champions New Zealand and would take on the All Blacks in Yokohama on 21 September 2019 in their tournament opener. Based on everything that had been seen over the last two years, they stood little chance in their current shape.

With Erasmus, not for the first time in his career, doubling up as both director of rugby and head coach, the first assignment was to assemble a management team. Jacques Nienaber, as expected, returned as Erasmus's right-hand man, while Welshman Aled Walters joined from Munster as the strength and conditioning coach. Walters had made a strong impression on Erasmus and Nienaber during their season together in Ireland, and he did not hesitate when asked by Erasmus to come and join the Bok revival.

There was also a return to the fray for Mzwandile Stick as assistant coach. This was the most eyebrow-raising of Erasmus's appointments given what Stick had endured under Coetzee. In many circles, Stick had been scapegoated for the Boks' poor performances in 2016 and it had cost him his job with the national side in 2017. Coetzee had not appointed Stick to his management team – that was an SA Rugby appointment – and after that woeful first year, the coach had enforced changes by relegating the former Springbok Sevens star to the youth structures and bringing in Franco Smith as his replacement.

It had been a difficult period for Stick, but Erasmus had often spoken about how highly he rated the young coach. In January 2018, he approached Stick about the prospect of rejoining the national setup. Stick had spent 2017 with the SA Under-20s, a side that included the likes of Damian Willemse, Curwin Bosch and Embrose Papier. A man who has always been confident in his own coaching ability, Stick acknowledges that it hurt being blamed for the Boks' failings in 2016, but he always kept the faith that he would be given another crack at the highest level.

'I wasn't happy with how it happened. Rugby is a team sport and when things didn't go very well, it looked like I was the scapegoat. It looked bad for me,' he says. 'I've never doubted myself, but the biggest thing is that somebody needs to give you that responsibility.

'As an assistant coach, you need to be clear on your roles and responsibilities so that you can be accountable in everything that you do. That is something Rassie did very well with me. He explained my roles clearly and I understood where I stood. In 2016 I felt like nothing was clear in terms of my role in the team.'

After accepting Erasmus's offer, Stick had to relocate from Port Elizabeth to Cape Town because Erasmus wanted the nucleus of his coaching staff to be together as he got to work: 'I moved and started working with Rassie and Jacques and I enjoyed it straight away, especially with people who respect your voice and the input you give. That's something I admire about them.'

As the months unfolded, Stick's value to the players and the management team under Erasmus would become clear. In addition to facilitating productive relationships with players, Stick was considered crucial to the aerial work the Springboks did up to and during the World Cup, while he was also heavily involved in the work the players did off the ball, particularly in their breakdown positioning. He went from being a Springbok outcast to a World Cup winner in 18 months, an evolution that was down to Erasmus's ability to identify potential and then nurture it.

The other somewhat complex appointment came in the form of scrum coach Pieter de Villiers, who had worked under Heyneke Meyer at the 2015 World Cup. De Villiers was still employed by SA Rugby and had been working in the High Performance structures, but his elevation to the Springbok side was complicated by the fact that the existing forwards coach, Matt Proudfoot, was still under contract at SA Rugby, having operated in the two years under Coetzee. Proudfoot and Erasmus also went back a long way together, with the former having joined the Stormers when Erasmus was in charge there. Less than two weeks after announcing his initial coaching team, Erasmus confirmed that De Villiers would be standing down from the role of Springbok forwards coach because of family commitments while Proudfoot was reintroduced.

Also around this time, Mark Alexander was re-elected as SA Rugby president for a second term. One of his first major contributions was to announce that the 30-cap rule on overseas-based players would be scrapped and that Erasmus could pick whomever he wanted. This opened the door to a range of players who were plying their trade abroad, though Erasmus was still selective about who he contacted to be a part of his setup. Getting the SA Rugby executive on board to change the policy on overseas-based players was a major part of Erasmus's initial presentation to the organisation, and once he had the buy-in from his bosses, he wasted little time in acting. Erasmus knew that he needed to build squad depth and have sufficient experience in the setup to launch a challenge in 2019, and this would guide him in his use of overseas players.

While the scrapping of the rule was an obvious help in World Cup preparation, it was also the beginning of a new SA Rugby contracting model. Erasmus would go on to facilitate a structure in which players based overseas would be paid by their clubs and not by SA Rugby. They would still earn match fees when playing for the Springboks, but SA Rugby no longer had to pay salaries to overseas-based players. It was a cost-cutting measure that ultimately benefited South African rugby when the coronavirus pandemic hit in 2020 and pay cuts ripped through the global game.

Erasmus got straight down to work, and he hosted three separate alignment camps for the country's Super Rugby franchises – the Stormers and Lions camp was conducted jointly – within the space of three weeks. Alignment would become a common feature of the Erasmus era, and one of his key strengths, players would later reveal, was his ability to have everybody on the same page. As the months progressed, it became clear that Erasmus wanted to be transparent with his players and staff. From the very beginning, everyone knew where they stood in the broader plan.

When match-day squads were announced, Erasmus would name the teams with the whole extended squad present, working through the names on a whiteboard and explaining why each player had been picked and why those on the bench had been left out. It created accountability – for him and the players – while it also ensured that there were no private selection chats that could potentially cause division in the ranks.

First and foremost, Erasmus prioritised restoring pride in the national jersey.

'I really believe we have the players and the rugby intellectual property to turn things around and mount a serious challenge at the

2019 Rugby World Cup,' he said straight after his appointment. 'We have 18 Tests and just under 600 days until Japan 2019 and a lot of planning has already gone into our Rugby World Cup preparations.'

As he began to shape the minds of the players in camp, trying to get them to buy in to his ideas of what it meant to be a Springbok, Erasmus identified three areas he believed were fundamental to Springbok success: results, transformation and public perception.

There had been an obvious dip in the results department under Coetzee, and Erasmus knew that fixing the scoreboard would be the first step on the road to redemption. He worried that, in recent seasons, the Springbok players had become concerned – and perhaps overly so in some cases – with public perception more than with results and performance.

At one of the alignment camps, Erasmus, who was seemingly always armed with a laptop and digital projector, showed the players two photographs. One was of the All Blacks performing their famous haka, and the other was of the Springboks lined up singing 'Nkosi Sikelel' iAfrika' before a Test. He asked the players to identify the difference between the two photographs. It wasn't racial diversity, nor was it size, nor facial expression nor level of commitment. Instead, Erasmus wanted his squad to notice the boots the players were wearing.

In the photograph of the All Blacks, every player was wearing black boots. In the Bok photo, the footwear provided a rainbow of colour, from pink to green to orange and black and white. It was a small example, but Erasmus used it to highlight what he perceived to be a lack of unity among the Springboks and, more importantly, too much emphasis on public perception.

Results, he stressed, had to be at the top of the list of priorities for the Springboks. Not public image. Results above all else. Erasmus challenged his players on their use of social media, asking what the purpose of it all was. He used one example of a player who had trained on Christmas Day and then posted images of his session on social media. What was the primary aim of the social media post? Hard work needed to be done with the aim of achieving the desired results, not to give off the perception of hard work. It was a fundamental mindset shift that Erasmus set about embedding in the Springboks from early on. Out of this was born the Boks' mantra: 'Let the main thing be the main thing.'

It was a simple line, one that Siya Kolisi would repeat many times during and after the World Cup to explain his side's mental state in Japan, but it carried a meaningful message to the players. The Boks needed to prioritise performance over all else, and they would hold each other accountable if they started slipping in making the 'main thing the main thing'. Everything else, Erasmus stressed, from public appearance to the Boks' being a beacon of light to South Africans, could only be achieved if they prioritised what they did together on the field. They could not inspire if they were not winning.

At those first alignment camps, Erasmus also emphasised the importance of conditioning. He challenged the would-be Boks to take ownership of their own preparation and performances, both on the field and off, and to get their heads to a place where they were prepared to put in the work, selflessly and without ego, that was needed to go the distance in Japan.

'The big working block he put in place was the identity of the team and what he wanted it to stand for. He hated entitled players and he said the only way to stop entitlement was for a player to take ownership of his career,' Matt Proudfoot remembers of those early camps. 'A cornerstone of that was his conditioning standards. The South African player wasn't conditioned to the level of the game he wanted to play, and he needed players to understand that.'

Erasmus was also quick to tackle the issue of transformation, and his plan from the onset, as with team selection, was to lay his cards on the table. Transformation was an area where many Bok coaches before him, none more so than Heyneke Meyer, had felt heat from both the South African public and the government. While there were many players of colour who had succeeded in national colours over the years, and some who had become greats, no Springbok coach had managed to field a World Cup side that was even close to demographically representative of the country.

Erasmus believed that, in previous regimes, very little had been said about transformation from within the team environment despite its being a massive talking point in the public space. This was something he sought to change, and he facilitated open, frank discussions on the need for the Boks to transform and how that could be achieved. His policy also ensured that no player of colour would ever feel he was being picked for any reason other than his ability, and if there were any players who had issues with their own involvement, there was now a forum where they could air those views in front of management and all their peers.

Erasmus would provide opportunities to everybody equally, but if a player did not have the right attitude then he would not play for the Boks, regardless of his race. Because he would discuss, in front of the whole squad, the strengths and weaknesses of the players he was selecting, and because he discouraged one-on-one conversations, there were never any question marks over the players he selected. 'Everybody got an opportunity and he was clear that by winning games we would change the perception around transformation. The best players played,' Elton Jantjies recalls.

With these frameworks in place, Erasmus began preparing for his first Test in charge – a unique trip to Washington, DC, for a one-off Test against Wales in June 2018.

In April it was announced that Lions head coach Swys de Bruin would join the side as an attacking consultant ahead of their trip to America. It was a partnership that would end up lasting 16 Test matches.

It was also around this time that questions over the captaincy began to arise. Erasmus had to be strategic with his squad selection for the Wales Test, with a three-match series against England starting the following weekend, and it led to his fielding something of a B-team in Washington. The looming encounter with Eddie Jones' touring side would be the new South African leadership's first real test and there was no obvious captaincy choice.

Warren Whiteley was considered one of the favourites for the role, with Erasmus acknowledging the Lions man as a 'strong contender' despite his still being sidelined by injury. Siya Kolisi was another option, having had a superb 2017 in Springbok colours, but his Super Rugby form in 2018 had dipped and he was no guarantee to start the first Test against England in Johannesburg.

Eben Etzebeth, meanwhile, was also battling injury, while Duane Vermeulen's chances, despite his being a popular public option, were seen as limited because he was based overseas (at French club Toulon). Flyhalf Handre Pollard was the other name coming up in that conversation.

Jake White suggested, in a column for All Out Rugby, that Erasmus should look to pick a side for Wales with 'a special emphasis on those that count towards transformation targets'. Erasmus acknowledged from the very beginning of his tenure that meeting a target of 45 per cent players of colour in all match-day squads was his mandate for 2018 and was specified in his contract. Knowing the numbers, Erasmus argued, was a positive because it meant that he, his players and staff knew where they stood. It quickly became apparent, however, that Erasmus would not be handing out caps that had not been earned in order to reach those numbers. Erasmus knew that there was enough talent in the country for the Springboks to be both highly competitive and transformed at the same time. The two goals were not mutually exclusive, and this was the message he delivered to his players.

As plans for the Wales Test and the England series continued, Erasmus was also facing an injury crisis with several high-profile players unavailable. Whiteley was eventually ruled out, while Etzebeth was in a race against time to be fit. Erasmus was also without star hooker Malcolm Marx, lock Lood de Jager and prop Lizo Gqoboka, as well as Jaco Kriel and Coenie Oosthuizen.

The coach named an unusually large squad of 43 for the four Tests, including 17 uncapped players, because of the travel demands of playing in America. It was an overwhelming statement that this was a clean slate and the beginning of a new direction for South African rugby. Among the potential debutants were RG Snyman, Thomas du Toit, Sbu Nkosi, Makazole Mapimpi and Aphiwe Dyantyi. All of those players, with the exception of Dyantyi – who was a shoo-in before his doping scandal in 2019 – would travel to Japan for the World Cup. Vermeulen, Willie le Roux, Frans Steyn, Faf de Klerk and Bismarck du Plessis were the overseas players picked.

The next announcement would make waves not only in South Africa but also around the world as Erasmus confirmed that Kolisi would be his captain for the three Tests against England. Pieter-Steph du Toit would lead a 26-man squad on their travels to Washington against Wales. In giving Kolisi the captaincy for the England series, Erasmus rocked the South African rugby community. The pair went back a long way, and Kolisi would later reveal that it was Erasmus who handed him his first professional contract at the Stormers back in 2010. Still, it was a decision that took many off-guard given Kolisi's lack of form in Super Rugby that year.

The social significance of South Africa's fielding its first black rugby captain was clear, and the decision was largely celebrated. Naturally, some cynics took the view that Erasmus was looking to score points of political correctness with his employers, the government and the public. Erasmus would later acknowledge that he was perhaps naive in making the appointment, saying that he had not expected such an intense reaction. For Erasmus, Kolisi was not a black captain but rather a rugby leader who earned the respect of the players on the field.

'I wouldn't like to look at it that way,' Erasmus said when asked about the significance of choosing the Boks' first black Test captain, adding that Kolisi had been a 'great leader' at the Stormers. 'I like him because he is humble, he is quiet, and the way he is playing at the moment is not flashy.'

Erasmus picked a total of 20 players of colour in his first 43-man squad. When pressed on his decision, he was quick to scotch suggestions that he was picking players to reach quotas. Looking back, flyhalf Elton Jantjies says, 'I don't know if it was genius or a miracle, but we actually had 20-odd players of colour that were representing the country and a black leader taking us to the World Cup.

'It had nothing to do with colour, it was just about what you put into the group. He got it right and I don't know what his secret was. If you were on form and would work hard, you would be in the squad, and we all knew that.'

Appointing Kolisi as captain may have been a simple rugby decision for Erasmus, but it would change the course of South African rugby forever. At the time, ahead of the series opener against England at Ellis Park on 9 June, it was perhaps too early to see this for the landmark moment that it was. By the time Kolisi was done, when he lifted the Webb Ellis Cup in Yokohama, he had changed the face of what had historically been considered a white man's game. It would become one of the most magical journeys South African sport has ever seen, and it started with a coach providing an equal opportunity without seeing colour as a factor.

A home series against an England side widely considered to be the biggest threat to the All Blacks' supremacy would be a baptism of fire for Kolisi. But he could not get pulled too far into his captaincy appointment and what it all meant. He, like every other Bok in the squad, needed to pull his weight on the field and earn his place. Erasmus and the Boks had to make it about the 'main thing', with the one-off clash against Wales an opportunity for South African rugby to take the first steps towards becoming a force in the global game once more.

That didn't happen.

It was a poor display in Washington from an inexperienced South African side, from which just two players – Du Toit and Mapimpi – would start the 2019 World Cup final. The Boks, all too familiarly, were dreadful on attack as they slumped to a 22–20 defeat in the wet. The scoreline, if anything, understated their poor play. Replacement flyhalf Robert du Preez, on debut, had two kicks charged down within the space of seconds towards the end of the contest to allow Welsh hooker Ryan Elias in for the match-winning try.

It was far from the inspirational start Erasmus was looking for. While he made no excuses in acknowledging the loss, the coach highlighted the positives of having blooded several new Springboks with an eye to the future. Few read much if anything into the result, and the England series was seen as the real litmus test. The point of the Wales fixture was for SA Rugby to receive a much-needed injection of funds, and the rugby dished up that day suggested as much. The result saw the Boks slide back down to number seven in the world rankings.

When the Boks returned home, it was clear that Erasmus was going to make wholesale changes to his side for the first Test against

England. Jones, meanwhile, opted to base the England squad in the humidity and heat of Durban for the duration of the series, with his side flying to Johannesburg, Bloemfontein and Cape Town on the day before each game. It was a tactical decision that took Erasmus by surprise.

When Erasmus named his side for the first Test in Johannesburg, all of the pre-game talk centred on Kolisi, but there was also the possibility that the Boks would field an all-black front row for the first time in their history, with Tendai Mtawarira, Bongi Mbonambi and Trevor Nyakane set to start. Nyakane, though, would withdraw just before kick-off with injury.

It was a very different-looking side from the one that had lost in Washington, but it was equally fresh. Nkosi, Dyantyi and Snyman were all handed Test debuts in the starting lineup. There were also starts for Willie le Roux, a returning Faf de Klerk, Handre Pollard and Duane Vermeulen. This was the spine of the Bok team against England that day, as it would prove to be in the months that followed and all the way up to the 2019 World Cup final. Erasmus had put together a side that, on paper, was both exciting and experienced.

From a transformation point of view, Erasmus included 11 players of colour in his match-day 23 for Ellis Park, and this also became a talking point in the build-up. While Kolisi was being celebrated by a huge section of the South African public, Erasmus was asked again before the first Test if it was difficult picking sides with quotas and transformation targets in mind. It was a line of questioning he had to get used to quickly, but because of the open-cards policy he had implemented in the change room and on the training ground, Erasmus could address the media in the same way he would his players. There were not different conversations happening in front of the cameras and behind closed doors, and his honesty and accountability were appreciated by the players – black and white.

'It was really not difficult. We have been following these players in Super Rugby closely and were in contact with them and their coaches,' Erasmus said. 'There was a lot we worked on with winning, building squad depth and transformation in mind. It wasn't something that we had to sort out last week; we've been doing this for the past four or five months. I'm very comfortable with the way we had to select the team.'

Regardless of the result, this would be a historic day for South Africa. Siya Kolisi, the young man from Zwide in the Eastern Cape, had been entrusted with leading his country. It may not have been that visible in the public space or on social media, but around braais and televisions, in pubs and at home, there was doubt over the decision. Many people were adamant that the colour of his skin and the opportunity to score political points had played a key role in landing Kolisi the captaincy. His peers, though, felt very differently, and their approval was all Kolisi needed as he embarked on an incredible journey.

It took Kolisi a while to get used to the responsibility. He certainly wasn't a polished product by the time the England series began, and Erasmus would later acknowledge that the Bok captaincy had at first negatively impacted on his form.

'He's a great choice. He's a good leader and I think a lot of guys look up to him,' were the words of Duane Vermeulen, one of the biggest characters in the Springbok dressing room and himself a candidate for the captaincy in the days leading up to the England series. 'I've got a lot of respect for him, on and off the field. He's a really great guy and a guy that can inspire this group of people.'

It was high praise from a man whom many considered to be Erasmus's strongest weapon and the natural leader of the pack. While it confirmed that Kolisi had the backing of his team-mates, it would do nothing to help the Springboks beat England on the field of play. Results and performance, after all, had to be the 'main thing', and Kolisi's captaincy would only truly inspire the nation if the Boks found a way to beat England. For a side that had reached new lows – and not long ago – it was the tallest of orders. Still, those initial steps needed to be taken, and they were in quite spectacular fashion on 9 June 2018, the day the Rassie Erasmus era of South African rugby provided its first glimpse of what could be achieved through unity.

Chapter 5
Kolisi

There was a palpable feeling of renewal by the time the 2018 inbound series against England got under way at Ellis Park on 9 June. Absolutely nothing had yet been achieved in the way of results, but Erasmus's squad selections and his decision to appoint Siya Kolisi as captain were refreshing and emphatically confirmed the dawning of a new era. Kolisi's appointment, at this stage, was for the England series only and Erasmus would re-evaluate the captaincy afterwards. Kolisi had led at Super Rugby level and had always been a popular figure in the dressing room, but he could not have been prepared for this trip into uncharted waters. At his first pre-match media briefing, Kolisi carried himself with a level-headedness and composure that would become familiar features of his leadership in the months to come.

He told the three Bok debutants – Aphiwe Dyantyi, Sbu Nkosi and RG Snyman – to trust in the fact that they had been picked for the Springboks because there was something special about them. He told them to enjoy themselves and savour the moment, recalling his own nerves during his Test debut – against Scotland in Nelspruit in 2013 – to reassure them that such feelings were natural.

In those early days of his captaincy, Kolisi realised that questions over the significance of being the Springboks' first black captain were likely to arise. In the months to come, it would become a line of questioning that Kolisi would have to tackle in every country the Boks visited, right up to the end of the World Cup in Japan. He never once backed down from what he considered a massive responsibility and, as the journey progressed, he began to understand the importance of his appointment more and more. He always brought the conversation back to rugby, though. He knew, as Erasmus had drilled home, that the Boks could not achieve anything special unless they were a winning side. Given his own struggles with form in Super Rugby 2018, Kolisi was more determined than ever to let his performances on the field do the talking.

Erasmus did not anticipate, nor was he prepared for, the reaction to the appointment. While he understood its social significance, he had simply never viewed the Springbok captaincy as something that could make or break a side.

'I was offered the Springbok captaincy twice in my career and I said "no" twice,' Erasmus says.

'Nick Mallett came to me twice and I turned it down both times. He asked me why and I told him that a captain had to set the climate in the team. I liked analysing, but I also liked a dop [drink] and I liked fun. A captain is the guy who sets the climate and I didn't think that was me.'

In his early days as Free State coach in 2005, Erasmus had not immediately appointed a captain. 'It was because, to me, it shouldn't be such a big thing in a team if everybody takes ownership,' he says.

'The fact that Siya was black and was captain was a huge thing, but the captaincy itself for me was never an issue. Other people look at captains and say the whole team revolves around him, and I didn't see it like that. I think that's why I was maybe naive.'

The images of Kolisi, in his 29th Test match, leading the Boks out in front of over 55 000 people in Johannesburg would be replayed countless times in the weeks and months to come. Wearing the iconic number 6 jersey – the same number that Francois Pienaar and Nelson Mandela had donned, at the same venue, when they lifted the Webb Ellis Cup together in 1995 – Kolisi was greeted with a roar as he took to the lush Ellis Park turf. In that moment, South African rugby showed progress. It had taken a long, long time, but the outpouring of emotion on the day suggested that it might have been worth the wait.

Kolisi was calm on the surface, taking it all in his stride as the cameras zoomed in on him to capture a moment in history. It was a lot for any 26-year-old to internalise, let alone one who had grown up in such difficult circumstances.

Kolisi's story is now well known. He comes from the township of Zwide, just outside Port Elizabeth, and to refer to his childhood as challenging would be a gross understatement. Kolisi, like so many in South Africa, grew up sidelined from the opportunities and privileges that others in more fortunate positions take for granted. With his father away working and his young mother – she was 16 when he was born – often unable to deal with life's challenges, Kolisi and his siblings were raised by his grandmother. Life was extremely difficult for them. Kolisi would later reveal just how tough the environment was during his time at Emsengeni Primary School, with stories of often going to bed hungry and not having necessities like school shoes and clothes. Rugby, quite literally, saved Siya Kolisi's life.

After making a provincial Eastern Province side at Under-12 level, Kolisi played in a tournament in Mossel Bay, where his superb performance drew attention. He had already caught the eye of the scouts at Grey Junior School while representing his local club, African Bombers, in a fixture against one of the school teams a few months earlier. On the strength of his performance in Mossel Bay, Kolisi was given a full scholarship to Grey Junior. He entered the school in Grade 7 and naturally progressed into Grey High School.

'I think this was a massive benefit for him,' Dean Carelse, one of Kolisi's coaches at Grey High, revealed in an interview with Rayder Media, 'as he had to be street-smart and think his way around the field as opposed to physically dominating everyone. He read the game extremely well and always found himself at the right place at the right time. In my opinion, his biggest strength during these early days was his ability and willingness to make his teammates look better than himself on the field. He was always eager to pass and let others take the shine through his playmaking and distributing, which to this day is still a big characteristic of his play and character.'

Kolisi's grandmother had already passed away, and his mother died soon after he started high school. It was a turning point in Kolisi's life. While it was difficult moving away from his family in Zwide, the move to Grey would shape the future of a man who was destined for greatness. While many of his township friends were turning to alcohol and drugs, Kolisi knew that rugby was his way out. He earned provincial honours throughout high school, playing Craven Week for EP for two years in 2008 and 2009.

The story of how Kolisi overcame the odds to rise to the top of his sport is inspiring enough. But the way he grew in the captaincy role, between that first Test against England and the World Cup final against the same opposition nearly a year and a half later, is equally remarkable.

'That was a very special moment,' assistant coach Mzwandile Stick recalls of Kolisi leading the Boks out for the first time. 'To see the change in our rugby in South Africa, where we have always talked about the opportunities that we didn't get in the past. There was a black captain leading our national team. It was something that was so good to see and not because I am close to Siya, but because of what it meant to our country.'

As the Boks lined up to sing 'Nkosi Sikelel' iAfrika', the cameras zoomed in on Kolisi. When he threw his head back, eyes closed, to belt out the closing line, 'Let us live and strive for freedom in South Africa our land,' the Ellis Park crowd erupted. The Boks would go on to win the World Cup, but this was as significant a moment as any in Springbok history.

Kolisi and the Boks, full of energy and emotion, then came crashing back down to earth as England raced to a 24–3 lead inside the opening 20 minutes. On the ropes and facing potentially another embarrassing result, Kolisi and the Boks gathered under their posts and had to find something from somewhere. Still quite reserved in those formative stages of his captaincy, Kolisi leaned on those around him, such as Duane Vermeulen, and senior players such as fullback Willie le Roux. They knew that they were better than the scoreline, and, more importantly, they knew that the South African public deserved better.

During that lull, a hush fell over Ellis Park, but there was one section of the crowd that was beginning to find its collective voice. At that point, few in South Africa knew of the Gwijo Squad, a group of Johannesburg-based fans who had started out supporting Varsity Cup matches. In the months to come, these passionate, mostly black rugby fans would take on a cultural significance previously unseen in South African rugby. They followed Kolisi and the Boks around the country, singing songs of celebration for what was a new dawn in the sport.

There were only 80 members of the Gwijo Squad present at Ellis Park that day, but they were loud enough to make themselves heard.

What followed was a comeback of astonishing proportions as the Boks ran in four tries in 19 minutes to go into half-time 29–27 ahead and eventually win the match 42–39. Sbu Nkosi, with two tries, was electric on the day, his raw pace and physicality shining through, while Faf de Klerk sparked everything from number 9. Dyantyi was another try scorer, and the combination of the Bok newbies with the experience of the overseas-based players gave South Africa a performance worth celebrating. It was the perfect start to Kolisi's captaincy. After the match, the skipper was praised for not panicking when things had looked bleak.

When the match ended, Kolisi conducted his pitch-side interview before running across the turf to celebrate with a group that was giving voice to a different sector of the rugby-loving public.

'We had accepted that these were environments that had become notorious for us not being welcomed in as black rugby supporters, and we had braced ourselves for a backlash,' Chulumanco Macingwane, founder and chairperson of the Gwijo Squad, remembers about that day. 'It was quite the opposite. There was quite a visible FOMO [fear of missing out] from other supporters, especially the white supporters, who felt the energy and wanted to be a part of it.'

Erasmus then called up 37-year-old hooker Schalk Brits, adding him to the setup ahead of the second Test against England. It was a surprising development given that Brits, who had last represented the Boks at the 2015 World Cup, had fully retired from all rugby following a ten-year career with English giants Saracens. With first-choice hooker Malcolm Marx still injured and Bismarck du Plessis also ruled out of the series through injury, Erasmus thought that including a player of Brits's experience and pedigree would be beneficial to the younger, less travelled players in the squad. When he received his call-up, Brits and his wife, Colinda, were quite literally sipping mojitos while on holiday in Ibiza to celebrate the end of his career.

'I first thought it was a joke from Vincent Koch, sending a few text messages around pretending I was the hottest new thing at the age of 37,' Brits remembers. 'After three or four text messages to Vincent, he came back and said, "No buddy, it isn't me." I came to the realisation that I was actually talking to Rassie.'

The initial decision was to include Brits for the last two Tests of the series given his decade-long experience in England. As it turned out, he would be a crucial part of the plans for the 2019 World Cup, and came out of retirement to play the 2019 Super Rugby season with the Bulls. The alignment that Erasmus had instilled among the Springboks meant that Brits had the same opportunities as every other player to push for a place in the squad.

While all the hype had centred around Kolisi ahead of the first Test, attention turned swiftly to Tendai Mtawarira for the second Test, in Bloemfontein, where he was set to earn his 100th Test cap for the Springboks. Few had experienced the effect of political interference in sport like the always smiling loosehead prop, who had been temporarily declared unavailable for the Boks by the national government in June 2010 because of his Zimbabwean nationality. That matter was cleared up quickly and Beast was back in green and gold soon enough, but it was another glaring example of the divisions that kept plaguing sport and society in South Africa. On this day, however, South Africa rose to applaud one of the greats of the game. Even President Cyril Ramaphosa, Mtawarira would later reveal, gave him a call on the eve of what would be a historic day for a man regarded as one of the most popular Springboks of all time. In an interview with the British & Irish Lions' official website in 2020, Mtawarira revealed how he had come close to signing a lucrative deal with French club Racing 92 in 2018 after the Boks' two woeful years. It was Erasmus who convinced him to stay.

The match fell on 16 June – Youth Day in South Africa and Kolisi's 27th birthday. The stars aligned for the Boks in the form of a commanding, clinical 23–12 win that wrapped up the series. Once again the Boks had trailed, going down 12–0 at one point, but they found the right gear when they needed it most. Fittingly for Mtawarira's milestone match, it was the Bok forwards who solidified their dominance over the English, even scrumming their way to a crucial penalty try that put the game to bed. Duane Vermeulen was brilliant for the hosts on the day, scoring a try of his own in a familiar display of big carries, brutal defence and relentless work at the breakdown. Kolisi, meanwhile, credited the Bloemfontein crowd for their role in another Bok comeback. Just two Test wins into his captaincy, he had already started to look more comfortable on the field and during his press conferences.

With Kolisi as leader, a different culture was developing, both in the stands and on the streets. It was the first sign that the Springboks were moving away from the problematic stereotype that rugby in South Africa was a sport that belonged, primarily, to white men. That shift was reflected in the increasing diversity at the stadiums, in social media commentary from fans and, most importantly, on the field for the Springboks, where black players like Kolisi, Mtawarira, Nkosi and Dyantyi were thriving and being celebrated. There was a unity developing – on the field and off. The rise of isiXhosa commentary, with SuperSport's Kaunda Ntunja becoming one of the most recognisable voices in South African rugby, was probably a direct result of Kolisi's captaincy and another shining example of how, under Erasmus, the Boks were changing the face of the game.

Ntunja had been working on isiXhosa commentary at SuperSport since 2009 and had seen a spike in interest during the 2011 World Cup, though nothing like what he experienced in Japan in 2019. As black interest in the Springboks reached new heights, more fans began tuning in to Ntunja's sometimes comical and always passionate accounts of a Springbok team that was changing the game. Clips of Ntunja's commentary went viral on social media, from the time he first introduced Kolisi as captain at Ellis Park to his description of Makazole Mapimpi's 'champagne moment' after scoring in the World Cup final.

'There was always interest in Xhosa commentary,' Ntunja remembers, 'but there was much more after we had a black captain. The ball started rolling. There was also the Gwijo Squad and it was all intertwined. The whole spirit of togetherness started gelling from then.'

As so many Springboks would later say, one of Kolisi's major strengths as a captain is his willingness to be guided by those around him. It was a trait that remained consistent from his first day as skipper all the way to the World Cup final. There was never any ego at play, and because of that, he had buy-in from the whole team. Where some had suggested that the captaincy should be handed to Vermeulen, Kolisi showed that there was greater strength in collaboration.

'He's huge, not only in supporting me, but in the player he is on the field,' Kolisi said of Vermeulen after the Bloemfontein Test, revealing a leadership style that was inclusive from the very start. 'There are times when I honestly don't know what to say and that's where he comes in.'

Kolisi had quickly turned to senior players in the Springbok squad who had experience of leadership or who he thought had leadership qualities, and he included them in discussions and decision-making. He wasn't interested in being right, but instead wanted the Boks to collectively come up with the best possible ways of implementing their plans. That was always the priority, and while Kolisi would grow more confident as a leader as his journey progressed, he never lost that selflessness and understanding that there was strength in putting minds together to come up with solutions.

'It's a genuine strength of any leader to be so self-aware that you understand your limitations and your strengths,' Francois Louw explains. 'To be so open and transparent in seeking the best views together and then to execute the best collective idea is what he did and that's how he got the respect of the most influential, senior guys in the team. The rest ultimately followed.'

The talk of Kolisi being a political appointment in those early weeks may have been unwelcome and unproductive, but if you speak to any player who has ever shared the field with Kolisi, you will know immediately that he is a captain who commands respect for rugby reasons alone. 'The real sign of a leader is how you treat others when success comes and, for me, that is one of Siya's greatest gifts,' Schalk Brits adds.

Kolisi himself, though, was still more focused on his own performance than anything else. The results in the first two Tests, and a series win over one of the best teams in the world, were obviously crucial for his captaincy, but even more pleasing was the fact that he was finding some form. His performance in Johannesburg had been solid, but he was much improved in Bloemfontein, where he worked tirelessly, was busy at the breakdown and remained composed with the sometimes difficult French referee Romain Poite. The early signs were that Kolisi was handling the responsibility of the captaincy, but he was never alone.

'There were a lot of opinions on him from the media and supporters that he wasn't the right man for the job at the Stormers and then he wasn't the right man for the Springboks,' Elton Jantjies, Kolisi's team-mate when they played together at SA Schools, remembers. 'He got a lot of external pressure ... we all had that, but for Siya it was double. We helped take the load off and I think Rassie handled it very well. He said we'd give Siya as much support as possible and allow him to be the best captain and rugby player he could be.'

The international media could not get enough of Kolisi, but with every media conference and interview he grew stronger. He hadn't yet been given the captaincy on a full-time basis, but with the England series in the bag and the country more optimistic about Springbok rugby than they had been in a long time, it did seem like Erasmus was onto something.

The third Test, in Cape Town, was an opportunity for Erasmus to tinker with his lineup. Giving players opportunities was important to the coach, who could easily have backed a winning combination in search of a series whitewash. Instead, he saw the value in building squad depth, and Test minutes under the belt was a metric he and his coaching staff planned meticulously over the full 18-month period to the World Cup. There were several changes for Cape Town, which included Brits coming in on the bench while Jantjies was given a run at flyhalf. Warrick Gelant, Jesse Kriel and Andre Esterhuizen also came in, while there was a start for hooker Chiliboy Ralepelle. Erasmus had created a culture where the World Cup was the goal, and because of his honesty when it came to team selection, the players knew where they stood and were on board with the plan to rotate.

On a wet and rainy day that did little to facilitate an entertaining game, Jantjies endured something of a horror show at pivot as the Boks slumped to a 25–10 defeat in the Newlands mud. England were far better than the Boks in managing the conditions, and it was a performance that provided a dose of sobriety to talk that the Boks were on their way to becoming World Cup competitors. Kolisi had tasted his first defeat as national captain. While the overall tone following the series was still positive, this was a stark reminder of the work that remained to be done. Erasmus, while acknowledging after the match that the Boks had been 'terrible', insisted that the signs over the course of the series meant they could still challenge to win the World Cup.

One of the biggest issues for the Boks on the day was their discipline, and they were penalised 14 times by New Zealand referee Glen Jackson. The analysis of referees would become a vital component of the Erasmus era, particularly at the World Cup, and after the match he acknowledged that the Boks had been poor in that department. Kolisi, meanwhile, had no issues with the officiating and offered no excuses.

While it was undoubtedly a poor performance, the Boks had made real strides in their efforts to restore the faith of the public. A series win over England, even at home, was not something anyone could have banked on following the experience of 2016 and 2017, and Erasmus was widely praised for having turned the Boks around, despite having won two and lost two since taking charge.

The locally based players would all return to their Super Rugby franchises to complete the 2018 tournament, but for Erasmus and his management team the work would never stop. There was data to analyse, plans on player workload to implement, tactics to discuss and performances at Super Rugby level to monitor. Erasmus, Nienaber, Proudfoot and Stick would enjoy a close relationship with the franchise coaches, and they would be in regular contact while Swys de Bruin returned to the Lions to guide them to their third Super Rugby final in as many years.

The Boks continued to hold training camps as Super Rugby wound to a close, and it was here that the philosophy of how Erasmus wanted them to play was further embedded. The England series showed that the Boks were more than capable of playing an attractive brand of rugby, but that would not be the priority. Instead, a strong set piece, an impenetrable defence and an intelligent, accurate kicking game would ultimately prove to be successful when it mattered most – at the World Cup. Erasmus had the franchise coaches on board early, and they knew what he and the Boks were trying to achieve.

'The way Rassie wanted to approach the game was the way we had approached it for the last couple of years at Saracens, so we were sort of coming from the same place. He didn't want to come and just play beautiful rugby; he looked at what was going to give us the best probability of success,' Schalk Brits says.

Brits, meanwhile, had discussions with Erasmus over his future. It was eventually decided that he would come out of retirement for another year with the aim of helping the Boks prepare for Japan. Nothing was guaranteed, though, and Brits would have to earn his place in the squad. After a potential move to the Stormers fell apart at the final hurdle, Brits signed for the Bulls for the 2019 Super Rugby season.

'He already had a plan until the first World Cup game against New Zealand. For any coach to plan 18 months in advance, it hasn't happened before,' Brits remembers.

The next major test for Erasmus and the Boks would be the 2018 Rugby Championship – a tournament dominated by New Zealand in recent years and one the Boks had not won since 2009. Erasmus knew after the England series that his side was still some distance behind the All Blacks in terms of performance, but he remained convinced they could close the gap by the time of the World Cup. The 2018 Rugby Championship would be a significant stepping stone in that process.

While the decision to back Kolisi as captain for the Rugby Championship would eventually come nearer the tournament, it was one that Erasmus acknowledged to be easy. South African rugby, having only ever known one way when it came to captaincy and leadership, now had a captain who was shattering the mould. One of the great South African sports stories of our time was under way, and Springbok rugby would never be the same again.

Chapter 6

Tears of joy in Wellington

Many people believe that the start of the Springboks' glorious run to the World Cup final came on 15 September 2018. This was the day on which the Boks, desperate in every department from start to finish, found something from somewhere to secure a stunning 36–34 Rugby Championship win against the mighty All Blacks in Wellington. It was a victory that shocked the rugby world.

It was South Africa's first win in New Zealand since 2009 and the most points they had ever scored against the All Blacks away from home. More important, though, was the belief that the result instilled in the players and the South African public. From AB de Villiers to Chad le Clos and former Springbok coach Peter de Villiers to President Cyril Ramaphosa, South Africans took to social media to pay tribute to one of the great days of Bok rugby. It was another powerful look at what this side could achieve in its unity. Images of Pieter-Steph du Toit, heroic on the day, in tears at the final whistle told their own story of how much this meant to the players. Exactly a year earlier, almost to the day, the Springboks had endured one of their worst outings in history as they were smashed 57–0 in Albany. The performance in Wellington proved how far they had come under Rassie Erasmus and suggested, perhaps for the first time, that they would be real contenders in Japan.

Following the June series against England, there were just three rounds of Super Rugby 2018 fixtures left. The Lions, once again, were in the title mix. They would finish top of the South African Conference and, for the third time in as many years, make it all the way to the final, only to lose 37–18 to the Crusaders in Christchurch and finish as runners-up. It just wasn't meant to be for the Lions in Super Rugby, but they had led the way for South African sides in the competition in recent years and, under Johan Ackermann, had shown what could be achieved through continuity and a plan. Ackermann had transformed the Lions, taking them from being relegated – to accommodate the Southern Kings in 2013 – to one of the most dangerous attacking sides in the competition. Swys de Bruin took over as head coach at Ellis Park for the 2018 season, with Ackermann leaving for English side Gloucester. Despite losing a couple of key players, De Bruin kept the momentum going, with the Lions comfortably outperforming the other South African franchises. The fact that De Bruin was doubling up as the attack coach for the Springboks made perfect sense and helped with the alignment that Erasmus had prioritised from the beginning of his tenure.

The Sharks, meanwhile, sneaked into eighth place on the combined Super Rugby log before going down 40–10 to the Crusaders in their Christchurch quarter-final. The Stormers and Bulls endured poor campaigns and did not threaten the playoff places, finishing 11th and 12th, respectively. With the Stormers already out of the running by the time the tournament returned after the June break, eyebrows were then raised when coach Robbie Fleck picked Siya Kolisi for a trip to Buenos Aires to take on the Jaguares immediately after the England series. Kolisi had endured an emotionally and physically draining few weeks in his first outing as Springbok captain, and the feeling was that he could do with a break. Fleck, though, picked Kolisi in his starting lineup for a match that the Stormers went on to lose 25–14. Very little was achieved, while the selection of Kolisi further highlighted the need for the franchises to manage their Boks.

Erasmus and his coaching team were in constant contact with the Super Rugby coaches throughout 2018 and 2019. The franchise coaches were under their own pressures to secure results, so Erasmus would never instruct them on how to play, but he would share his Bok plans with them in detail and also offered his coaching staff to lend assistance where they could. The alignment Erasmus was seeking needed to be achieved between the national setup and the franchises, and as a result the Bok coaching staff would spend time with the players and coaching teams from all over the country.

Erasmus and the Boks were looking at between 45 and 50 players at any given time, and throughout Super Rugby they monitored all of them. The Boks were together in camp for a limited time throughout the year, which made the relationship with the franchises a crucial one.

Erasmus was particularly concerned with how his players would be managed and conditioned when they were at their franchises, so Aled Walters was given the task of knowing in detail, and at all times, the state of the players, and reporting their progress back to Erasmus. The level of detail was filtered down to every minute the players spent on the field. When they went back to their Super Rugby teams, the players in the Bok mix knew exactly what the expectations were from a Springbok point of view in terms of conditioning and the physical attributes they needed to improve. The onus was on the players themselves, with the help of the conditioning experts at the franchises, to help them hit those metrics. The players needed to take ownership.

De Bruin was the only member of the Springbok coaching team who was tied to a Super Rugby franchise, but that did not stop the others from being actively involved. Erasmus did not want his coaching staff tied down in the office during Super Rugby, and he

Allister Coetzee and the Springboks looking despondent after the 57–0 thumping they suffered against the All Blacks in Albany, 16 September 2017. MICHAEL BRADLEY/AFP VIA GETTY IMAGES

Rassie Erasmus addresses the Free State Cheetahs during their 2004 Currie Cup semi-final against Western Province at Newlands. The Cheetahs won the match 17–11, displaying impressive conditioning standards in the oppressive heat and humidity. TERTIUS PICKARD/GALLO IMAGES

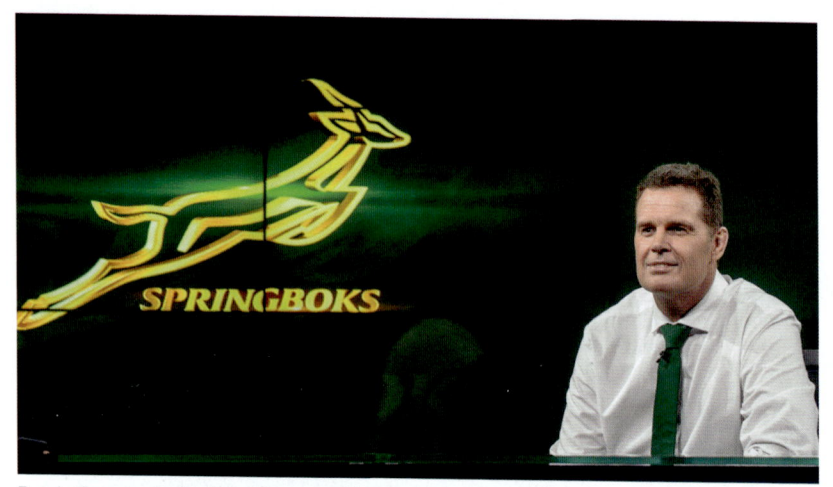

Rassie Erasmus in the SuperSport studios after being unveiled as the new Springbok coach, 1 March 2018. SYDNEY SESHIBEDI /GALLO IMAGES

Siya Kolisi leads the Springboks out for the first time against England at Ellis Park in Johannesburg on 9 June 2018. It was a historic day for South African rugby, with the Boks winning 42–39. DAVID ROGERS/GETTY IMAGES

Pieter-Steph du Toit and Bongi Mbonambi embrace after beating the All Blacks in Wellington on 15 September 2018. The 36–34 win stunned the rugby world, and many consider it to be a turning point for the Boks on their journey to Japan. HANNAH PETERS/GETTY IMAGES

Aphiwe Dyantyi celebrates after scoring a try against the Wallabies in Port Elizabeth in September 2018. The Lions wing enjoyed a stellar year, but he would become the centre of much controversy in 2019. GIANLUIGI GUERCIA/AFP VIA GETTY IMAGES

ABOVE: Scrumhalf Herschel Jantjies, in just his second Test match, scores off the bench to secure a 16–16 draw for the Boks against the All Blacks in Wellington on 27 July 2019. The Boks went on to win their first Rugby Championship in ten years.
MARK TANTRUM/GETTY IMAGES

LEFT: Eben Etzebeth at the 2019 World Cup squad announcement in Johannesburg on 26 August, just a day after news of the alleged Langebaan incident first broke.
SYDNEY SESHIBEDI /GALLO IMAGES/ GETTY IMAGES

Siya Kolisi shares a photograph with Springbok fans at OR Tambo International Airport. The Boks departed for Japan on 30 August, and were the first of the visiting sides to arrive in the host country. LEFTY SHIVAMBU/GALLO IMAGES/GETTY IMAGES

Franco Mostert competes for the ball in South Africa's World Cup warm-up against Japan in Kumagaya on 6 September. The Boks won 41–7, displaying impressive conditioning standards in the oppressive heat and humidity. MATT ROBERTS/GETTY IMAGES

LEFT: Siya Kolisi takes a hard knock in the 2019 Rugby World Cup opener against New Zealand on 21 September. The Boks were not at their best and lost 23–13, but they were mentally prepared for the possibility of defeat in the match.
STEVE HAAG/GALLO IMAGES

BELOW: Schalk Brits, captain on the day and playing at number 8, scores a try for the Boks in their pool game against Namibia in Toyota on 28 September. The Boks won 57–3.
MUHAMMAD AMIR ABIDIN/NURPHOTO VIA GETTY IMAGES

LEFT: Elton Jantjies running water duties during the Springboks' Pool B clash against Italy on 4 October. While not in the first-choice match-day 23, Jantjies was a valuable member of the Bok squad and played a key role in preparing for the final against England.
STEVE HAAG/GALLO IMAGES

BELOW: Willie le Roux, pictured here in South Africa's crucial 49–3 win over Italy at Shizuoka Stadium, endured increasingly tough criticism from fans back home as the tournament progressed.
STEVE HAAG/GALLO IMAGES

Eben Etzebeth, RG Snyman, Lood de Jager and Franco Mostert – South Africa's power locks – celebrate after the Italy match. WARREN LITTLE – WORLD RUGBY/WORLD RUGBY VIA GETTY IMAGES

This was the 'Bomb Squad' celebration after the Italy game that caused so much controversy for the Springboks. ANNE-CHRISTINE POUJOULAT/AFP VIA GETTY IMAGES

encouraged them to visit the franchises whenever they could.

'Monday we would meet in the office, Tuesday we would fly to a franchise, and then Wednesday we would fly back. On Thursday we would report back, so every week we were at a franchise,' Matt Proudfoot reveals. 'We met the franchise coaches, touched base with the players individually, told them what we were looking at and, where we could, assisted them.'

The coaching staff worked individually on these trips. Mzwandile Stick would visit franchises and show them what the Boks were doing in terms of their aerial and kick-chase work, while Jacques Nienaber spent extended periods with the coaches and the players explaining his defensive structure at the Boks. Nienaber even accompanied the Lions on their trip to Singapore to take on the Sunwolves on 23 March 2019. At any given stage, there was a good chance that a member of the Springbok coaching staff would be present with a Super Rugby side. The form and condition of the players in Super Rugby, of course, would go a long way towards determining their potential role with the Springboks.

'It was a breath of fresh air. In the previous regime we never had that. They would come and talk to the players and there was no daily communication', De Bruin recalls. 'If you wanted any guy at any stage for a coaching session, Rassie would make him available.'

Every player the Boks were looking at was given a road map to selection, which served to monitor their progress while they were at their franchises. This included a list of attributes that the player needed to excel at if he was going to fit into the Boks' plans. Progress in those categories would be discussed at the report-back meetings held on Thursdays at the SA Rugby offices in Plattekloof, Cape Town. The metrics ranged from physical, position-specific attributes to the mental and emotional state of the player, and they were monitored continually and in minute detail.

'I spent a lot of time individually with the forwards on the fundamentals of what they needed to do,' Proudfoot remembers. 'I looked at their different skill sets – scrum, lineout, maul, contesting and maul stop. Those were the five big areas I focused on. On a more detailed level, and as assistant coaches, we had to monitor the improvement of players on an individual basis. We would discuss them weekly, particularly how they managed stress, how they managed setbacks, how resilient they were, how much ownership they took, their leadership ... these were qualities we spoke about to understand how they would handle the pressures of a World Cup.'

On the basis of those discussions, Erasmus and the coaching staff would play 'selector' every week. If they had to choose a starting XV and a squad right now, what would it be? This was a process that continued throughout the Super Rugby season.

For the 2018 Rugby Championship, Erasmus named a squad of 35 that included three uncapped players – Damian Willemse, Marco van Staden and Cyle Brink. All had featured prominently with impressive campaigns for their Super Rugby franchises, and they had been rewarded. The 20-year-old Willemse, in particular, was an exciting prospect who played with freedom and skill as an emergency flyhalf for the injury-hit Stormers. Notable returnees from injury were Eben Etzebeth, Warren Whiteley and Malcolm Marx, while Bath-based veteran Francois Louw was also included. Duane Vermeulen, meanwhile, was absent due to his club commitments in Japan (he had signed for Kubota Spears in June).

Most of the squad had been in camp in Stellenbosch for a couple of weeks while Super Rugby was winding down, with the Lions players set to arrive later due to their participation in the tournament final. While Erasmus knew that results would always be crucial for the Springboks, he re-emphasised the need to build squad depth with the World Cup in mind.

'It's a difficult balancing act. We know there are only 15 Test matches [until the World Cup] and we want to win as much as possible, but you also want to get them ready for the World Cup to have a realistic chance,' the coach acknowledged ahead of the 2018 Championship.

Behind closed doors, however, Erasmus was eyeing a win over the All Blacks away from home. He would only have two cracks at it before the World Cup, but it was something he knew would give the Boks exactly the injection of confidence and belief they needed before heading off to Japan. But first they had to get through home and away legs against Argentina as the 2018 tournament got under way.

First up were the Pumas in Durban on 18 August. In announcing his team for the clash, Erasmus boasted serious firepower in the pack, with Whiteley, Louw, Etzebeth and Marx all included in the starting lineup. Pieter-Steph du Toit partnered Etzebeth in the second row, highlighting a physicality that would be a feature of the Bok forwards all the way to the World Cup. On the bench, Willemse was set to make his Test debut.

It was the backline, however, that stole the show, as the Boks scored six tries – two each for wings Aphiwe Dyantyi and Makazole Mapimpi – on their way to a 34–21 bonus-point victory. Man of the match Dyantyi could have scored a hat-trick, but he selflessly offloaded to Mapimpi when he almost certainly could have scored himself. The Boks were firing in a way that South Africans had not seen for a while. Mapimpi was scoring whenever he was given opportunities, but much of the hype centred on Dyantyi, who had enjoyed a stellar Super Rugby season with the Lions and was finding his feet at international level too. While the Boks were comfortable in victory and scored some exciting tries along the way, Erasmus was cautious, describing the performance as 'dominant but not crisp'. The Boks had lost a few lineouts, and flyhalf Handre Pollard's performance had been erratic, but the fact that they had won with a bonus point without hitting their straps was pleasing.

The away leg in Mendoza took place the following week. Fixtures in South America had become tougher in recent years, given the constant improvement of the Pumas and the rise of the Jaguares in Super Rugby, and the balancing act that Erasmus had spoken about would be tested here. He wanted to keep securing results, but he needed to rotate his players to build depth. The trip to Argentina was identified as an opportunity to do exactly that. Initially, Erasmus said he would look to make a number of changes to his side, but when the time came there was only one, with Franco Mostert coming in at lock for Pieter-Steph du Toit, who moved to the bench.

Du Toit's role was becoming an interesting one given his ability to operate at flank as well as lock. With quality in abundance, Erasmus needed to find the perfect balance, especially between his second row and loose forwards, where there were plenty of attractive options. Du Toit, wearing the number 7 jersey, would eventually go on to become the 2019 World Rugby Player of the Year and the 2019 SA Rugby Player of the Year and was a potent weapon for Erasmus and the Boks on their road to glory. Proudfoot believes the decision to move Du Toit out of the second row was one of the catalysts for the Boks' ultimate success.

'The roles of 4, 5 and 7 are so similar in rugby. People don't understand the similarities. They tackle the same, they carry the same, they all jump in the lineout. The only difference is that the number 7 defends the blindside of the scrum,' Proudfoot says. 'Pieter-Steph has an incredible engine and physique. I said to Rassie that I felt the scrum was overpowering his athleticism. We needed to release his athleticism. That was his point of difference and if we allowed him to express that in a game, he was going to get the numbers we were looking for.'

That move opened the door for Mostert, who had become a star for the Lions and was highly rated for his unrelenting physicality and work ethic. It also meant that, later, Erasmus would not have to rely almost solely on Vermeulen to provide the physicality in his loose trio. It was the first step towards striking that perfect balance.

Having emphasised continuity in team selection, Erasmus then looked on as Kolisi and the Boks, once again, crashed back down to earth with a poor showing and a 32–19 loss. It would perhaps have been an easier result to stomach had Erasmus not placed his faith in the very players who had been comfortable in victory just a week before. After the match the coach acknowledged that the performance had been 'embarrassing'.

Pollard again came in for some heat for failing to command proceedings from flyhalf, the Boks slipped back down to number seven in the rankings and – because the All Blacks had already secured back-to-back wins over the Wallabies – the 2018 Rugby Championship was considered wrapped up after just two rounds.

Ahead of the Australasian leg, Erasmus sprang a surprise by calling up the uncapped Cheslin Kolbe to his squad. It was a move that few saw coming given that Kolbe had slipped off the radar somewhat, having left the Stormers for Toulouse in 2017. A player with a devastating burst of pace and a natural X factor, Kolbe had often been touted as a future Bok, especially by the Cape media, but his small size always counted against him. Former Bok coach Nick Mallett once famously suggested that, because of his frame, Kolbe's future could be as a scrumhalf. Erasmus, though, had been impressed by Kolbe's form for his French club, and in the months that followed it became clear that what Erasmus saw was far more than a player with pace and a sidestep.

'He wasn't in the picture, but then we started analysing a lot of overseas-based players,' Erasmus remembers. 'We didn't really want to take a player to the World Cup who had under eight or nine Test caps. To make sure we had that depth, we had to delve more into overseas clubs. Cheslin didn't have a lot of time and preparation with us, but he got into it so quickly.'

As the Boks jetted off for Australia for their clash against the Wallabies in Brisbane, Erasmus acknowledged that they were hurting. He knew the pressure was on to secure results and he was challenging his Boks to respond. There were six changes from the side that had lost in Mendoza, including Du Toit starting at number 7, Jantjies replacing Pollard, and Damian de Allende returning to the number 12 jersey. Kolbe, meanwhile, was set for a Test debut off the bench.

The Wallabies had been struggling themselves under coach Michael Cheika – going down 38–13 and 40–12 to the All Blacks in the opening two rounds – and they needed a win as much as, if not more than, the Boks. For the South Africans, this was a chance to prove that they were closer to the All Blacks than they were to the Wallabies. Instead, a poor second-half showing, characterised by individual handling errors, saw the Boks go from leading 18–17 at half-time to losing 23–18. This was the match in which starting hooker Bongi Mbonambi launched a long lineout throw into no-man's land that cost the Boks a try and led to his being substituted ahead of the half-time whistle. That alone raised eyebrows, but Erasmus would later explain that the substitution was down to Mbonambi's physical state and not the mistake. The knives were out in the Brisbane aftermath. Kolisi, too, came in for some heat for his own performance – he was also at fault for the botched lineout – as well as for his handling of referee Glen Jackson.

Erasmus had always known the job would come with pressures, and that the South African public would be ruthless in demanding results, but with just three wins from seven (42.85 per cent), this was the first time that the public really started to raise questions about where the team was heading. Second-guessing the coach never takes long in South Africa, and the following week saw headlines suggesting that the Boks, still ranked seventh in the world, were on a hiding to nothing heading into their Test against the All Blacks in Wellington on 15 September. Instead, the Boks put in a performance that instantly turned those negative perceptions around.

Erasmus, in naming his side for the All Blacks, had gone back to something resembling his first-choice XV, with Pollard returning at flyhalf and Lukhanyo Am at number 13, while Jesse Kriel, surprisingly, moved to the right wing and Mapimpi dropped out of the squad altogether.

Erasmus desperately wanted a win in New Zealand, but he knew it would take something special. He acknowledged ahead of the match that another defeat could cost him his job.

Looking back, it is clear what a mammoth effort it took to beat the All Blacks on their own turf. Everything had to go the Boks' way, and it did. They had more than their fair share of good fortune, but the win was ultimately down to a heroic effort from every Bok on the park. It gave them proof that they could beat anybody in the world, in any conditions.

When the All Blacks scored two tries to open up a 12–0 lead after 17 minutes, thanks to a couple of beautifully executed, free-flowing attacking moves to which the Bok defence had no answer, the contest looked to be heading in a familiar direction. But then came a period of around 12 minutes that stunned the All Blacks and the world as the Boks ran in three tries through Aphiwe Dyantyi, Willie le Roux and Malcolm Marx to surge into a 21–12 lead. The Dyantyi try was simple in its execution, with work done by the forwards to make the yards before a move through the hands out left; Le Roux pounced on a howler of a quick lineout throw from Jordie Barrett; while Marx finished off a rolling maul that Proudfoot had been working on tirelessly since arriving in Australasia. The Boks were turning their opportunities into points – something you simply had to do to win in New Zealand. The All Blacks then hit back through Rieko Ioane, but the Boks took a surprising 24–17 lead into the break.

Shortly after the restart, Kolbe announced himself on the Test stage with an intercept try out of nowhere. His finest qualities of speed, X factor and sparking something out of nothing were on display, and the Boks stretched their lead further as the impossible began to look possible. Ioane then scored again for the hosts, but the Boks' fifth and final try on the night was perhaps their best as Jantjies and Warren Whiteley combined to send Dyantyi over in the left corner for his second.

The All Blacks were easily the stronger side, but after tries from Codie Taylor and Ardie Savea, and a horrible missed conversion from Beauden Barrett, the Boks led 36–34. With the pressure raining down in wave after wave of Kiwi attack, South Africa also lost Le Roux to a yellow card for a professional foul on the line. He was back on the park for the closing minutes when the Boks had to defend with everything they had as the All Blacks continued to bash away relentlessly. There were many times when it looked like the All Blacks would score, but somehow the Boks kept them out. That desperation on defence would be seen again in the 2019 World Cup final against England, but this was about the Springboks' restoring their place alongside the All Blacks in one of the game's great rivalries.

When Dyantyi forced a knock-on from Damian McKenzie three minutes after the hooter, it was all over.

Not given a sniff before the match, these Boks gave South Africa a performance to remember. The ensuing celebration shook the country. In an instant, belief in what Erasmus was doing was restored. While the Rugby Championship title may have been out of reach for 2018, this was a day that played a critical role on the World Cup journey. Du Toit, again in the number 7 jersey, and Kolisi put in inspirational performances for the Boks, but a triumph of this nature required a team effort, and that was the message from the skipper afterwards. Francois Louw had replaced Kolisi on 66 minutes, setting the tone for how the balance of the loose forward trio would look in the future. The defensive statistics were staggering, with the Boks making 235 tackles to New Zealand's 61. Heart, as much as anything, got the Boks over the line, and it was exactly the attitude Erasmus had been seeking from his players since his appointment.

'For Argentina away and Australia away, the focus was already on Wellington,' Erasmus says. 'That game was so big and something we had worked towards. The only way people – fans, the media, referees and the opposition – will believe that we can win the World Cup is if we beat New Zealand, in New Zealand. That gave everybody the belief.'

The win also saw the Boks jump up two places to fifth on the world rankings ahead of their home leg of the Rugby Championship, where Tests against Australia in Port Elizabeth (29 September) and the All Blacks at Loftus (6 October) awaited. De Allende, Am, Mapimpi and Whiteley were all ruled out with injury for the Wallabies game, allowing Erasmus to try a few fresh options as Sikhumbuzo Notshe and Kolbe were both handed their first Test starts in PE. Willemse, meanwhile, was the fullback cover on the bench after Erasmus asked Western Province coach John Dobson to play him there in a Currie Cup clash against Griquas the week before. It was far from the blockbuster performance the world had witnessed from the Boks in Wellington – they had less than 40 per cent of both possession and territory – but the hosts did enough to secure a 23–12 win in front of an electric PE crowd of over 40 000, thanks to tries from Dyantyi and Faf de Klerk.

Later that night, the All Blacks wrapped up the Rugby Championship title with a 35–17 victory over Argentina in Buenos Aires, but Erasmus emphasised that growing as a team, and not winning the tournament, had been the Boks' goal in 2018. With back-to-back wins over New Zealand and Australia, that growth appeared to be taking place. A clash against the All Blacks at Loftus was a dead rubber in the context of the log, with the Boks set to finish second regardless of the result, but given what had happened in Wellington, the fixture was still a mouth-watering prospect.

Le Roux, who had been granted the window to represent his country by his English club, Wasps, earned a 50th cap, while De Allende returned again and Louw started in place of Notshe at number 8. Ahead of the match, Erasmus shared an interesting story about how he had passed up an opportunity to sign Le Roux from Boland during his time at the Stormers, essentially telling him he wasn't good enough and, in so doing, paving the way for the fullback's success with the Cheetahs. Le Roux would become a central figure in Erasmus's World Cup plans, and would be the subject of controversy during the tournament, but by this stage he had the full backing of his coach, and that would last all the way to the final in Yokohama.

Whereas the Boks had relied heavily on the bounce of the ball and a powerful defence to get the job done in Wellington, they were more clinical at Loftus. They dominated in most areas and looked set to secure another win against their biggest rival. Pollard and De Klerk had kicked accurately all day while tries from Kriel and De Allende had given the Boks a 30–18 lead going into the final ten minutes. But the All Blacks ended up scoring 19 unanswered points in the final quarter of the match to secure a stunning 32–30 win thanks to a late try from Ardie Savea. As former Bok flyhalf and SuperSport pundit Naas Botha noted after the match: 'We controlled the game for 79 minutes.'

It was a devastating end to what could have been another magical outing for the Boks, but the result could not dampen the positivity that had re-emerged in South African rugby. The Springboks had received some hidings from the All Blacks in recent years, especially during the tenures of Allister Coetzee and Heyneke Meyer, and the gap in quality had widened during that time. These two results under Erasmus proved that the gap had closed and that the Boks were on track for 2019. The improvement couldn't have come at a better time for the Springboks, and Erasmus was getting closer to knowing what his best XV was. He still hadn't publicly backed Kolisi to lead the Springboks at the World Cup, but the skipper was growing into his role with every outing, while his form in the latter stages of the Championship began to touch the heights of what he had reached in 2017.

The pieces were beginning to fall into place for the Boks, and the public could see it. The idea of winning a third Rugby World Cup, all of a sudden, did not seem that far-fetched.

Chapter 7

Never stop learning
IIIIIIIIIIIIIIIIIIIIIIIIIIIIIIIIIIIIIIIIIII

South African rugby, at Springbok and franchise level, went through something of an identity crisis after the 2015 Rugby World Cup. The All Blacks won that tournament in relatively comfortable fashion, enhancing their reputation as the dominant force in the global game. Under Steve Hansen, the New Zealanders had continued to show incredible skill with ball in hand in a philosophy that was characterised by pinpoint execution at the breakdown, physical outside backs and offloading capabilities. This approach filtered through the country's Super Rugby franchises. It was always fast-paced, always accurate and, at times, provided jaw-dropping entertainment. The conditioning levels of the New Zealand players were also a marvel, with the All Blacks almost always finishing games stronger than their opposition.

With the Boks having bashed their way to a semi-final loss to New Zealand in 2015, following that shock loss to Japan in Brighton in their tournament opener, it was widely accepted that something needed to change in South African rugby. As a result, the franchises began taking some drastic measures in an effort to up their skills and offloading abilities. The plan, it seemed, was to try and replicate the All Black style. In doing so, South Africa's Super Rugby sides – the Bulls and Stormers in particular – began running the ball from deep and employing a fearless approach. The Lions had been working on this philosophy since 2013 under Johan Ackermann. This gave them a head start over their South African rivals, which bore fruit in the years to come, but for the other franchises it did not come as naturally.

Allister Coetzee entered the Springbok fold fully aware of the desire of the public to see a more enterprising, expansive game, and it was something he certainly tried to facilitate during his early months in charge – before the pressure to secure results took precedence. By the time Coetzee was sacked, the Boks did not look like they had taken any forward steps in terms of identifying a playing philosophy that could take them to the World Cup. There was, however, one match in which Coetzee's charges implemented a game plan that was noticeably effective. It came in the final Rugby Championship Test of 2017, on 7 October, when the Boks went down 25–24 to the All Blacks at Newlands, having been hammered 57–0 in Albany just three weeks earlier. On this day, the Boks employed a direct, forward-driven game plan that was based on a strong set piece, and it kept the All Blacks on the back foot for much of the contest. It still wasn't enough to get a much-needed win, but it was arguably one of the best performances of the Coetzee era, largely down to the execution of a simple yet effective strategy.

For forwards coach Matt Proudfoot, the only member of Erasmus's coaching staff to have operated between 2016 and 2019, that Newlands performance gave the Boks a blueprint against New Zealand that would lead to success against their 'old foes' in 2018 and 2019. 'In 2017 we looked at the two teams and decided we were better than them from number 1 to number 8,' he explains, 'so we made them confront our forwards as much as possible. That was difficult for them to handle. They didn't realise where the change had come from, but all we were doing was playing to the South African strengths.

'The world had fallen into a belief that rugby must be played the way New Zealanders play, but New Zealanders play the best way that New Zealanders play. To a large extent, the world was trying to follow that because they had been so successful. We stopped trying to play like them and decided to play like South Africans. That has historically been a model that they have struggled to handle. Strong set phase, strong defence, strong kicking game, strong in the tackle, releasing devastating counterattacks ... that is the way South Africans enjoy playing rugby. We don't have powerful outside backs, but we have devastating outside backs.'

Unfortunately for Coetzee, it was a case of too little, too late, and his disappointing end-of-year tour in 2017 sealed his fate.

When Erasmus arrived in 2018, it was important for him to get the Springboks on the same page, not only in terms of their mental state, but also in what they were doing on the field. What was the Bok style going to be under Erasmus? As the first Test matches of 2018 unfolded, there were signs that it would be a multifaceted approach. In the England series, particularly in Johannesburg and Bloemfontein, the Boks scored some dazzling tries and their wings featured on the scoreboard. Aphiwe Dyantyi was a world-class find, but in Sbu Nkosi, Makazole Mapimpi and, later, Cheslin Kolbe, Erasmus had some lethal finishers at his disposal, and they all possessed serious pace.

It was also telling, initially, that he had lured Lions head coach Swys de Bruin on board as his attack expert. De Bruin had been a part of the Lions evolution under Johan Ackermann, when the franchise became easily the most naturally attacking side in South Africa, playing with freedom and confidence with ball in hand. Erasmus's desire to bring De Bruin on board, combined with the approach shown in those first two England Tests, suggested that he would employ something similar with the national side. Erasmus had fought hard to get De Bruin, having sat with Lions CEO Rudolf Straeuli to make the pitch. Straeuli eventually agreed, as long as the Lions remained De Bruin's priority.

De Bruin would end up staying with the Boks for 16 Test matches – his last was the 16–16 draw against the All Blacks in Wellington in the shortened 2019 Rugby Championship – before standing down from his role due to stress-related illness. De Bruin was honest about his struggles with anxiety throughout the 2019 season, and he returned to South Africa during the Lions' Super Rugby tour of Australasia as a result. Doubling up as head coach of a Super Rugby franchise and a member of the national setup took its toll, but De Bruin's eventual decision to step away from his Springbok commitments was not down to his mental health alone.

Soon after he joined the Bok coaching team, De Bruin began to sense that Erasmus would prioritise a forwards-driven, kick-heavy game plan with the World Cup in mind. This was confirmed by Erasmus's first Test in charge – the trip to Washington against Wales that the Boks went on to lose 22–20. 'I started realising that it was not going to be like the Lions where we were just going to play this free-flowing, attacking style,' De Bruin recalls. 'That Test was there for the taking, but he [Erasmus] felt that it was because of over-running that we lost it.'

After the first two Tests against England, where the Boks scored seven tries in two games, De Bruin began to feel that perhaps he was wrong, and that Erasmus would encourage his side to play an attacking brand of rugby. He would later realise that this was not the case. 'Rassie is a cunning old fox and he knew from Washington that we would get everything out of attack we possibly could early on, but he knew what he wanted in the long run,' adds De Bruin.

De Bruin would often have long conversations with defence coach Jacques Nienaber, discussing the merits of playing a running-heavy or kick-heavy game. There were certainly differences of opinion over how the Boks should play, but there was never anything but respect between the two. Their conversations would even extend to selection. When Erasmus asked De Bruin for his thoughts on the loose trio, for example, he would suggest light-footed, quicker options such as Kwagga Smith and Warren Whiteley, players who De Bruin felt could be more mobile in getting around the park and aiding an attack-minded approach.

As the months went by, De Bruin accepted his fate. Eventually, Erasmus was clear in his view that if the Boks were going to win the World Cup, they would have to make dominating the aerial battle a priority. It was a tactical decision that worked a treat for the Boks in Japan, but it ultimately left De Bruin feeling like he was facing a losing battle in his endeavours to instil all-out attack. It was obviously still important to be able to score tries, and the work on attack remained crucial, but as the Boks evolved under Erasmus they started playing with less of the ball, prioritising territory over possession while relying on their rock-solid set piece, forward carries, impenetrable defence and the pace of their outside backs to counterattack for their points. It was a game of attrition that was far more traditional than De Bruin's approach at the Lions, and while he would always try and encourage more running, he knew that was not the way Erasmus and Nienaber wanted to go.

Erasmus knew about De Bruin's struggles with anxiety and stress before the side left for New Zealand for their Rugby Championship Test in 2019 and he was supportive. When the time came, De Bruin told Erasmus that he thought it would be best for him to return home instead of travelling to Argentina for the final match of the 2019 Championship. Erasmus, who called De Bruin 'dad', accepted the decision. He brought in the defence-minded Felix Jones, whom he had also worked with at Munster, as De Bruin's replacement. It was perhaps indicative of the game style he would emphasise in the run-up to Japan.

'I felt my stress levels were not where they were supposed to be. If I stayed on, I'm not so sure it would have been the right thing,' De Bruin says. 'There was never a fight and there was never an incident and Rassie always treated me with the utmost respect. I was going back and forth between Super Rugby and the Springboks, and I was spending 24 weeks a year away from home and in hotels. Then, with the Springboks not playing the brand that I loved, it was a decision I had to make, and I did. I had already got the message that if we wanted to win the World Cup, we were going to play this style.

'Rassie's tactics and the philosophy he went with was absolutely the right call and he achieved something incredible for this country. If I had gone to Japan, I'm not so sure we would have won the World Cup.'

The Boks, with a pack that had evolved into the envy of world rugby, would rely on their forwards for a dominant set piece and a defence that could not be breached. Through Faf de Klerk and Handre Pollard, they would kick themselves into the right areas of the field. The chasers would look to win the aerial contests, the carriers would secure simple, clean go-forward possession, and the backs, when the opportunity arose, would look to stretch a defence that had been sucked into a breakdown battle. The kick-heavy approach would come in for some passionate criticism from South African supporters during the World Cup, particularly directed at De Klerk, but Erasmus and Nienaber knew that if the Boks played to their traditional strengths, they could beat anybody in the world. They had proved as much.

Erasmus had already started refining his tactical approach by the end-of-year tour in 2018, where fixtures against England, France, Scotland and Wales awaited. He knew how the Boks would need to play to win the Rugby World Cup, and northern-hemisphere conditions would be the ideal platform for them to improve their kicking game. Nienaber's focus on defence was also beginning to take centre stage. He had spent time with all of the Super Rugby franchises throughout the 2018 season, educating them on his philosophy, so that by the time players arrived at a Bok camp, they were up to speed with what they needed to do. The Boks were still conceding tries in Test matches, but the nature of their rushed defensive lines meant that opposition sides were being placed under severe pressure on attack.

'They would only pick players who love to tackle,' Swys de Bruin remembers. 'Jacques was meticulous, and it was very important for him to have enough time on defensive stuff at training. At one stage there were not even separate attack and defence sessions anymore; they were combined so that he could really focus on defence in a game situation.'

After the Sharks were crowned 2018 Currie Cup champions, Erasmus named a 36-man squad for the northern hemisphere tour. He had been in camp with around 20 players as the Currie Cup drew to a close, again looking for every possible opportunity to spend time with players in the name of alignment. Sergeal Petersen, Ruhan Nel and JD Schickerling were the uncapped players included, while there was also a recall for 36-year-old former Stormers fullback Gio Aplon, who was playing his rugby at Toyota Verblitz in Japan. Schalk Brits returned, while Whiteley was also included, having recovered from a groin strain. Duane Vermeulen was also back, which made the number 8 position an intriguing one, with Whiteley still considered a strong leadership presence in the group. With Willie le Roux and Faf de Klerk unavailable because the fixture fell outside the official international window, the Boks would be tested in depth in two key positions for their tour opener against England at Twickenham on 3 November. Erasmus's solution was to play Damian Willemse at fullback and Ivan van Zyl at scrumhalf, while Vermeulen started at number 7 in a move that saw Pieter-Steph du Toit return to lock despite his loose forward heroics in the Rugby Championship.

It was a day that would end in controversy as England flyhalf Owen Farrell's hit on Andre Esterhuizen after the hooter was ruled to be fair after referee Angus Gardner consulted the television match official. It gave the hosts a 12–11 victory, but South African supporters were livid, in the belief that Farrell had not used his arms. Sbu Nkosi scored the only try of a match that, for large parts, the Boks dominated through their physical forwards. There were more concerns at lineout time, too, where Malcolm Marx endured a tough outing by overthrowing three times.

In the week following the England Test, Erasmus made waves with a tongue-in-cheek video that found its way onto social media. The video showed Erasmus conducting a tackling drill with Esterhuizen, encouraging him to hit a tackle bag high and with no arms. It was a light-hearted dig at the refereeing decision, which the public enjoyed, but it became a moment that Erasmus would look back on with regret. He soon realised that his approach to officiating needed to change, and the reaction to the Farrell tackle became the catalyst for a major shift in how Erasmus and the Springboks approached referees in the months to come.

'Our first thing we had to get right was for referees to understand that we respected them,' he says. 'That was maybe a mistake we had made in earlier Test matches, like the one we lost against England with the Farrell tackle and my actions after that. That was one of the lessons for me and the players. What a coach believes of the referee, the players believe of the referee. The moment you as a coach start respecting the referee and looking at how you can help him make the game work, the players do too. It's about the referee feeling comfortable and understanding that you don't look down on him.

'I can be so egocentric, but then you're actually hurting the whole of South Africa because for that one second that you're being nasty to a referee or treating him badly, then the whole team feels that and you lose the Test match because they don't handle the referee well. I had to make a massive mindshift, the other coaches had to make a massive mindshift, and then we had to convince the players to make that mindshift. If we didn't do that and didn't respect the referee, we wouldn't have stood a chance.'

Erasmus felt that the Springboks, given their form towards the end of the Rugby Championship, were gathering momentum at the perfect time. When Gardner ruled that the Farrell tackle should go unpunished, Erasmus was mortified. His reaction in the form of the video suggested as much, but the coach began to re-evaluate his position after the Boks got the rub of the green the following weekend against France. Referee Nigel Owens noticed that the Stade de France clock was incorrect and took the time back by a few seconds, which allowed the Boks to win the game with a late try.

'I almost took it personally when I thought, "How can a referee make a mistake like that?" But he can,' Erasmus says. 'You have to accept that. In the next game, we should have lost against France and then Nigel Owens saw that the clock didn't stop, and he took it back by 25 seconds.

'That made me realise that none of these guys want to screw us over. All of them want to get the game to work and the moment you help them to get the game to work – not to win always – you will get much further than calling them cheats or pointing out all their mistakes. That 2018 November tour helped me a lot with that.'

Erasmus, like his players, was learning all the time.

With his record having slipped to five wins from eleven (45.45 per cent), he needed a positive result against France in Paris on 10 November.

The Boks received a major boost ahead of that Test, with their overseas-based players – Le Roux, De Klerk, Kolbe, Francois Louw, Vincent Koch and Franco Mostert (who had been the subject of a nasty contract battle between the Lions and his new club, Gloucester) – available inside the Test window. All six were included in the match-day 23 for Paris. In what would prove to be Whiteley's final Test match, the Boks needed a Bongi Mbonambi try off the back of a rolling maul to secure a 29–26 win, having been 23–9 down at one stage. It was an important moment in Mbonambi's Springbok journey. While the Boks were far from their best, this was a vital win that was again characterised by some sterling work from the forwards and a flawless kicking display from Handre Pollard. Mbonambi may have scored the winning try, but he also delivered some pinpoint lineout throws when the Boks were under intense pressure. Siya Kolisi, though, endured a second poor outing of the tour as concerns over his workload and form resurfaced.

For the Test against Scotland at Murrayfield on 17 November, Whiteley's absence with a calf strain opened the door for Vermeulen to shift to number 8. It meant that Du Toit could return to blindside flank, with the Boks fielding what would be their loose trio for the World Cup final – Kolisi, Du Toit and Vermeulen. With De Klerk released to Sale, Erasmus gave a first start to scrumhalf Embrose Papier, who was impressive on the day. There were far fewer box kicks from the Bok number 9, who sparked numerous attacks with crisp service, and Erasmus's men bagged a pleasing 26–20 victory. Pollard, with 18 points, was superb again and his return to form was ideally timed with the World Cup in mind. For Erasmus, one of the more pleasing aspects of the game was a developing maturity in the Boks' ability to close out the game. It would be a valuable tool at the World Cup.

It was after this match that De Bruin recalls another chat with

MIRACLE MEN

Nienaber: 'We had a long meeting in Edinburgh after we beat Scotland at Murrayfield, and I felt this was the way going forward because we ran well against them that day and we did not go for the kicking game as much.' While the Boks were settling on their style, they had one Test remaining in 2018, and it came in the form of an exacting trip to Cardiff for a clash against Wales on 24 November. The Boks had lost on their last three visits to the Principality Stadium, and Erasmus identified the fixture as potentially the toughest of the tour. De Klerk was available again, but Erasmus opted to reward Papier for his showing against Scotland as he named an unchanged starting lineup. Kolisi, meanwhile, had been lucky to escape punishment following what looked a rather sinister headbutt against Scotland centre Peter Horne.

In a brutally physical clash, the Boks had two tries disallowed but were outmuscled by Wales as they slipped to a 20–11 loss. These sides would meet again in the World Cup semi-finals, but this was Wales' ninth Test win in a row as they confirmed their status as genuine World Cup contenders. It was a disappointing end to 2018 for Erasmus and the Boks, but they had achieved much over the course of the year.

The Boks had won seven and lost seven under Erasmus, for a win rate of just 50 per cent, but they had gone a long way towards restoring the faith of the public. The win against the All Blacks in Wellington was critical, and was undoubtedly Erasmus's biggest result of 2018, but the growth was about more than just one match.

Kolisi was looking more comfortable with each outing as skipper, and Pollard was also starting to find his feet at flyhalf. The Bulls pivot had endured a tough, long battle with injury under Allister Coetzee, but towards the end of 2018 he was showing exactly why he had been so highly rated since his youth. It helped, of course, that the Boks had now settled on a game plan. With territorial dominance now paramount, Pollard and De Klerk could prioritise field position, and this helped the flyhalf settle into the role Erasmus wanted him to play as the team's general.

The defensive capabilities of this side had also shone through in 2018, with the work of Nienaber rightly praised. Defence, almost singlehandedly at times, won Test matches for the Boks and would be the backbone of their success in Japan the following year. With a pack of forwards that could dominate any in the world and that found its strength in physicality, the Boks were tapping into the attributes that had historically made them one of the most feared and respected sides in the world.

They weren't all brawn, though, and the Boks scored some wonderful tries in 2018. They had also unearthed a few deadly finishers out wide: Dyantyi, Nkosi, Mapimpi and, towards the end of the year, Kolbe could hurt any side on the counter.

'We had a clear game plan. It was very basic, but you could still express yourself and have a go when you saw space,' Elton Jantjies explains. 'You could play your own rugby because that is why you got picked for the Springboks. Rassie encouraged us to use our own skill sets, but around the game plan. When things didn't go our way, it meant we actually knew how to find solutions because our game plan was so simple.'

At the World Rugby Awards, held in Monaco the night after the Wales Test, Dyantyi was recognised for his stellar debut season by scooping the coveted Breakthrough Player of the Year award. After a superb season for the Lions in Super Rugby, he had proved his worth on the international stage too, with six tries in his opening eight Test matches, including two in the famous Wellington win. A relatively late bloomer who graduated to Super Rugby through the Varsity Cup with the University of Johannesburg, Dyantyi's rise to the top was a story as inspirational as any. He had not been scouted as a youngster and had to go the long way around, but it had seemingly paid off, and Dyantyi was a shoo-in for the number 11 jersey in Japan and comfortably ahead of the other wings. The doping saga that followed was tragic for him on a personal level, but Erasmus had used 2018 to build squad depth and this was particularly true on the wing.

While Erasmus was getting closer to identifying his best possible starting side, there were still positions where uncertainty remained. Whiteley's future participation was in doubt as he continued to be plagued by injury, but with his leadership valued within the Bok squad, was it possible to accommodate him and Vermeulen in the same side? That would almost certainly mean that Pieter-Steph du Toit would have to move back to lock, but Proudfoot and Erasmus had accepted that he was more effective at flank. Striking that loose trio balance was key. There was also uncertainty in midfield, where Damian de Allende and Jesse Kriel appeared to be the preferred pairing. Both players still had their fair share of critics, though, and the centre pairing always felt like an area where the Boks were not completely settled. In the front row, Mbonambi was starting to make a case for being picked ahead of Marx, while the two prop positions were also still wide open. Erasmus had created a culture in which players were given opportunities to challenge for their positions. It bred healthy competition and, as a result, improved performance. Building squad depth was something the coach had always identified as being hugely important, and he achieved this in 2018 while maintaining the standards. There had certainly been poor displays and results along the way, but the broader picture appeared healthy. These Boks, transformed in their racial make-up, mental state and physical approach, were onto something.

While the international season was over, 13 of the touring Springboks stayed on in Europe for an extra week to play for the Barbarians against Argentina at Twickenham. Erasmus was the coach of that side. Most who have played Test rugby will tell you that being a part of a Barbarians week is a special time, and for these Boks it was a therapeutic way to bring the curtain down on a season that had been long and testing but also very rewarding. Eight Springboks started that match, with the other five on the bench, before a late Elton Jantjies drop goal secured a 38–35 win for the Baa-Baas. Kolisi, De Allende and Lood de Jager were all try scorers that day.

Erasmus was still in England when he confirmed to the UK media that he was backing Kolisi to lead the Boks at the 2019 World Cup. In terms of his actual transformation target of 45 per cent in 2018, Erasmus had fallen just short. That did not matter to any of the players, though, who knew that opportunities were being given and the rest was up to them. Kolisi had skippered the Boks in 13 of their 14 Tests in 2018 and won more than he lost. More significantly, he was growing into the role, and was employing a unique leadership style of inclusivity. While that selfless approach earned him the buy-in of his team-mates, it also gave him the backing of the country's rugby public. With a shortened 2019 Rugby Championship to come, the Boks did not have time left for experimentation. There could realistically be no other man to lead them in Japan.

The sleeping giant of South African rugby began to stir in 2018.

Chapter 8
Reconnaissance

The level of planning and detail that went into the Springbok recovery in 2018, combined with results and performance on the field, restored a level of public faith in the national side. Winning the World Cup still seemed a stretch given the strength of New Zealand, Wales, Ireland and England, but the Boks had at least put themselves back into the conversation. For coach Rassie Erasmus and his management team, however, there was even more hard work ahead.

Following the 2018 end-of-year tour, Erasmus and the players involved in the Barbarians match at Twickenham returned home, but there was little time to rest. The planning for 2019 continued, and Erasmus organised a pre-Christmas trip to Japan to scout the conditions his players would be exposed to during the tournament.

Accompanied by conditioning coach Aled Walters, head of operations Charles Wessels and logistics manager JJ Fredericks, Erasmus left for Japan on 1 December to conduct a seven-day reconnaissance mission. World Rugby, the sport's governing body, had allocated hotels and training venues for the sides to choose from, but because the Boks were seeded second in Pool B behind the All Blacks, they had second option on accommodation behind the world champions. Erasmus and Walters wanted to see the hotels at first hand. Wessels and Fredericks had already been on one mandatory trip to Japan, at

World Rugby's expense, following the draw in Kyoto in May 2017, when Allister Coetzee was still coach.

The Boks would play their pool games in Yokohama (All Blacks, 21 September), Toyota (Namibia, 28 September), Fukuroi (Italy, 4 October) and Kobe (Canada, 8 October). Erasmus, Walters, Wessels and Fredericks visited all four cities during their stay, examining everything from the comfort of the hotel rooms to the quality of the training venues and gym facilities. Walters was a central figure on the trip, applying everything he saw to his plans for conditioning and player recovery. He met with the chefs and food and beverage managers at the hotels, ensuring they were committed and able to provide the Boks with their necessary nutrition levels over the course of the tournament.

With great attention to detail, the Bok management also used the trip as an opportunity to explore the Japanese transport system. Travel would be a major factor for all 20 sides competing at the tournament, and Erasmus was looking for any possible way to get an edge over his competitors. Instead of travelling by hired car, the reconnaissance team made use of public transport – buses and trains – to get from city to city. They wanted to experience what the Boks would experience on travel days during the World Cup. This exercise led to a major logistical decision: the Boks would travel exclusively by train and bus during the World Cup, avoiding air travel completely. After doing their research, the reconnaissance team had calculated that flying would add on unwanted travel hours. Given Japan's state-of-the-art rail system, the Boks could save time by taking the train.

'The thinking around that was that on the train there is more freedom of movement, which aids in recovery. There are some big boys, and sitting on a plane can be very uncomfortable with the limited leg room,' Fredericks explains.

MIRACLE MEN

Allowing the players to stretch their legs, walk around and enjoy a more relaxed journey, even if it sometimes took longer, factored into the decision, with Walters scrutinising every detail in determining what would be physically best for the players. Given that travel days came soon after game days, these were crucial hours of recovery in his conditioning programme. As the players would later confirm, recovery was as important to Walters as the work they did on the field. The players were also encouraged to do their own analysis on the train trips, which would be more difficult on a flight. Fredericks noted that at the start of the World Cup most sides were flying between venues, but as the tournament progressed, he saw more and more realise that the train was the more logical option. It was another example of the level of planning it took to get the best out of the Boks when it mattered most.

It was also on this trip that Erasmus decided the Boks would base themselves in the seaside city of Kagoshima, nestled on the southwestern coast of the island of Kyushu, for their tournament build-up. They would have to travel to Kumagaya, north of Tokyo, for a warm-up match against the tournament hosts, but this would be their one and only flight until they left for home. And so Kagoshima became their home away from home. Erasmus's decision, upon inspection, to make Kagoshima the Boks' pre-tournament base had much to do with the weather conditions. The city is one of Japan's most consistently humid and hot places, and Erasmus wanted his players to become accustomed to the change of climate as quickly as possible. While other cities expressed an interest in hosting the Springboks, Erasmus's mind was made up after visiting Kagoshima.

'The city went out of their way to make the boys feel at home. Everything was there for us and the people opened their hearts to the players. It was a masterstroke from Rassie,' says Fredericks.

With the Boks having enjoyed their Christmas break, Super Rugby 2019 became the main focus, and the franchise coaches, led by Swys de Bruin, accepted the fact that the Springboks would be the priority for the season. The coaches were under their own pressures to secure results – Robert du Preez from the Sharks and Robbie Fleck from the Stormers in particular – but the broader picture meant that they had to factor in Erasmus's plans and the Springbok alignment. The players' workloads, at training and during matches, would have to be closely monitored, while the Super Rugby coaches might also have to be flexible in terms of fielding some players in positions where Erasmus was considering them for the Boks.

There were returns to South African rugby for Duane Vermeulen and Schalk Brits, who signed with the Bulls, having both been linked initially to the cash-strapped Stormers. Vermeulen's committing to South Africa was a win for Erasmus in the context of the World Cup given his importance to the Boks. By playing Super Rugby, it meant the bruising number 8 could share valuable time with his Springbok team-mates throughout the year instead of just when the European club window allowed. Brits, meanwhile, hit the ground running at the Bulls as he set about proving that he still had the ability to warrant a place in the Bok setup despite having retired from rugby the year before.

The Stormers confirmed that Siya Kolisi would stay on as captain for 2019 despite there being continued concerns over his workload. The Bok skipper ruffled a few feathers at the beginning of the year when, in an interview with Japan's Kyodo News, he was asked how he felt Nelson Mandela would have reacted to quotas in sport. In response, he suggested that South Africa's first democratically elected president would not have been on board with picking players because of the colour of their skin. The ensuing storm blew over quickly, and Kolisi was seen as being misunderstood, but it was another reminder to him that he was always on the record and representing a diverse, divided group of passionate South Africans every time he played for the Boks or spoke about them.

Over at the Lions, Warren Whiteley made another recovery from injury and was named 2019 captain as he looked to remind Erasmus of his own World Cup credentials. There was also a lot of focus on how star wing Aphiwe Dyantyi would go in his second full season with the franchise. Dyantyi, the 2018 World Rugby Breakthrough Player of the Year, had become a fan favourite in South Africa and was determined to keep delivering the goods with Japan in mind. After just two rounds of fixtures, Whiteley's stop-start career suffered another setback, this time with a pectoral injury – another setback in an injury-plagued career.

In those early stages of Super Rugby 2019, Erasmus went public in applauding the tactical styles of the South African franchises. If his desired approach for the Springboks at the World Cup had not been blatantly obvious before, it certainly was now.

'Last year you saw a lot of attacking, running rugby from our franchises and this year it feels that a lot of the guys are grabbing the Test match mould, if I can call it that, and they're trying to apply a lot of pressure through territory and a tactical game,' Erasmus said in the press.

'For a national coach, that can be a positive where it is not just a free-flowing, running game. I don't want to harp on kicking, but if you think of World Cups and Joel's [Stransky] drop goal to Stephen Larkham's drop goal to Jonny Wilkinson's drop goal … a World Cup final has never been won by eight tries. It's always been high-pressure games with a penalty or drop goal deciding it. It's suddenly this game where it isn't all about X factor and brilliant moments. It's almost like the teams are trying to squeeze each other out tactically. I enjoy that.'

Throughout the 2019 Super Rugby season, the Bok management

team continued their visits to the franchises, providing constant updates on the selection road maps of all players whom Erasmus was considering. It meant that every weekend of Super Rugby action was an opportunity for a player who potentially was not on the World Cup radar to put up his hand. Unfortunately, as the season progressed, the local franchises were not at their best and the South African Conference would eventually be won by Argentina's Jaguares, who progressed all the way to the tournament final in Christchurch. The Crusaders won the competition for a third year running, a quite superb achievement given the tragic mosque attacks that had rocked Christchurch on 15 March.

Back in South Africa, Tendai Mtawarira made history by overtaking Adriaan Strauss as the most-capped South African Super Rugby player of all time with his 157th appearance in the competition, while hookers Schalk Brits and Akker van der Merwe were both red-carded after a punch-up when the Bulls met the Sharks in Durban at the end of March. Brits, banned for four weeks, had contributed massively to the Bulls being the form South African franchise at that point, and was playing himself into the Bok squad with every performance. At the Stormers, Robbie Fleck came in for criticism over his management of players, with Kolisi and Damian de Allende having featured throughout the season without a rest. Fleck eventually sent the Bok skipper home, despite his squad being ravaged by injury, ahead of the final fixture of their Australasian tour against the Rebels. There was also drama at the Sharks when hooker Chiliboy Ralepelle's B-sample from a doping test in January returned positive, effectively ending the professional career of a player who had been on the fringes of the Bok setup the previous year. It would be the first, and less significant, of two doping scandals to hurt South African rugby in 2019. The Lions, meanwhile, were not in a good place, and after they were hammered 42–5 by the Sharks at Ellis Park, De Bruin called an emergency meeting with the franchise's leadership.

As the pool stages developed, the South African Conference was wide open, with all four local franchises having delivered encouraging performances along the way. Consistency, though, was an issue for all of them. There were, as a result, few individuals using the tournament to make a serious Springbok statement.

One youngster who was doing just that, however, was Stormers scrumhalf Herschel Jantjies. A product of Paul Roos Gymnasium in Stellenbosch, Jantjies was given an extended run in the Stormers' number 9 jersey in 2019, thanks largely to an injury to Jano Vermaak in week two. Just 22 at the time, Jantjies made an immediate impact and developed into the form South African scrumhalf in Super Rugby during the group stages. He earned the praise of fans, critics and the country's Super Rugby coaches as he played himself into the Springbok conversation.

It came as no surprise when Jantjies was included in a Springbok alignment camp when the Stormers had their bye weekend over 10–11 May. Jantjies, a kid from a modest family background who still lived at home with his parents and brother in Kylemore, outside Stellenbosch, was in the process of breaking through in what would be a whirlwind year for him. At the start of 2019, there were many South Africans who had never heard of Herschel Jantjies. He had never played a full Super Rugby season and was not his franchise's first-choice option in his position. Before the end of the year, however, Jantjies would find himself on the field when referee Jérôme Garcès blew the final whistle to crown the Springboks champions. Few players have gone from relative obscurity to global superstardom so quickly.

In 2019, everything Jantjies touched turned to gold, and he would become one of the stories of the World Cup, despite being well below Faf de Klerk in the pecking order. If it was a gamble to back a player of Jantjies' inexperience at a World Cup, it was one that certainly paid off. The likes of Ivan van Zyl, Embrose Papier, Ross Cronje and Louis Schreuder were all ahead of Jantjies in the race to the World Cup when Super Rugby 2019 got under way, but midway through the competition he had jumped ahead of all of them. Erasmus would monitor Jantjies closely on the field and at the Bok alignment camps, and he was impressed by what he saw. Size, as Cheslin Kolbe had already demonstrated in 2018, was not the be-all and end-all.

'He is another player up there with one of the best in terms of the South African teams. He is one of the best number 9s in the country at the moment. He is playing outstanding rugby and has just grown from strength to strength as the competition has gone on. His service is quick and effective, he is dangerous around the fringes and the biggest jump in his game has been his defence,' Robbie Fleck said of Jantjies during a press conference at the halfway point of the season.

While a number of Springboks suffered injuries throughout the 2019 Super Rugby season, few were serious enough to threaten their World Cup participation. Whiteley, though, continued to struggle. He made every effort and was often touted for a return to the Lions lineup, but he could not recover, and his World Cup place was in jeopardy.

Then, on 25 May, Springbok skipper Kolisi injured his knee during the Stormers' 34–22 win over the Highlanders at Newlands. Initial predictions were that Kolisi would be sidelined for six weeks, but the injury would prove significant enough to rule him out of the entire 2019 Rugby Championship, while his World Cup participation was also touch and go. While the seriousness of the injury was perhaps downplayed at the time, it came close to ruining Kolisi's fairy tale. Even as the Springboks departed for Japan later that year, doubts lingered over his preparedness given how much rugby he had missed in 2019. Had the injury happened just a few weeks later, and given the timelines, Kolisi could very easily have been left out of the World Cup squad.

Eben Etzebeth then broke his hand the following weekend and, suddenly, the Boks had two serious injury concerns out of Cape Town.

The Bulls and Sharks were the only two South African sides to make the Super Rugby playoffs that season, but there would be no run to a tournament final as had been the case with the Lions in the three preceding years. The Bulls went down 35–28 to the Hurricanes in Wellington, while the Sharks limped to a 38–13 loss to the Brumbies in Canberra, and with that the curtain came down on South Africa's participation in the tournament. It was not the worst news in the world for the Springboks and Erasmus, who would now have the full attention of his players on the upcoming Rugby Championship and plans for the World Cup.

Erasmus and a group of 39 players gathered for a camp in Pretoria to prepare for the Rugby Championship. By 1 July, the Sharks and Bulls players who had featured in the Super Rugby playoffs had joined the group and the Boks had three weeks to prepare for their tournament opener against the Wallabies at Ellis Park. Every day, every training session, every team and individual meeting for the next 20 weeks, both in South Africa and in Japan, had already been mapped out by Erasmus.

Francois Louw, who was finishing off his club duties with Bath, was the last to arrive in Pretoria. 'It's a hell of a long time,' he recalls. 'Even in South Africa, you're still technically on tour because you don't stay at home. You're in hotels and training and together the whole time. I might be wrong, but I think it's the longest tour the Springboks have ever been on.'

One man who was in that camp, and about to go through a journey from hell, was the Boks' find of 2018, Dyantyi. The star wing was first ruled out of the Championship opener against the

Wallabies at Ellis Park on 20 July with a hamstring strain. He was sent back to the Golden Lions where he was due to undergo rehabilitation. It was an injury that kept Dyantyi out of the entire 2019 Rugby Championship, with Erasmus eventually confirming that it would be difficult to pick him for Japan given his lack of game time. Then, just two days before the Bok World Cup squad announcement on 26 August, it became public knowledge that Dyantyi had tested positive for three banned substances – methandienone, methyltestosterone and LGD-4033 – following a test done at the beginning of July during the Springbok camp in Pretoria. Injury or no injury, this was a devastating blow to a player who, just months before, had the world at his feet and the brightest of futures. When the 31-man squad for the World Cup was announced, Erasmus said that the injury, and not the doping scandal, was the reason that Dyantyi had been excluded. In truth, there was no way Dyantyi could have travelled to Japan under such a cloud of uncertainty.

Devastated, Dyantyi denied ever taking any banned substances knowingly, and vowed to prove his innocence. With his professional future at risk, he could only look on as his team-mates carried on without him and achieved something special, something that he had been agonisingly close to being a part of. Nobody was more despondent than Dyantyi himself, but few took it harder than his Lions mentor, Swys de Bruin. It was De Bruin who had pulled Dyantyi out of the Varsity Cup wilderness at the University of Johannesburg and given him the tools to become a Springbok. 2019 was a difficult year for De Bruin as his battles with stress and anxiety affected his coaching. He returned to South Africa during the Lions' Australasian Super Rugby tour that year, but the news of Dyantyi's Springbok career going up in flames provided a different feeling of despair.

'I'm in this game for different reasons than most,' De Bruin reflects. 'I want to coach to score tries, glorify God and make a difference in players' lives. When that happened to Aphiwe, I took it tough. It was very hard on me and I know how he battled. I know the journey we walked together.'

As Dyantyi's star dimmed, another was about to explode in the form of Herschel Jantjies. There were only four more Tests to play until the World Cup squad was announced, and the little pocket-rocket scrumhalf from Kylemore was about to enter the Springbok fray in a way that nobody had ever done before.

Chapter 9
The final cut
|||||||||||||||||||||||||||||||||

It had been ten years since the Springboks last won a Rugby Championship. That success had come in 2009 under Peter de Villiers, when the tournament was still called the Tri-Nations and Argentina was yet to join the fray. The Boks famously beat New Zealand three times – twice at home and once away – on their way to five wins from six and an eight-point victory on the log.

In 2019, while winning the Rugby Championship was certainly desired, it was far from the priority for coach Rassie Erasmus and his men. Instead, the tournament would serve as the side's final preparation for the World Cup in Japan, and if results had to be sacrificed now for the benefit of the bigger picture, then that was a sacrifice worth making. South African rugby lovers had gone a long time without silverware, though, so when Erasmus's Boks sprung a surprise by actually winning the 2019 edition, it was the perfect tonic for supporters who now fully believed that something special could be achieved in Japan.

The Springbok camp in Pretoria towards the end of June ahead of the 2019 Championship marked the beginning of the 20-week journey that would end in Yokohama on 2 November – the day of the World Cup final. While there was much hard work done on the training field, a hallmark of Erasmus's coaching style was the work done indoors, where team meetings brought everybody on the same page, mentally and emotionally. It was at one of these meetings, a few days before South Africa's Rugby Championship opener against Australia at Ellis Park, that Erasmus sprang a surprise on his players by revealing the starting lineups for all three fixtures in the tournament. The Boks would host the Wallabies in Johannesburg on 20 July before travelling to Wellington, as they had in 2018, for a clash against the All Blacks on 27 July. Their final match of the shortened campaign would be a trip to Salta to take on Argentina on 10 August. Before a ball was even kicked, the extended Springbok squad knew what the plans were for all three matches.

'He just put up an Excel spreadsheet and gave the three teams,' Francois Louw remembers. 'A few guys were a bit concerned that their names weren't there, but he said that those were the teams, and that if we wanted to know why you were not there, he would tell us why. You had to accept that it was the pecking order, but by being so open and transparent he got the guys buying into it. We were all on the same page from day one, whether it was selection or buying into the strategy.'

Form was not going to be a factor in selection during the Championship. Erasmus accepted that players would make mistakes, but he gave them the platform in 2019 to play with freedom and put up their hands for a place in the World Cup squad. Managing the workloads of the players was also a major factor in the predetermined lineups, with conditioning boss Aled Walters having monitored every minute of playing time over the course of the Super Rugby and European seasons.

'He said the teams would only change for two scenarios: a player being injured or a player acting like an arsehole,' forwards coach Matt Proudfoot adds. 'He hated players who became entitled, and that was a reason he would change a team. If a player didn't play well or made mistakes, that wasn't something that upset Rassie. He would want to understand why and then it would be for the coaches to fix. If a player got entitled or dropped his work rate or didn't have a positive attitude, then he would change the team for that.'

Because of the week's turnaround between the Wallabies and All Blacks matches, Erasmus decided that he would send the bulk of the players who had been selected for the All Blacks game to New Zealand early, effectively splitting up his squad. He was that certain in his planning.

With captain Siya Kolisi still sidelined with the knee injury he had sustained in Super Rugby, and still a real concern for Erasmus, Eben Etzebeth, who had recovered from his hand injury, was given the captaincy for the Wallabies game. It was the 12th time in Etzebeth's career that he had captained his country, having done the job for Allister Coetzee in 2017. Much of the hype ahead of the Boks' first Test of the year centred on Stormers scrumhalf Herschel Jantjies, who was named in the starting lineup. There was also a starting debut for former Stormers bruiser Rynhardt Elstadt, who was making a late play at a World Cup place, having excelled since joining French club Toulouse in 2017. Bulls prop Lizo Gqoboka, meanwhile, was set for his debut off a bench that was littered with overseas-based star power. Vincent Koch, Marcell Coetzee, Cobus Reinach and Frans Steyn were all included as Erasmus explored his options.

At Ellis Park, in front of more than 51 000 screaming fans, the Boks dominated the contest from start to finish on a day that Jantjies will never forget. The atmosphere in the iconic stadium was overflowing with emotion, as it had been during Kolisi's first Test as captain (against England in 2018), following the tributes to former 1995 World Cup-winning Springbok wing James Small, who had died tragically just ten days earlier. Small's children were present as a moment of silence was observed, and when the Boks took to the field, they looked like they were possessed. It perhaps was not the most polished performance from the hosts, and Erasmus fielded a somewhat experimental side, but the Boks blew the hapless Wallabies away by scoring five tries to just two from the visitors to claim a commanding 35–17 win. Herschel Jantjies had a perfect day, bagging two tries for himself on his way to a man-of-the-match performance and one of the most explosive Bok debuts ever seen. His first try came in the 11th minute when he finished off a superb attacking move that saw Elton Jantjies show the deftest of touches, but his second provided a moment that would be replayed again and again in the week ahead as he sniped around the blindside of a scrum to score a classic scrumhalf's try. It was a dream start for the youngster, and while his tries stole the show, it was his all-round game that impressed Erasmus most.

'To come straight from Super Rugby and play like that – his service, his box kicks, his technique, his grit on defence and of course his marvellous attacking ability were awesome,' Erasmus commented, justifying the decision to hand the newbie a Bok debut so close to the World Cup.

The Ellis Park triumph also saw Frans Steyn back in a Springbok jersey for the first time in over two years. He came off the bench, operating at centre, and his versatility would become crucial to the Springbok cause in the months ahead. Steyn's presence would ultimately cost Elton Jantjies his place in the World Cup match-day 23, but it also opened the door for Erasmus to employ a 6/2 forwards/backs split on the bench in Japan. This was a tactical move that would be widely praised, since it allowed the Boks to unleash greater firepower in the form of their replacement forwards, but it would not have been possible without Steyn, who covered every position in the backline except scrumhalf, even if he was far from the quickest in the squad.

With the plan to split the squads for the Rugby Championship in operation, 14 Boks had travelled to New Zealand on the Thursday before the clash against the Wallabies at Ellis Park. After that match, Erasmus, the coaching team and another eight players flew out of Johannesburg on Saturday night while a further ten players left on the Sunday. The logistics of who needed to arrive in New Zealand, and when, were made easier by the fact that Erasmus already knew who was playing. The All Blacks had edged Argentina 20–16 in Buenos Aires in their opening fixture of the tournament and were in the process of their own experimentation with the World Cup in mind, but a clash against the Springboks would always have a certain gravitas. The fact that this one would be played in Wellington, the scene of the Springbok heroics the year before, made the fixture all the more tantalising.

As part of the rotation policy, Etzebeth, Pieter-Steph du Toit and Makazole Mapimpi were the only survivors from the starting lineup at Ellis Park, though Erasmus handed the captaincy to the returning Duane Vermeulen in an effort to build leadership depth. By this stage, Erasmus was already close to knowing what his best side was, as evidenced by the fact that the backline for Wellington was exactly the same as the one that would start the World Cup final in Yokohama. In the forwards, Kwagga Smith started in the number 6 jersey, with Kolisi still injured, while the rest of the pack had a settled and familiar feel to it. The Boks had already identified their blueprint against the All Blacks, and they would once again take them on in the physical exchanges.

This time around, there was a confidence about the Boks that stemmed from what they had achieved in 2018. It may not have been as exciting a contest in terms of free-flowing, counterattacking tries, but the 16–16 draw that Saturday confirmed that the rivalry between two of the game's giants was fully restored. The Springboks had closed the gap to the point where they no longer feared playing in New Zealand. It was an arm wrestle of epic proportions, with the Springbok forwards once again huge. Handre Pollard was superb on the day, nailing some pressure kicks off the tee, including a match-levelling conversion after the hooter, but it was Herschel Jantjies once more who stole the headlines. With the Boks 16–9 down entering the final minute of play, Cheslin Kolbe found some space down the right flank before kicking ahead. Jantjies, who had replaced Faf de Klerk, was the man chasing, launching himself skyward in a challenge against New Zealand substitute scrumhalf Aaron Smith. Jantjies won the battle, with the ball bouncing off his own shoulder and then looping up perfectly into his arms as he dived over for the try, silencing a Westpac Stadium crowd that had already started celebrating a hard-fought victory. Pollard slotted the extras, and the Boks were rewarded with a draw in a match they had dominated in the first half before being outplayed in the second. After the match, Erasmus said that his side had been lucky, but it did not change the fact that the Boks were now in the hunt for the Rugby Championship title. The World Cup clash between these sides on 21 September in Yokohama would be the game that mattered, and the Springboks had done enough against the All Blacks in 2018 and 2019 to ensure that the result was now almost impossible to call.

This was attacking coach Swys de Bruin's final Test with the Boks before he stood down. 'In my stint against the All Blacks,' De Bruin remembers, 'we got the score to 82–82 in three Tests, and given what had happened before, I am proud of that.' This highlighted the improvement the Boks had achieved under Erasmus against the world's best.

De Bruin may have felt that he could no longer add value to the Boks because of the difference in opinions over playing style, but Erasmus had been prepared to manage that through to the end of the World Cup and was sad to see him go.

'There was never any fighting about that,' Erasmus says. 'A lot of things that he brought into general play, like the "beat your man" thing that he always measured guys on, was fantastic. "Beat your man" is still one of the fundamentals in the sense that Swys taught us that. There are so many things that Swys taught us in those first games that he was with us.

'I had made peace with the fact that Swys would want to run and Jacques would be leaning more towards being structured and organised and I would be the balance between the two. That's actually the way you want your attack and defensive coaches to operate … you want them to fight for their departments and then somebody must settle the two.

'A lot of the fundamentals that Swys taught us helped us win the World Cup final, like seeing the space on the blindside. There was a difference of opinion, but it is something we would have managed without a problem if he hadn't moved out.

'Swys was a massive loss. I would have managed his style of play. We missed him.'

With a weekend off before the tournament-deciding trip to Salta to take on Argentina, the Boks based themselves in Auckland for their preparation instead of returning home. A bonus-point win would guarantee the Boks the Rugby Championship title, but as attractive as that was, the World Cup was still the priority. The good news for South Africans was that Erasmus's plan was to field close to his full-strength side again, seeking continuity, with on-field match preparation time becoming limited ahead of the World Cup. While the coach was almost settled on what his 31-man World Cup squad would be, he acknowledged that it would be a difficult task to whittle down the current group, which consisted of 36 to 38 players at any given time, depending on fitness. Half the Boks left Auckland for Argentina on Friday 2 August, while a second group left that Sunday, leaving the

MIRACLE MEN

squad around a week to prepare for the clash with the Pumas.

The only changes for the Pumas Test came in the front row, where Erasmus brought in Tendai Mtawarira, Bongi Mbonambi and Trevor Nyakane for Steven Kitshoff, Malcolm Marx and Frans Malherbe, respectively. By this stage, the issue of transformation had been dealt with internally in the Springbok dressing room and players knew that if they were good enough, trained hard enough and showed the right attitude, they would be given their opportunities.

'That was the way it was since the very beginning,' centre Lukhanyo Am remembers. 'We all knew where we stood. We just wanted to prove our worth on the field and we knew that if we put in the yards, we would get that chance.'

Fielding an all-black front row, though, was still significant as a reminder of how far the side had come under Erasmus. All too often, black players had been associated with being speedsters in the backline, yet here was a first-choice Springbok side with an all-black front row and a black captain in the forwards (albeit still sidelined by injury). Mbonambi, with every opportunity he got, had started edging ahead of Marx in the race to the number 2 jersey. It was a remarkable feat, since in 2017 and 2018 Marx was considered by many to be the most impactful hooker in the world.

Vermeulen retained the captaincy for Salta, with Kolisi starting his road back to the Boks by featuring for Western Province in the Currie Cup that same weekend. With Australia stunning the All Blacks 47–26 in Perth, the Boks knew that a win – bonus point or not – would be enough to land them the title.

The Boks had endured some tricky trips to South America in recent years, but this was not one of them. Instead, they flexed their muscles in every department, showing off their World Cup credentials by delivering a 46–13 hiding that handed them their first Rugby Championship crown in a decade. Pollard scored a staggering 31 points in that match, while Kolbe and Mapimpi bagged a try each to solidify their positions out wide for the Boks in Japan. The front row collectively dominated the Pumas at scrum time, while Nyakane in particular gave his best performance in Bok colours and made an impressive 15 tackles on the night. The celebrations that followed showed that winning the Championship actually meant a lot to these Springboks, who looked more than ever like they were primed to make a run at higher honours in the weeks and months to come. The Boks had a depth of quality in their squad that South Africa's national side had not seen in years. There were a couple of pieces of the puzzle still to ponder – the fitness of Kolisi being the most obvious – but by the end of the 2019 Rugby Championship the Bok machine had started to take shape beautifully. The strides that had been made were obviously pleasing to Erasmus and his team, but there was the feeling in the Bok management group that there was more to come.

'When we hit 2019, we knew we were prepared, but we didn't quite fire in the Rugby Championship as much as we had wanted to,' Matt Proudfoot remembers. 'We didn't hit the intensities we wanted to. That was a little bit concerning for us, but we knew it would turn.'

The Boks had two more Test matches before their World Cup opener against the All Blacks – against the Pumas at Loftus and Japan, in Japan, two weeks before the start of the World Cup. It may not have been in the original plan, but Erasmus decided to pull back completely for the one-off Test against Argentina at Loftus, which came the weekend after South Africa's Rugby Championship celebrations in Salta.

'Things changed in the Rugby Championship because we actually won the thing,' recalls Francois Louw, who had slotted into his role as a leadership figure off the bench. 'He [Rassie] was conscious that we were going to melt. In that last Argentina game, he completely rotated the side and gave some guys a run there that were third, fourth or fifth in the pecking order.'

Most of the first-choice Boks – Louw included – were then given a few days off. 'I managed to go to a family wedding, which was fantastic – to break away for three or four days, and then come back into camp,' he says. 'Rassie was very aware of the emotional side and understanding when guys needed a break. At the end of the day we're all human, we're not robots, and he saw that side of us.'

The big news ahead of the Loftus Test was that Kolisi was set to feature for the Boks for the first time that year, having finally recovered from his knee injury. Others, however, were not so lucky. It began to look almost certain that Warren Whiteley's seemingly never-ending struggle with injury would rule him out of World Cup contention. It was a bitter pill for Whiteley to swallow, given that at the start of the Erasmus era he had been considered by many as the favourite to lead the Boks in Japan. Damian Willemse and Aphiwe Dyantyi (before the doping case surfaced) were also racing to get fit.

For a host of other Springboks, the clash against the Pumas at Loftus was one final opportunity to convince Erasmus that they should be on the plane to Japan. Erasmus drafted in Scarra Ntubeni for a long-overdue Springbok debut, while Wilco Louw, Marco van Staden and Dillyn Leyds were also added to the squad. Ntubeni had been called up to two previous Springbok squads without ever earning a cap, and for years there had been a running joke at Western Province that while he owned a Springbok blazer, he was never able to wear it. That all changed on 17 August 2019, though, when he earned a Springbok Test cap off the bench against the Pumas.

It was also an emotional day for Schalk Brits, who was named as captain for the fixture despite Kolisi's having been named in the starting lineup. Erasmus wanted Kolisi to focus completely on his game without any distractions, and he was also not sure how long his skipper would last on his return. So it was Brits, at the age of 38 years and three months, who led the Boks into battle in what was his first Test start since 2008. The Boks were far from their best as they relied on two Sbu Nkosi tries to secure a laboured 24–18 win, but the more important news was that Kolisi had played 53 minutes and had looked sharp. The energetic Brits, meanwhile, proved beyond doubt that he still had the goods to perform at Test level with a flawless lineout throwing display, while he made serious metres with ball in hand too. His inclusion for the World Cup was largely down to the experience he offered on the training field and in team meetings, but at Loftus he showed he could do the job on the field if called upon.

Erasmus, his coaching team and a group of 36 Springboks then made their way to Bloemfontein. This would be their final camp in South Africa before the 31-man World Cup squad was announced and they left for Japan. It would mean bad news for five players who were part of the extended squad, but upon closer examination of the desired balance, it was not difficult to figure out who was likely to miss out. Marcell Coetzee had already been ruled out with an ankle injury that required surgery, but when Erasmus released Marvin Orie, Thomas du Toit, Lizo Gqoboka and Andre Esterhuizen from the camp to represent their provinces in the Currie Cup, the writing was on the wall. It was particularly difficult for Esterhuizen, who had run Damian de Allende so close for the number 12 jersey under Erasmus. The arrival of Frans Steyn, though, meant that Erasmus now had sufficient cover in that position. Coetzee, too, was left gutted, having been very much in the mix before his injury. That still left 32 players together in Bloemfontein, and only one would not make the cut.

The Springbok squad for the 2019 Rugby World Cup was announced on Monday 26 August live from SuperSport's Randburg studios. It had been widely accepted that loose forward Rynhardt Elstadt would be cut, and that proved to be the case, but by the time the squad was announced the South African public was digesting a story that would make waves all over the world: star Springbok lock Eben Etzebeth had been accused of a serious assault outside a Langebaan pub in the early hours of that Sunday morning.

The initial accusations came from social media, and reports suggested that the alleged altercation had been fuelled by racial tension, and that Etzebeth and his friends had badly injured the man in question.

A story of this nature, considering Etzebeth's Springbok standing, inevitably commanded media attention, and the timing could not have been worse. The Bok World Cup squad, including 12 players of colour, was the most transformed in the country's history. With Kolisi confirmed as skipper, the side was about to represent South Africa in a way that no Bok outfit had ever done before. This should have been the talking point that day, but instead the South African rugby public found itself divided along racial lines once again. The squad was duly announced, but the headlines were all about the Etzebeth controversy. It was impossible to know exactly what happened that night in Langebaan – the case needed to follow the course of the law – but the mere accusation would hurt the Bok image.

It was a development that required urgent attention, and Erasmus tells the story of how Eugene Henning, CEO of the South African players' union, MyPlayers, was pulled off the aircraft just before it was due to leave for Japan. The Boks did not have a team psychologist or mental coach in their ranks, and Henning was tasked with all issues related to the well-being of the players.

'He was actually on the plane already, having gone through customs. We got Eugene off that plane and he handled that whole situation for us with the right lawyers,' Erasmus says. 'He handled a lot of stuff for us. I'm not a very personal guy who spends time with players one-on-one. They know I'm not like that. We had Eugene. If somebody's house got robbed from roof to carpet in 15 minutes, and then somebody needed to help him while he was busy with training, Eugene would handle that. If one of the players' wives had a problem with something, Eugene would handle it. He helped us out with all kinds of things, and for a players' trade union to work so closely with us and for the SA Rugby leadership to allow that for us was fantastic. Usually, player unions are the enemy, but he went with us as a player affairs manager.'

It was not the last controversy management would have to extinguish before the end of the World Cup, but it was one that had the potential to disrupt what had become an impressively united group of players.

In Australia, Israel Folau had been dropped from the Wallabies World Cup squad and stripped of his professional contracts because of a social media post, based on his strong Christian beliefs, that suggested that homosexuals were sinners. The action of Rugby Australia CEO Raelene Castle effectively ended Folau's career, and had been widely applauded. Given the seriousness of the allegations against Etzebeth, there were many respected critics in the public and media spaces who felt that the SA Rugby bosses should do the same, and that Etzebeth, despite denying the allegations and with nothing tested in court, should not go to Japan. Instead, SA Rugby stood by their man, with both president Mark Alexander and coach Erasmus expressing their confidence that Etzebeth was telling the truth. The importance of Etzebeth to the Springbok cause was obvious, but Erasmus's position did not stem from that logic. He understood the human element of the situation, and it was important for him as a coach to show faith in his players when they needed it.

'If there was any truth in it, it would have been a massive issue for us,' Erasmus said, shortly after naming his squad. 'After speaking to Eben and hearing his side of the story, there is obviously trust between a coach and a player. I must trust him to do stuff on the field for me and win Test matches for us, and he must trust me to believe him when he tells me something.

'I'm pretty comfortable with what he's told me and obviously you can't just believe what someone else says on social media.

'Until something like that gets proven, it's just a rumour, in my opinion.'

Because of the sensitivities surrounding racial division and the ongoing problem of crime in South Africa, this was indeed a bold stance from the SA Rugby leadership. It would have been easy to completely distance themselves, as an organisation, from any behaviour that was potentially rooted in racism or violence. Instead, the members of the Springbok squad – black and white – stood alongside one of their own and believed in him. The unity that had been created within this group was not about to be shattered by a social media post.

'We supported the guy,' Louw recalls. 'In today's society, it's bizarre to make accusations without having all the facts. You can have an opinion, but keep your opinion to yourself. I wasn't there, I don't know what happened, and the fact that politicians got involved and expected certain things was also quite bizarre. Thankfully, we were shut out from it all, being so far away. We had to get on with the job and that's what we did.'

It was a story that simply would not go away. Etzebeth met with representatives of the South African Human Rights Commission (SAHRC) the day before the Boks left for Japan, but the allegations would continue to surface in the early stages of the World Cup, particularly in South Africa as developments were reported. The complainants, who were dubbed the 'Langebaan Four', were reportedly seeking damages in the region of R1 million, and there were allegations that Etzebeth had had a firearm in his possession. The SAHRC lodged a formal complaint against Etzebeth following the Boks' clash with Italy on 4 October, and he followed up by confirming that he would be taking the SAHRC to the High Court. It was messy, and not the kind of discussion Etzebeth, Erasmus or anyone involved in SA Rugby wanted during a World Cup campaign.

On the field, however, the Boks were as prepared as they could possibly be, and they had achieved much in their time together under Erasmus. These Boks were hungry, capable, united and full of belief as a result of their performances over the previous two years, particularly against the world-champion All Blacks. Knowing that they could once again compete with their fiercest rivals was a major confidence booster for a squad that was now rich in depth and full of world-class players. It had not happened overnight, but was the direct result of many hours of sacrifice – on and off the field – and working together in the collective belief that, in Erasmus, the Boks had a coach who knew what was best for them.

'Obviously, we hit speed humps and the plan was tweaked,' says Louw, 'but we were all completely exposed to what was going on and how we were going to do it. Everyone was in sync with each other. We clashed. We bumped heads all the time, but we were constructive in coming out with solutions that we all bought into.'

On Friday 30 August 2019, the Springboks departed from OR Tambo International Airport for Japan. It was a vibrant affair, with Kolisi a central figure as around 2 000 screaming fans saw him and his side off. Had South Africa known what was going to unfold in the weeks to come, however, there would certainly have been more supporters present.

The Etzebeth story, and the various reactions to it, was a reminder of the divisions embedded in South African society, but it also revealed just how tight the bond was between Erasmus and his players. To them, at this stage anyway, these uniquely South African issues were not a factor. The 'main thing' was winning rugby matches at the World Cup. What happened over the next two months, though, brought these very South African issues of racial tension, division, strife and inequality to the forefront for this group of players. When the Boks left Johannesburg that day, with future heroes like Kolisi, Kolbe, Am and Mapimpi on the plane, rugby was their main story. But when they returned nearly two months later, every player on that plane – black or white – knew that there was so much more at play.

Chapter 10
Body and mind

Before the Springboks arrived in Japan, a touching video was posted on social media. It showed a group of around 400 people from the city of Kumagaya, including the mayor, learning the words to the South African national anthem. Kumagaya Stadium was the venue for the Boks' warm-up clash against the tournament hosts on 6 September – two weeks before their tournament opener against the All Blacks in Yokohama. The Japanese public embraced being the centre of the rugby universe, and they made every visiting side feel as welcome as possible. The Brave Blossoms would do their country proud on the field too, making it all the way to the tournament quarter-finals for the first time in their history.

After the Boks arrived in Japan, and just over two weeks out from their World Cup opener, a photograph posted on social media went viral. The post included a large percentage of the 31-man Springbok squad posing shirtless for a team photograph during a gym session in Gifu ahead of the Japan game. It was obviously meant as a lighthearted moment for the Boks, but the impressive physiques of the players made instant waves on the internet, with online news websites quick to point to what looked a superhuman group of players.

The shirtless photograph sent two important messages. The first was that, clearly, the Springboks were at their physical peak. Bongi

Mbonambi, in particular, looked monstrous, but even smaller players such as Cobus Reinach, Cheslin Kolbe and Herschel Jantjies were a picture of strength. Physicality had always been a strong point of successful Springbok teams in years past, and opposition coaches would have expected nothing different from the Bok class of 2019.

The second clear message was in the smiles. The Springboks were enjoying themselves in Japan. By this time, unity was sky-high and a belief existed within the group.

From team selections to playing styles, to work in the gym and on the training ground, these Boks were as prepared as they could possibly be. Erasmus had been vocal during the build-up on his 20-week plan to win the World Cup – the Boks were just over ten weeks in by the time they played against Japan – but in truth that plan had started the second he returned to South Africa in 2018.

While Erasmus hoped his side's early arrival in Japan would help them acclimatise to the severe heat and humidity, he also wanted the Boks to feel comfortable in what was a very different culture. Many of the squad had visited Japan at some point with their Super Rugby franchises, while others had enjoyed extended stints there playing club rugby, but spending more than two months away from home in the intense environment of a World Cup presented a different kind of challenge.

The warm-up match against Japan had both countries' supporters intrigued. It would be their first meeting since that stunning World Cup night in Brighton four years earlier. Erasmus placed a lot of value on this fixture, which the Boks went on to win 41–7, thanks largely to a hat-trick from Makazole Mapimpi, as it gave his players the opportunity to play a competitive match in the Japanese humidity against the side most comfortable in those conditions. As the clash unfolded, and particularly towards the end, it became clear that the Boks had plenty in the tank and were primed.

The pressure of playing a World Cup was something the players had to experience for themselves, and as the tournament unfolded, both the mental and physical strength of the squad would be pushed to their limits. Erasmus knew this and had done everything in his power to ready the Boks for any eventuality on the field, but there were off-field matters that would become significant too. Erasmus could not guarantee results, but he could ensure that, physically and mentally, the Boks gave themselves the best possible chance of success.

In Aled Walters, the Springboks possessed a fitness guru whom Erasmus and Nienaber had rated highly during their time together at Munster. From the very first alignment camps in 2018, Walters began drawing up individual plans for the Boks. His strength was in his relationships with Erasmus and Nienaber, and he knew intimately what the coaches wanted to get out of their players. This was dictated by the type of game Erasmus wanted to play. Having established a relationship at Munster, Walters could quickly identify what physical attributes needed to be prioritised or improved to fit into Erasmus's plan. When he arrived in South Africa, he was immediately struck by the sheer size and physicality of the players, but he quickly went to work, and the Boks realised that they were dealing with a different kind of fitness expert.

Conversations with players reveal that, under Walters, there was never any wasted energy. Every fitness exercise mattered, whether in the gym or on the training field, and contributed towards a certain trait that would be needed on game day. Walters had a skill for managing the players' workloads, and this was shown in 2019 when the Boks were rested strategically – during Super Rugby and the Rugby Championship – as part of a long-term rotation plan for the World Cup.

'There is a big difference between working cleverly and working hard,' Schalk Brits remembers, 'and that's where Aled came in. We worked extremely hard under Aled, but also extremely cleverly.

'My previous experience was that those two things didn't always go hand in hand, but with Aled, he made sure that they did. He emphasised recovery, making sure that it was just as important as what we did on the pitch.'

Flyhalf Elton Jantjies, who had been intimately involved with the Springbok setup during Allister Coetzee's tenure, remembers clearly the first alignment camp under Erasmus and Walters. What stood out for him was the level of detail in the planning, and specifically with regard to conditioning. 'We didn't count the days, we made the days count,' Jantjies says. 'Aled wasn't stupid in making us run for the sake of running. It was all position-specific and centred around the metres we were going to run on game days. There was a lot of technology behind it. We all had different requirements and different standards and that's what Aled got right.'

The physical requirements were unique to the Bok game plan, with each player's role different to that of the man next to him. Were the Springboks the fittest team in Japan? There are no metrics that can prove that, because every side made different demands of their players, and they prioritised different things.

The Boks were, however, at the optimum physical level for the type of game they wanted to play. Clinical, physical and dominant defence would be the key weapon in the Springbok arsenal, and these players had the muscle. Relentless tackling also required endurance, and these players were lean enough to ensure that there would be no signs of fatigue, such as hands on heads or sucking in air. The balance between raw physicality and stamina had been perfectly cultivated, and it was all down to a Welshman whom many in South Africa had never heard of before 2018.

'It wasn't a walk in the park. We took proper shots, nothing like

Kamp Staaldraad, but very proactive,' Francois Louw remembers of his sessions under Walters. 'In my opinion, Aled has the most important trait that a conditioner can have, and that's to get the buy-in from the players. You get guys who can shout at you until they're blue in the face, but if you don't get guys buying into your system, what are you actually going to get out of the person?'

Walters would push the Boks hard on the training ground, but he understood the human element and the players appreciated him for it. 'When Aled asked for something, the guys listened. When it was time to go off and relax, he gave the guys the freedom to go and do that,' Louw adds. 'He was a Welshman coming into quite a hardcore South African culture that is massively diverse, but before the end he was speaking Afrikaans and Xhosa and the guys loved him. When he said, "Get on your horse and go!" the guys did that.'

Japan did not give the Boks the biggest test on the scoreboard in that warm-up match, but the scoreline failed to tell the whole story. The Springboks spent a large chunk of the game tackling, but as the final whistle drew nearer, they were the ones who finished with comfortably more energy. The Japanese, playing in their home conditions, seemed to be running on empty. It was not a result that meant anything in the greater context of the tournament, but it was perhaps the first sign of exactly how fit these Springboks were.

'That warm-up game against Japan was a massive unknown for us with the conditions and the environment. We really did well in that game and that almost launched the team … we were flying after that,' Matt Proudfoot remembers.

During the tournament, the Boks would have their run-ins with injury, and would lose Jesse Kriel (hamstring) and Trevor Nyakane (torn calf) early on. It was particularly devastating for Nyakane, who had booked his ticket to Japan after a tireless season of training, on and off the field, and a stellar performance in Super Rugby 2019 and the Rugby Championship. The images of him in tears after leaving the Yokohama turf during the All Blacks game confirmed that his journey had come to an end.

Thomas du Toit replaced Nyakane while Damian Willemse jetted over from Saracens, where he had been on a short-term loan, to replace Kriel. Star wing Cheslin Kolbe missed the semi-final against Wales with an ankle injury, but other than that, the Boks were largely unscathed in the injury department. Walters was rightly praised for achieving a level of conditioning that was crucial to the ultimate success of the Boks.

Erasmus later revealed that there were only a couple of instances where players with niggles had to sit out of training. One of them was Siya Kolisi. The coach was keen on managing his skipper carefully, and he gave Kolisi 66 minutes in the Japan game. The skipper grew stronger as the tournament progressed, but it was a gamble to take him to Japan in the first place given his lack of game time in 2019. It was a gamble that ultimately paid off, though, thanks to superb management from Erasmus and Walters.

'The moment you get a conditioning coach that understands that he mustn't just get the players fit, but fit for the way we want to play, then you're on the right track,' Erasmus says. 'He must understand what player is where and what he is doing at his franchise. How old is he? How must you manage him? How do you get him fit to play the way we want to play?

'Aled has got that ability. He sits in at every coaches' meeting and the next morning you will see that the warm-up drill contains what we are trying to get out of the training session. After every meeting he would go and work out how he could help the coaches get their coaching points across the next day. He was brilliant at that.'

The test of mental strength was a different matter entirely and was even more intriguing because the mindset of the squad shifted as the tournament progressed. As Kolisi has said numerous times since lifting the Webb Ellis Cup, Erasmus did not initially ask the Springboks to play to lift the country and unify the people back home. Rugby was always the primary focus; it had to be if the Boks were going to achieve anything. Erasmus knew that if the Boks were going to leave a legacy and become a story worth telling, they first needed to win. And that was his message. But as the World Cup reached its business end, and as the Boks drew closer to realising an impossible dream, the significance of what they were achieving back home became more obvious. This World Cup was no longer only about rugby. This was about a nation, divided in so many ways, coming together.

As they progressed further together, how could they not think about what success would mean to the country? It required mental strength, particularly in that week between the semi-final and the final, not to let the social significance of a potential World Cup win impact on performance.

There was, and had to be, a mental toughness about this squad. As the tournament progressed, there were criticisms from the rugby public back home, particularly aimed at Faf de Klerk and Willie le Roux, for what was perceived as a lack of form. Eben Etzebeth's Langebaan case was another distraction, while, later on, the side would be absurdly accused of being divided along racial lines when the infamous 'Bomb Squad' story unfolded. Throughout all of these sideshows, the Boks remained united, bound together by a common goal.

More important than any of this, though, was the situation at home. South Africa was burning: gender-based violence, xenophobic attacks and crime of all kinds continued to ravage communities; service delivery was patchy at best; the economy was at a standstill, with unprecedented levels of unemployment; and loadshedding was making life difficult for everybody. There was a feeling that South

Africans had put up with just about enough. All of this was happening while the Boks were in Japan trying to win a World Cup. They were far from the most important South African story of 2019, but these Boks left South Africa as rugby players and it is no exaggeration to say to say that they returned home as social warriors. They were role models, beacons of hope in the darkest, toughest times, and it took emotional and mental maturity to deal with that responsibility, both in winning the final and in dealing with the astonishing response when they returned home.

The measure of mental strength in elite sport is the ability to deliver high-level performances consistently and when the pressure is at its most suffocating. And while Erasmus's definition of what pressure is to South Africans ahead of the final was perfectly timed, it took emotional intelligence and social awareness to embrace what they heard from home. When they took to the field for the final, they did so as South Africans before they were Springboks. Together, these Boks had a role to play in something far bigger than rugby, but Erasmus's emphasis on prioritising performance above all else over the previous 18 months meant that the Boks understood that they had to win in order to inspire. The Boks could not allow themselves to get carried away, and their mental state, despite all the emotion, had to be focused exclusively on their plan. They needed to strike a balance.

Many analysts believe that the Boks were so good against England in the final that they would have beaten anybody on the day, thanks largely to the fact that they were mentally, tactically and physically prepared for any scenario.

'The Boks won before they got on the field,' says mental conditioning expert Mike Horn. An explorer at heart, Horn has worked with the Indian cricket team that won the 2011 World Cup, the Proteas when they became the number-one-ranked Test side in the world in

2012, the German football side that won the 2014 World Cup and the Kolkata Knight Riders in the Indian Premier League.

Horn's résumé is extensive, and he has been tasked with motivating the best in the world to find something extra from somewhere in the pursuit of victory.

In an unexpected role reversal, it was the Boks who inspired Horn in 2019. While the Boks were in Japan, the 53-year-old Horn was on an expedition to the Arctic with his Norwegian counterpart, Boerge Ousland. The pair crossed the frozen Arctic Ocean on foot via the North Pole, a gruelling journey of some 1 650 kilometres. Horn and Ousland were starting to run low on supplies, having taken a few wrong turns along the way and lost valuable time. Both were losing weight, Horn started to develop frostbite, and the families of the men were extremely worried and on the verge of sending out an emergency rescue team. With around a month and a half still to go, and with no guarantee he would reach his destination, Horn clearly remembers receiving a satellite message from his brother informing him that the Boks had beaten England to become 2019 world champions. That message, he says, changed the course of his mission.

'That was the only news I got in four and a half months on the ice,' he recalls. 'It was inspirational to me. The Boks had come such a long way since the last World Cup when they lost to Japan in their first game, to winning the World Cup in Japan, and that was something that meant so much to me as a South African. It gave me the motivation to keep going.'

Horn and Ousland somehow completed their expedition in one piece. Upon watching the Springbok games when he got home, Horn said the mental strength of the Boks grew as they moved through the group stages and knockouts.

'They had that progression that leads to your self-belief growing and that is very important in a World Cup campaign,' he says. 'If you look at their body language and the way they moved on the field, it looked like they moved as a unit. I think Rassie speaking to the boys about entitlement and the process and what a World Cup win means helped a lot.'

According to Horn, the Boks simply wanted it more, particularly in their final against England: 'It is he who has the strongest belief that will conquer. I think that's what is so important in sport, and what the Boks had.'

Tactically, the Boks were prepared for the World Cup. They had their game plan, and because it was a simple one, they could adapt if the situation demanded it. They were physically ready, something that was down to the relationship between, and the work done by, Erasmus, Nienaber and Walters.

Much of the build-up to the tournament, from the very first alignment camps, saw the Boks around a table and away from the training ground. The mental component of this journey was as important to Erasmus as anything else. He needed his players to know exactly what was expected of them. He needed them to believe that through the right levels of hard work, sacrifice, accountability and togetherness they could achieve the unthinkable in Japan.

It is no coincidence that the Springboks of 2019 were able to unite a nation. They were a diverse group of players who were united themselves, and this came as a result of countless hours spent together, singing from the same hymn book to understand the same message. Together, they reviewed philosophies and tactics, analysed opposition, studied referees and understood the immense privilege they had in representing their country. It was the planning necessary to achieve a level of mental and emotional maturity that would translate into success.

The senior players in the side, such as Francois Louw, were treated exactly the same as the youngest, such as scrumhalf Herschel

Jantjies. This was Erasmus's way – open cards, an open platform for anyone to raise any point or discussion, and complete transparency. It created a culture in which these players quickly rallied around a common cause. If you wanted to be a part of this World Cup group, then you needed to show that you were on board with the plan.

It was important, though, for the Boks to enjoy themselves along the way, and Erasmus knew that better than anyone. 'We've got a strong drinking culture in the team,' Louw adds, 'which I'm not afraid to say. That's what kept the guys sane. When we had an off day, we enjoyed each other's company and had a bit of a blow-out, but when it was time to work and get back to it there was a complete buy-in.'

The Boks arrived in Japan fresh, energised, in superb physical condition and, most importantly, confident and full of belief that they could do something special. All that was left now was to transfer that confidence into performances on the field, and for that they would not have to wait long. The defending champions, the All Blacks, were first up.

Chapter 11
A losing start

The Japan game ticked all the right boxes for the Springboks in their commanding 41–7 victory. Their defence and fitness levels in the extreme heat were superb and they scored six tries on the day – five belonging to their two wings, with Makazole Mapimpi bagging a hat-trick and Cheslin Kolbe scoring two. Three of the tries came from counterattacks and two were off the back of a dominant set piece – exactly according to the Bok blueprint. With the side at full strength, the Boks were in another league to their Japanese opposition, and the win boded well for the start of their World Cup charge.

Just hours after the match ended, news came that 1995 World Cup-winning wing Chester Williams had died suddenly after suffering a heart attack in his Cape Town home. Williams was due to travel to Japan for the World Cup, where he planned to promote his Chester's Lager and IPA beer range. As South Africa mourned a man who had paved the way for players of colour in rugby, in Kumagaya the Boks internalised the news. In the space of less than two months, both starting wings from that famous Springbok team of 1995 had passed away unexpectedly. The legacies of Chester Williams and James Small were celebrated at the 2019 World Cup final, though, when the Springbok numbers 11 and 14 both scored tries to make history for their country. At Williams' memorial service at the University of the

LEFT: Cobus Reinach's hat-trick in the Springboks' 66–7 win against Canada in Kobe on 8 October was the fastest in Rugby World Cup history.
MIKE HEWITT/GETTY IMAGES

BELOW: Makazole Mapimpi scored two tries for his side in their 26–3 quarter-final victory against Japan in Tokyo on 20 October. Mapimpi's road to World Cup glory was inspiring.
BRENDAN MORAN/SPORTSFILE VIA GETTY IMAGES

Beast Mtawarira was shown a yellow card for this tackle in the quarter-final against Japan. Mtawarira would announce his retirement from international competition after the tournament, leaving as a true great of South African rugby. ANNE-CHRISTINE POUJOULAT/AFP VIA GETTY IMAGES

Flyhalf Handre Pollard was faultless off the tee and was named man of the match in the 19–16 semi-final win against Wales in Yokohama on 27 October. Pollard got better and better throughout the tournament and was vital to South Africa's success. Behind Pollard are centre Lukhanyo Am and conditioning coach ALED WALTERS. THE ASAHI SHIMBUN VIA GETTY IMAGES

Siya Kolisi, Bongi Mbonambi and Cheslin Kolbe (foreground) and the rest of the Springboks celebrate their semi-final win over Wales. CRAIG MERCER/MB MEDIA/GETTY IMAGES

Lukhanyo Am and Makazole Mapimpi combine to score the Boks' first try in the World Cup final against England in Yokohama on 2 November. CAMERON SPENCER/GETTY IMAGES

Cheslin Kolbe beats England captain Owen Farrell to score South Africa's second try in the World Cup final. Kolbe was one of the stars of Japan 2019 and became a South African fan favourite. SHAUN BOTTERILL/GETTY IMAGES

Man of the match Duane Vermeulen (holding the ball) was magnificent in the final, where the Springbok pack dominated. Also pictured here are (from top left) Tendai Mtawarira, Malcom Marx, Frans Malherbe, Pieter-Steph du Toit, Franco Mostert and Eben Etzebeth.
WESSEL OOSTHUIZEN/GALLO IMAGES

LEFT: Siya Kolisi and President Cyril Ramaphosa lift the Webb Ellis Cup together as the Springboks celebrate making history.
WESSEL OOSTHUIZEN/GALLO IMAGES

BELOW: The Springbok captain takes a moment for himself after the final.
DAVID ROGERS/GETTY IMAGES

Pieter-Steph du Toit and Duane Vermeulen share a beer after the World Cup final. Du Toit would go on to be named the 2019 World Rugby Player of the Year. JUAN JOSE GASPARINI /GALLO IMAGES/ GETTY IMAGES

Prince Harry and Francois Louw in the change room after the final. Louw's leadership during the World Cup was later hailed as being crucial by coach Rassie Erasmus.
JUAN JOSE GASPARINI /GALLO IMAGES/GETTY IMAGES

The arrivals hall at OR Tambo International as fans greet the returning Springboks. It was the beginning of a South African celebration that would last for weeks. GUILLEM SARTORIO/AFP VIA GETTY IMAGES

Siya Kolisi and Rassie Erasmus speak to the media after the team's arrival at OR Tambo International. The smiles tell their own story. SYDNEY SESHIBEDI /GALLO IMAGES/GETTY IMAGES

Makazole Mapimpi, Lukhanyo Am and Siya Kolisi were all greeted as heroes on the entire Eastern Cape leg of the trophy tour. AUTHOR PHOTO

Author Lloyd Burnard shares a light moment with World Cup winner Schalk Brits on the Port Elizabeth leg of the trophy tour. AUTHOR PHOTO

Western Cape, where he worked as head coach of their Varsity Cup side, PJ Powers belted out 'World in Union' as a hall crowded with people, including 1995 captain Francois Pienaar, broke down under the weight of the emotion.

Erasmus's attention to detail in preparing his side for the World Cup had by now been accepted as the norm by every member of the Bok setup. Every possible eventuality, and every possible area where the Boks could find an advantage, had been examined and then re-examined by Erasmus. This level of planning extended to the refereeing, too, and the Bok management team had gone out of their way to analyse the men who would oversee their fixtures at the World Cup. Frenchman Jérôme Garcès, who had been involved in some controversial decisions in matches involving the Springboks in previous years, was tasked with blowing South Africa's tournament opener against New Zealand. Garcès, by the time the World Cup was over, would have refereed the Springboks in three matches, including the 2 November final and the semi-final against Wales the week before. The Boks could not have known this at the start of the tournament, so they were fortunate to have carried out such extensive homework on Garcès in particular.

Erasmus's new approach to officiating had come months ahead of the tournament, in response to the controversial Owen Farrell tackle during the 2018 end-of-year tour. The coach had set up a panel to provide feedback on the referees the Boks would have in Japan. The plan, simply, was to know as much about the referees as possible so that, on game day, the Boks could be in the best possible position to manage expectations, and they hoped to get the rub of the green when it came to a marginal decision. The research included analysis on how the referees blew games of rugby, from scrummaging to the dark arts at the breakdown and the offside line. But it went much deeper than that.

The level of detail in the refereeing reports included personality traits, all with the hope of finding an edge. The Springboks would role-play at team meetings and at training sessions, practising what they would say to the match officials with the research in mind. The report compiled on Garcès, for example, revealed that he responded well to being complimented on his physical appearance. If the match was fast-paced, the Boks would make a point of praising Garcès on his condition and his ability to keep up with the players, hoping to rub him up the right way.

The Boks identified different role-players for matches involving Garcès. Siya Kolisi, as captain, was tasked with treating Garcès with respect throughout the contest, working with him to keep the game moving. If there were any issues with how Garcès was blowing the game, those concerns were to be raised by Duane Vermeulen. There were many observers, specifically during the early stages of the World Cup, who suggested that Vermeulen was running the show on the field for the Springboks. That was never the case. It was a predetermined plan from Erasmus and the Boks to keep Kolisi on Garcès' good side throughout the match. Vermeulen was simply playing his role.

Another role was reserved for whoever the hooker was on the field – Bongi Mbonambi or Malcolm Marx – and his job was to ensure that the set pieces were as structured as possible throughout. The research suggested that Garcès took kindly to sides that provided a clean set piece. He didn't want people wandering around aimlessly at lineout and scrum time; he wanted the players to be in their positions and ready to proceed with the game. He wanted structure, and the Springbok hookers would check in with him throughout the match to make sure they were in the right places at the right times for a set piece, doing their bit to make the game as clean as possible.

The Springboks talked about their plans for each referee, and those plans would involve certain tactics that would have escaped the attention of most onlookers. In some instances, the Boks would deliberately tie their shoelaces or place their hands on their knees when being addressed by the referee, because their research had suggested that certain referees felt intimidated when having to look up at larger, more physically imposing players. Speaking down to a player made some referees feel more powerful or more in control. Every management team at this level would devote time to preparing for the referees, but it is difficult to believe that any team at the 2019 World Cup went to the same level of detail as Erasmus and the Boks.

The Springboks' intricate planning was to be immediately tested as they left their base in Kagoshima and headed off to Tokyo to prepare for the All Blacks game on 21 September. This was the blockbuster attraction of the group stage given the quality of the two sides and their history. Conditions were extreme, but the Boks' early arrival in Japan certainly helped them. Conditioning guru Aled Walters confirmed that Vermeulen lost three kilograms in training due to the heat and humidity. 'I play in Durban and I'm kind of used to the heat, but this was on another level,' Sharks and Bok number 13 Lukhanyo Am remembers.

Much of the pre-match talk in South Africa centred around Garcès. The Boks had won just four of their 14 Tests under the Frenchman, including five straight Test defeats against the All Blacks. The South Africans had more detailed plans for Garcès this time around, but they were more interested in their own performance. This fixture would have a major influence on whom the Springboks would face in the quarter-finals. If the Boks won and finished top of their pool, then Scotland would be their likeliest opponents in the last eight. If they lost, and finished second in the pool, then a clash against heavily fancied Ireland awaited. As it turned out, neither of those scenarios materialised, thanks to Japan's stunning performance in Pool A, where they finished ahead of both Ireland and Scotland.

MIRACLE MEN

There were no surprises when Erasmus named his side for the match against the All Blacks: it was the exact same match-day 23 that had beaten Japan in the warm-up. As Kolisi led the Springboks out onto the field at International Stadium Yokohama, millions of South Africans huddled around their television sets. It had been a long journey to the World Cup, filled with highs and lows, but the waiting was finally over. The Springboks were Rugby Championship winners, and the prospect of taking on the might of the Kiwis in their very first assignment was tantalising.

There was no clear favourite, but the All Blacks emerged victorious on a day on which the Boks, with Chester Williams' face imprinted in the numbers on their jerseys in tribute, probably felt they deserved more. A tight start, characterised by kicking from both sides and strong, safe ball-carrying, saw the first quarter locked at 3–3, with the Boks dominating territorially. A vintage counterattack, against the run of play, then saw wing George Bridge give the All Blacks the lead with a try. Just a couple of minutes later, Scott Barrett went over for New Zealand's second, following another period of sustained, albeit free-flowing attack that penetrated the Bok defence. Having been as good, if not better, than the All Blacks for most of the match up to that point, the Boks found themselves down 17–3 after 27 minutes. While they came close, they could not recover.

Pieter-Steph du Toit scored after a frantic period of open play early in the second half to close the gap, but there was just too much left for the Boks to do. A Handre Pollard drop goal narrowed the deficit to 17–13 going into the last quarter, but the All Blacks held on and added two further penalties to claim the win. Ultimately, a period of five minutes in which the Boks slipped two tries cost them, and so they started the tournament with a loss. If the Boks were going to win the World Cup, they would need to become the first side in history to do so after losing a match at the tournament.

The nature of the rivalry between South Africa and New Zealand dictates that their contests will always be intense. The fact that this was a World Cup encounter only heightened the tension. The Boks were visibly disappointed when, after a mix-up between Willie le Roux and Makazole Mapimpi, Garcès blew his whistle to bring the match to a close. They had been waiting for this day for months and had prepared to win. That was and had always been the mindset against the old foe. But, because of the message from Erasmus before the fixture, the Boks did not dwell on the result and moved on almost instantly. This was not the match, win or lose, that was going to define their World Cup charge, and Erasmus had made that perfectly clear in the build-up.

'If we had beaten New Zealand, then against Italy we could have played almost a second-string team. You can't really manipulate who you want to play in the quarter-finals because you don't know what is going to happen,' Erasmus explains.

'You have to win that one big game. We wanted to beat the All Blacks and we couldn't, but we still knew that we could beat Italy. The other two – Namibia and Canada – were really warm-up matches.

'Winning a World Cup is easier than winning a Rugby Championship in terms of the number of matches you need to be well prepared for.'

Garcès, as expected, figured in the ensuing backlash, with many South African supporters feeling their side had been hard done by. The Boks conceded nine penalties to just four from the All Blacks, with the Boks coming out on the wrong side of a few calls that looked to be touch and go. It was the All Blacks, however, who made headlines over the refereeing, with captain Kieran Read labelling as 'gutless' Garcès' decision not to sin-bin Mapimpi, who was caught lying over the ball to slow down the play.

The Boks, meanwhile, noted the decisions that had gone against them and sought feedback from World Rugby's refereeing panel on where they had gone wrong. Never once did Erasmus or Kolisi criticise a referee, either publicly or during a match. With the emphasis that had been placed on adapting to the officiating, the disciplinary return against the All Blacks was still disappointing for Erasmus. What he could not fault, however, was the commitment of his players, nor, for the most part, their execution. The Boks had been nowhere near outplayed on the day and, although they went down by ten points, the performance confirmed a belief that they could go the distance.

'The reality was we knew we could afford to lose that game,' Francois Louw remembers. 'We had beaten them the year before and drawn to them that year. We gave everything and prepared as best we could, but the reality was that we knew it didn't matter. What mattered was the next task, which was the next three games in our pool. We didn't change anything for the next game in terms of our outlook or approach to training. Every pool game was approached the same way that the final was approached. We were methodical to the point where it became monotonous, but in a positive way.'

The Boks had lost, but they kept faith in what they were doing and in their preparation. As they left International Stadium Yokohama that day, most of the players believed that they would meet the All Blacks again before the tournament was done. England and Eddie Jones, of course, had other ideas, but at the time the Boks felt that they had unfinished business with their southern-hemisphere neighbours.

Erasmus had created an atmosphere in which the expectations for that first All Black match did not lie in the result, and because of this the Springboks were able to bounce back quickly.

'He completely took the pressure off the players for the All Blacks game,' forwards coach Matt Proudfoot says. 'He said we were going to go in hard for it, but win or lose it didn't matter. He just wanted a performance out of that game. He didn't allow them to start the competition under pressure. He told the players that all he cared about was the work rate and how hard they worked for each other. He said the result was on him, not on anybody else. I think there were two bad kicks in the game, and that probably cost us. They countered from their own half and scored two tries, but we looked at the game structurally and we were actually really happy.

'Everything we wanted to do, we did. There were a few areas we wanted to improve on, and we spent the next three weeks doing that, but the big game for us was always going to be Italy. That was the game we prepared for, because that would put us into the quarter-final and give us a chance.'

While it hurt to lose to the All Blacks, the Springbok reaction to the defeat was enough to convince assistant coach Mzwandile Stick that they were very much on the right track: 'I knew exactly why we lost, and I never doubted us. I could see we were in the right space. Yes, we had been hurt by our interpretation of the laws against the All Blacks, but I knew that the boys were in the right space,' he recalls. 'If you had to ask me for a point where I realised that we've got what it takes to win, I would say it was after we lost against the All Blacks.'

Proudfoot also believes that the match against the All Blacks was the day Kolisi took a giant step forward in his captaincy. All Black captain Read got the better of Garcès and, as a result, was influencing the match far more than Kolisi was.

'I think he was struggling to get back to full fitness. He wasn't at his best in that All Black game. When you're not fully fit, it's difficult to concentrate on the referee that much,' Erasmus says.

From that point, however, Kolisi really grasped the importance of controlling the refereeing as much as possible, and the role-playing the Boks had worked on together kicked in. Every inch of space needed to be fought for in the pursuit of victory. While the Boks felt they had lost a few because of their reaction to the officiating, they would not let that happen again.

'That's the game where Siya really understood: "It's me against the opposition captain here. Who is going to control this game? It's either going to be me or him."' Proudfoot says. 'That was when he realised he needed to take it on board and bring in guys like Duane, Bongi and Malcolm ... they knew they needed to support Siya and allow him to do his job. That gave the team extra teeth, in that we could start controlling the five or six grey penalties in a game, and those are the penalties that could win or lose you a World Cup final. That was phenomenal.'

Trevor Nyakane, meanwhile, received the devastating news that he would be returning to South Africa after sustaining a torn calf against New Zealand. He would be replaced by Thomas du Toit, who was rushed over from Toulouse, where he was on loan.

This was also the match in which scrumhalf Faf de Klerk started receiving heat from back home for his persistent box kicking. The territorial element was crucial to Erasmus's game plan, and De Klerk was a central figure in that plan, but a large section of the South African rugby public laid into the blond number 9 on social media. Admittedly, De Klerk had struggled with his accuracy against New Zealand. The criticism of De Klerk would last for the duration of the tournament and was only forgotten once the Boks were crowned world champions, but the need for him to kick had been identified by Erasmus and Jacques Nienaber as the philosophy that was most likely to bring about success. It was a stark reminder to the Springboks that the South African rugby public, first and foremost, wanted results. It had only taken one defeat, on the biggest stage and against the world champions, for the pressure to start building from the home supporters.

Another topic of discussion was Kolisi, who was the first player substituted by Erasmus against the All Blacks, getting through 50 minutes before he was taken off. It sparked further debate over the skipper's physical state and match readiness. When Kolisi left the field, Vermeulen took over the captaincy, prompting questions over who the real leader of the group was.

The Boks' second match, against Namibia in Toyota on 28 September, seemed an ideal opportunity to get some valuable playing minutes under Kolisi's belt. It came as a shock, then, when Erasmus included him as one of the substitutes for the clash at City of Toyota Stadium. It was one of 13 changes to the Springbok starting lineup as Erasmus backed the quality of depth that he had spent a year and a half building. With Mapimpi and Am the only two players to retain their places, the captaincy was given to Schalk Brits, who started at number 8. Not only was Brits experienced and more than capable, but he also added an element of versatility, shifting from the front of the scrum to the back. Since his comeback, Brits had captained the Boks at Ellis Park against Australia, and now he would have the honour of leading his country on the grandest stage of them all.

Frans Steyn came in at number 12 for his first Test start in over seven years, while the two Jantjies – Herschel and Elton – were named as the halfback pairing. Elton Jantjies was becoming an increasingly important figure for young Herschel, and had taken the Stormers scrumhalf under his wing. Herschel, having joined the Boks relatively late, had a lot of catching up to do. Looking back, he identifies Elton, his room-mate throughout the World Cup, as having been key in that regard.

'Elton really helped me a lot and I think it showed in the games we played together,' Herschel Jantjies says. 'We had a good understanding of what we needed to do. Every time we had a conversation it would help me with something, and if I didn't get something, he would be the first guy that I would ask.

'He went to bed every night with a laptop, analysing the opposition, and fell asleep most nights with the laptop on his chest. He did everything he could and then brought that intensity to the training in emulating the opposition. He'd have to know our stuff and their stuff, and it was just amazing. I learnt a lot from him.

'He would say to me once or twice, "Flip, I really want to play," but you would never see that impact his training or his attitude. He was the ultimate team man.'

Elton Jantjies was one of many players in this Springbok squad, Brits included, who knew their role. If everybody was fit, he would not play the games that mattered most. Pollard was comfortably the first-choice number 10, and given Erasmus's desire to field six forwards on the bench, there was no room there for Jantjies either. It did not stop him, though, from doing all he could to help the Boks win the World Cup. In the week of the final, England were believed to be in two minds over whether to play Owen Farrell or George Ford at flyhalf. Jantjies' job for the week was to replicate both styles of play at training and to run the Springbok 'B-backline' as close to what the Boks could expect from the English on match day. Thanks to many hours on the training field and in front of his laptop analysing, Jantjies gave Pollard and the rest of the Boks as close to the real thing as they could have hoped for that week. If you speak to any member of the Springbok coaching staff, they will tell you that Jantjies' work ethic is near-unrivalled and add how important his work on replicating the English plays was in the build-up to the final.

Every player wanted to start every match; that is the way it has always been in professional sport. This could not happen at the World Cup, and there was a natural pecking order. What every player had in common, however, was the desire to leave Japan as world champions.

'We had such good meetings with guys who I thought were going to be reserves and there were even some who I told they might not even play a game at the World Cup,' Erasmus says.

'It's a bitter pill to swallow, but all of them sucked up their pride and committed to working together to win this tournament. I called Schalk Brits, Francois Louw and about seven guys when we landed in Japan. I told Schalk he was probably going to play two games – one at number 8 and probably the other one at hooker – and that he was probably going to captain in both of them. That was his part of the World Cup and we're going to be there for eight weeks and the guys needed to accept that, and they did.'

It also helped that every player, regardless of how much he played (or did not) at the World Cup, had the same financial incentive from SA Rugby. This was another Erasmus masterstroke in his efforts to foster unity.

'If I played one minute or every minute, we would all get the same financial bonus if we won,' Brits remembers. 'That was something that every player bought into. Even the players that got injured at the World Cup, like Jesse and Trevor, got the same amount of money as I got and that Siya and Pieter-Steph got. That made a big difference.'

With Kolisi struggling to return to full match fitness, another player who would have been thinking about starting berths as the tournament progressed was veteran Francois Louw. Considered one of the shrewdest loose forwards in world rugby, Louw had to accept early on that if he wanted to go on this journey with the Springboks, and to improve on the semi-final place he achieved under Heyneke Meyer in 2015, he would have to accept his role.

'You want to play, but that was Rassie's plan and he was very open about it. I knew from the outset that my role was going to be a support player in the back row,' Louw says. 'It was a role that I fully embraced and towards the end we had formed a tight unit on the bench in the Bomb Squad. We really lived up to that reputation and genuinely saw ourselves as the guys that would make the difference and win the games. I fully accepted it and it made for an unbelievably enjoyable tournament for me. It was a decision out of my hands and all I could do was play as well as I possibly could.'

Despite his assigned role, Louw would go on to be one of the key members of the Springbok class of 2019, both on the field and off. 'People talk a lot about Schalk Brits and he did have a massive role, but Francois Louw played just as big a role. He helped Siya so much with his leadership,' says Erasmus.

In the knowledge that they were effectively Erasmus's second-choice side, the Boks prepared to meet Namibia. In Pool D, Uruguay had stunned Fiji a few days before to land a 30–27 win, and then, hours before the Bok match, Japan knocked over Ireland. It was one of the great results in Rugby World Cup history, with the hosts bringing tears to the eyes of their passionate fans at Shizuoka Stadium. That 19–12 win meant as much to the Brave Blossoms as their stunning night in Brighton against the Boks in 2015. More importantly, it threw the quarter-final race in Pool A wide open. A tournament that most had expected to be predictable in terms of results had already provided two major upsets, and these served as a timely reminder to the Springboks that anything was possible.

The Boks, as expected, were far too strong for their southern African neighbours as they ran in nine unanswered tries in a dominant, if not spectacular, 57–3 win. Mbonambi and Mapimpi scored two tries each, while Louw, Am, Warrick Gelant, Kolisi and Brits all got over the line for their slice of history. While Lood de Jager was the official man of the match, Brits was one of the standout players for the Boks, slotting in seamlessly at number 8 in a move that allowed Mbonambi to take further strides towards making the number 2 jersey his own. Kolisi entered the fray in the 53rd minute of the match, getting nearly 30 minutes of game time. Elton Jantjies did not have his best day, however. The Boks were expected to be far more of a threat with ball in hand, but they ended up relying on the dominance of their pack for most of their rewards on the scoreboard. Given the overall philosophy of the Boks, this was nothing that Erasmus and his management team needed to lose any sleep over.

The story of that weekend, though, was undoubtedly what would become known as the 'Shizuoka Shock' and Japan's fairy-tale triumph over the Irish. For months before the tournament, Ireland had been tipped as potential title challengers at the World Cup, and they arrived at the showpiece having moved to the top of the world rankings. While the rugby world marvelled at the efforts of the Japanese, it was a result that also had a direct impact on the Springboks and their path to the final. With the Boks having lost to New Zealand, they knew that their quarter-final would almost certainly be against whoever topped Pool A. That was expected to be Ireland, but now it seemed that Japan were in with a shout. A quarter-final against the tournament hosts was not something that Erasmus would have thought likely at the start of the World Cup. While he could never acknowledge it publicly, it was surely a more attractive proposition than squaring up against the Irish.

First, the Boks had to take care of their own business, with fixtures against Italy and Canada. Italy, long before the World Cup, had identified the match against the Springboks as their pathway to the quarter-finals. They had, after all, beaten the Boks once since the last World Cup, and that night in Florence would serve as the motivation for a belief that they could do it again. It represented the ultimate banana peel for the Boks, but this side had come a long way since the disastrous end-of-year-tour in 2016. It would mean nothing if they did not deliver the goods on the field, though. All of the planning, the preparation, the hours on the training field, in the gym and around a table at team meetings ... it was all for this. The World Cup final was still the dream, but until they had knocked over Italy, the Boks could not afford to think that far ahead.

Chapter 12

The Bomb Squad

The Springboks were in high spirits during the short train ride from Toyota to Shizuoka. The performance against Namibia had been far from flawless, but the Boks were on the board at Rugby World Cup 2019 and had used all their second-string players during the match, highlighting the depth of quality in the squad. The mood was optimistic back home. It was more than just support, though; there resonated a tangible belief that Rassie Erasmus's Springboks could go the distance.

Erasmus had spoken in the build-up to the tournament about the Springboks potentially flying under the radar, with sides such as New Zealand, England and Ireland more heavily fancied. But at this point in the competition all the talk was about the performance of Japan's Brave Blossoms, who were stealing the show. Their win over Ireland had rattled the tournament. Rugby in Japan had grown tremendously since 2015, but the national side was still far from being considered a powerhouse of the game, while in Super Rugby the Tokyo-based Sunwolves franchise had underachieved. Japan's effort at their own World Cup in 2019, though, echoed that of a top-tier nation, and every bit of praise was fully deserved.

The Springboks could not pay attention to any of that – not yet, anyway. Japan would be a part of their World Cup journey, but a slippery clash against the Italians awaited. After the loss to the All Blacks, a win against Italy was now South Africa's ticket to the quarter-finals and Erasmus treated the fixture as if it was a knockout game. Absolutely nothing could be taken for granted.

Based on the information gathered on their pre-tournament reconnaissance, the Springboks isolated themselves as much as they could for a week that Erasmus knew could define their campaign.

'We had a specific location for that week, which was on a golf course, and it was only us in the hotel,' Erasmus says. 'The closest takeaway shop was 30 minutes away, and the players could only think rugby. As much as I believed that we could beat New Zealand, and as much as we wanted to, I always knew it was a 50/50 game. The Italy game was a difficult game mentally because we had lost to them in 2016. That was actually our big pool game.'

Erasmus returned to his full-strength side for the match at Shizuoka Stadium – the same venue where Japan had beaten Ireland just a week earlier – and his selections were telling.

It would have seemed almost impossible as recently as a year earlier, but Bongi Mbonambi displaced Malcolm Marx as the first-choice hooker. Marx had been a dominant figure in both Springbok rugby and world rugby, but Erasmus was staying true to his word. Opportunities would be provided, and it was up to the players to make the most of them. Mbonambi had been in superb form throughout the 2019 international season and now he had his reward.

Marx was still a key figure, giving an already powerful bench even more in the way of physicality and aggression. As had become the norm under Erasmus, the decision to pick Mbonambi ahead of Marx was explained in front of the entire squad and there were no one-on-one chats. Mbonambi had grown increasingly accurate with his lineout throws, but one of the main reasons for his elevation was his efficacy at scrum time. Dominating the set piece was a vital component of the Springbok game plan, and in Mbonambi the Boks had a player who gave them a solid foundation in the front row. Tendai Mtawarira also returned to the starting lineup for the Italy match, coming in for Steven Kitshoff, who had started against the All Blacks. Lood de Jager was the other change, replacing Franco Mostert. All three of those changes would stick until the World Cup final.

'People look at Beast and underestimate him, but the players respected him for who he was,' Matt Proudfoot says. 'When he said, "Boys, I want to scrum," the rest of the pack would buy in and do it. Between him, Trevor and Bongi they created a nucleus around the identity of what the scrum would be.'

The injured Nyakane had been ruled out of the tournament by this stage, and his absence meant a place on the bench for Vincent Koch. In every position, the Boks were well stocked with two world-class options who had been given the opportunity to prove their worth over the last 18 months. They never lost anything with any of these tactical shifts. The performance of the bench, with Erasmus favouring a six/two forwards/backs split against Italy for the first time in the tournament, was considered as important as what the starters did.

Shortly after the team was announced, the Springboks confirmed that Jesse Kriel had also been ruled out of the tournament following the hamstring strain he had picked up in coming on as a substitute against the All Blacks. The exciting and versatile Damian Willemse was his replacement, in another show of Springbok depth.

In their most clinical performance of the group stages, the Springboks scored seven tries as they thumped the Italians. It was the regular offenders who did the damage, with Cheslin Kolbe scoring two tries, while Makazole Mapimpi, Lukhanyo Am and Mbonambi also scored again. RG Snyman and Marx scored off the bench. The Boks were far too powerful for Italy in every department, but especially among the forwards. If Italy had any chance, it was extinguished when their loosehead prop Andrea Lovotti was red-carded for tipping over Vermeulen dangerously after the whistle had already blown for a penalty. Italy were 17–3 down at this stage, with the second half having just kicked off, and there would be no way back for them. The match also saw uncontested scrums employed from just the 18th minute after Italy lost both of their tighthead props to injury. With the Bok scrum one of their major weapons, this would have been a worry for Erasmus, but the gulf in quality between the sides ensured that the Boks came away 49–3 winners.

More pleasing than the result against Italy was the performance. Kolbe, once more, was sensational as his World Cup star continued to rise. It took him just five minutes to dazzle his way past two Italian defenders on the right flank for his first try, which again came after the Boks provided the go-forward continuity with their big, physical ball carriers before throwing it out wide. His second was the result of a Handre Pollard cross-kick that sat up perfectly for him, but Kolbe showed a burst of pace to finish. While the foundations were being laid by South Africa's incredibly strong defence, their set piece and their kicking game, Kolbe was starting to emerge as the star of the Springbok charge. There was a worrying moment when he left the field limping towards the end of the contest with what looked an ankle injury, but it was quickly confirmed that he would be fit and ready for the quarter-finals.

The Boks still had to play Canada in their final Pool B match, and they were expected to field a second-string side again. Vermeulen was the other injury worry, with a tender shoulder following that tip tackle, but he too was quickly cleared. Another pleasing return from the Italy game was that Kolisi played the full 80 minutes in what Erasmus described as his best performance since returning from injury. Erasmus said he had a few butterflies heading into the match, not only because of the importance of the fixture to his side's World Cup progression but also because of what had transpired in Florence in 2016. Defence guru Jacques Nienaber, meanwhile, acknowledged a few sleepless nights in preparation. As it turned out, there was no need for such nerves.

By the next day, when the Bok performance should have been making headlines, attention was instead focused on one of the most bizarre stories in South African World Cup history. It would become known as the Bomb Squad saga.

After the Italy game, a video circulated on social media that would present a serious challenge to Springbok unity. The video in question consisted of television footage from the end of the match showing players shaking hands and the Springboks celebrating after the final whistle. A group of Boks were forming a huddle together when Mapimpi walked towards them to join in. Frans Steyn, who had come off the bench for the Boks, then appeared to dismiss Mapimpi. Given that the players in the huddle – Steyn, François Louw, RG Snyman, Franco Mostert, Vincent Koch and Steven Kitshoff – were all white, accusations of racism in the Springbok squad were immediately ignited on social media. After Mapimpi walked away from the tight ring of replacements, Steyn had seemed to break away and make a dismissive hand gesture in the wing's direction. It did not look good at all, but the later explanation provided context to the incident that would leave everybody who had taken issue with the video, and those who had brought race into the conversation, looking foolish.

'It was a massive thing. Players don't come to my room and I don't do one-on-ones, but that week I had about five or six guys come to me,' Erasmus recalls.

Steyn, in particular, was lambasted.

'Frans Steyn was the key to going to a six/two split. He is the nicest guy and helped wherever he could. He played such a big role and he was the gel that bonded the players and calmed them,' says Erasmus. 'He had such a good vibe about him – with black, coloured and white guys – and he really helped the players buy into the fact that they had certain roles.'

In the video, the players in the huddle may have all been white, but they were also all substitutes and this was the sole reason for their celebration together. The Bok bench was becoming an increasingly vital cog in this World Cup machine, particularly since Erasmus had taken the decision to go with a replacements bench top-heavy with forwards. It was turning into the most physically intimidating bench in world rugby, and the players who were assigned the responsibility of closing out games had formed a special bond that was centred on that duty. Along the way, the Bok substitutes had dubbed themselves the Bomb Squad. They would be the guys sent in to get the job done when the stakes were at their highest, when games were on the verge of being won or lost. At training and at warm-ups on match days, the Bomb Squad would group together, focused on how to deliver the goods under extreme pressure.

'I told Frans that he was only going to start two games but that he was probably going to be involved in every single game. That's why we slowly built his fitness up so that he would be ready for the semifinal and final,' says Erasmus. 'You had to say those things to those guys, and they embraced it and formed the Bomb Squad.

'Within the team, it's so tough sometimes to accept it when the coach tells you something that is not nice to hear. But they accepted it, made a plan around it, and made it positive. And then somebody else, on social media or Twitter who is not even part of it makes it a negative thing, and that's what pissed off the guys.'

In hindsight, the reaction to the video was ridiculous and unnecessary. What it did highlight, however, was the divisions that persist in South Africa. It was an unfortunate distraction that impacted negatively on several Springboks, but the response of the group to power through and keep the 'main thing the main thing' told its own tale of exactly how close this squad was. They broke down racial barriers not through words but rather through their performances together on the field.

'There was someone who tweeted that Duane was the real captain in the team and that I was deceiving people,' continues Erasmus. 'There were also times when people said that they had heard confidentially, the previous year, that Siya was going to get dropped. But we already knew the team on the Monday internally. Those things can piss you off.'

Context, and the absence of context, was a key factor in the controversy created by the video. When viewed from a second angle, it could be seen that Steyn's dismissive hand gesture, which had appeared to be directed at Mapimpi, was in fact aimed at Lood de Jager in jest. De Jager had been promoted to the starting lineup for the match against Italy, with Mostert dropping to the bench. It was a tactical shift that Erasmus had made, with Mostert's hunger and firepower adding even further venom to the bench. De Jager, who had been a long-serving member of the Bomb Squad, having been below Mostert in the pecking order, was making his way over to the huddle that had formed, probably out of habit. It was then that Steyn gestured for him to leave. De Jager, now a starter, was no longer part of the Bomb Squad. This should have been a light-hearted, comical moment between him and his team-mates. Instead, the reaction of the South African public forced SA Rugby into action, and the next day Mapimpi posted a video to his Instagram account to explain what had transpired.

'As I was walking towards them, I realised that they were about to do their call, and that I wasn't part of it, so I decided that I needed to move away. I wasn't part of it, but there was nothing wrong there with what they were doing – we are united as a team,' Mapimpi said.

Erasmus, too, was quizzed about the incident at a press conference.

'It's so sad that somebody could see something negative in that because I can give you my word that, as a head coach, I would not allow anything like that in the team. There is nothing like that in the team,' he said.

'For those who want to see something negative in that, I guess they will find something. But I can guarantee to the other 95 per cent of the people in South Africa who want to know the truth, that that is the truth. This team is such a closely knit team that there will never be something like that where a team member can't be in a huddle.'

Even then, after Mapimpi had set the record straight himself, there were those who said he was only doing so because he had been instructed to. This Springbok team, more transformed and demographically representative than any that had gone to a World Cup before, was still having to overcome obstacles of race and division – even when they did not exist.

Because the match against Canada would take place just four days after the win over Italy – the Springboks' shortest turnaround at the tournament – there was little time to dwell on the negativity coming from home. The task at hand needed to remain front and centre for the Springboks, but this was not made any easier by the distractions that kept popping up.

The day before the Italy match, SA Rugby gave in to some of the public pressure surrounding the Eben Etzebeth case by issuing a statement acknowledging that they would be launching their own internal investigation into what had transpired in Langebaan. The Springbok leadership and players still backed Etzebeth fully, but as an organisation SA Rugby needed to be objective and it had a responsibility to seek the truth and act accordingly. The SAHRC had committed to bringing a criminal prosecution against Etzebeth, and the story was not going away at a time when the Springboks needed all attention on the World Cup.

'Following our discussions with the South African Human Rights Commission, we have instituted an internal process to address the matter, the details of which remain an employment matter between SA Rugby and the player,' the SA Rugby statement read.

Looking back, SA Rugby president Mark Alexander acknowledges that the organisation was under considerable pressure to act. Alexander was instrumental in the decision to keep Etzebeth in Japan, but he had the full backing of the minister of sport and recreation, Nathi Mthethwa.

'We took a lot of shots from the media,' Alexander recalls. 'But how could we take this decision before the boy [Etzebeth] had been proven guilty, or even charged? Who were we to do that? Imagine we had acted and ruined his World Cup dream, something that he had worked his whole life for, for nothing.'

Whenever a member of the Springbok squad was asked about the Etzebeth story, they downplayed it, with Kolisi insisting that it was not having any impact on his charges. The Bomb Squad story, too, was quickly brushed aside and the Bok group tried, publicly at least, to move on.

Inside the squad, however, some of the players were taking it hard. Louw was a core member of the Bok bench, with his experience and pedigree a luxury for Erasmus in the second half of matches. Over the past few months, going back to the 2019 Rugby Championship, he had embraced his role in the squad fully and had seen the Bomb Squad individually take ownership of their duties.

'Honestly, we were actually furious,' Louw says. 'We were really upset by it. We chose not to make a big deal about it, but it was the fact that we were sitting on the other side of the world as South Africans, as proud as we could be to represent our country, and there were people that still wanted to divide and destroy rather than to understand.

'It was almost undoing what we were as a team, with the diversity we had within that side. It was made bigger than it really was because a few arseholes looked for something that wasn't there, and it pissed us off. But there is always a positive to everything and perhaps that pulled us together a little bit tighter.'

Mapimpi, a naturally cool character, was also not spared. His journey to the World Cup was a phenomenal achievement of talent shining through when, at times, it looked like talent alone would not be enough. A product of the Eastern Cape township of Mdantsane, Mapimpi's career looked to be going nowhere slowly. He was stuck playing for Border until as recently as 2016, when he was not on the Springbok radar. A move to the Southern Kings in 2017 was his breakthrough year, and he scored 11 tries in Super Rugby – more than any other South African that year – to spark the Kings to a fifth-place finish in the South African Group ahead of the Cheetahs, Bulls and Sunwolves. Most South African rugby followers had not been aware of Mapimpi before that season, but they were quickly introduced to a player with raw pace and an uncanny finishing ability.

The Kings and the Cheetahs lost their places in Super Rugby 2018, and both franchises opted to join the newly expanded PRO14 league in Europe. Mapimpi relocated to Bloemfontein to join the Cheetahs, where he would be exposed to northern-hemisphere opposition and a fundamental change in style. It did not hamper his try-scoring, though, and he bagged another ten to finish second on the try-scorers' list for that season. Mapimpi was then off to Durban to join the Sharks in a return to Super Rugby, and he held his own in a side that was not playing the free-flowing, attacking style he had enjoyed at the Kings and Cheetahs. His Springbok debut came in Erasmus's first Test in charge – the trip to Washington, DC, where the Boks lost to Wales – and he has not looked back. Mapimpi had to quickly adjust to the demands of Springbok rugby, with his aerial ability and defence requiring swift, significant improvement. With the help of Jacques Nienaber and Mzwandile Stick, Mapimpi made the strides he needed to, and after Aphiwe Dyantyi was ruled out of contention, he convinced Erasmus that he could be entrusted with a World Cup starting place.

'Coach Stick was always honest with me,' Mapimpi remembers. 'He would congratulate you if you did something well, but he would tell you when you did something wrong and show you how to fix it. After training, he would take me and all the outside backs and spend extra time on the high ball. It was good for me.'

By the time the 2019 World Cup ended, Mapimpi had scored 14 tries from his 14 Test matches – a remarkable return. He also became the first South African in history to score a try in a World Cup final, etching his name into the country's proud rugby history. It made for an enthralling individual success story. And yet, when the Bomb Squad video surfaced, after a day in which he had scored another World Cup try for his country and should have been celebrating, Mapimpi found himself embroiled in a racial incident of which he was totally unaware. He had become an innocent victim overnight.

'It was tough for me,' he says. 'People were looking at me to explain what was going on and to say if there was racism, or something like that. People were expecting me to lie. There was a Bomb Squad, but a lot of people didn't believe that.'

Mapimpi found comfort in his team-mates, both black and white, whom he knew he could rely on. Despite the reaction on social media, which became brutal, the Boks knew that they had created a culture of unity within the squad. This was the time to put that unity to the test, even if resistance was coming from the very people they were representing.

'It didn't make sense for us to listen to people from the outside who didn't know what was going on within the squad,' Mapimpi adds.

What was more important, and what would be more helpful to the greater cause, was how the Boks felt about each other. In that regard, there were never any issues. With Kolisi as their leader, these players had embedded the philosophy that, regardless of their different backgrounds, they were all equals. Mapimpi and Steyn never felt like they had done anything to impact the relationship between the players. The bond was too strong for that to happen. The Boks addressed the issue in a team meeting and made a collective decision to move on from it quickly.

When one looks back at what the Springbok class of 2019 accomplished, not just on the field but also in the context of what the World Cup triumph meant for South Africa as a country, then the Bomb Squad story does feel out of place. This Springbok squad, under Kolisi, was breaking down barriers all the time. They would continue to do so into the final, where Mapimpi and Kolbe scored magical tries, and beyond on a trophy tour celebration that showed off the country's best qualities of unity and inclusivity. Those are the stories that matter. While the Boks were starting to hit their straps on the field, this was a week in which they endured distractions off it. All the planning in the world could not have prepared the Boks for these scenarios, but Erasmus quickly brought them back to a place of common ground where winning rugby matches was the most important topic of conversation.

'We felt like some people just didn't want us to succeed as the Springboks,' Schalk Brits remembers, 'and they wanted to make it a racial thing. What Rassie did there was phenomenal. As players we thought that we had to send something out to the public to say that there is no racism, but he just told us to play rugby and use that to give hope to our nation.'

A black coach who had been scapegoated under the previous

regime – Mzwandile Stick – was thriving and earning the respect of his peers and the players. A black hooker – Bongi Mbonambi – had dethroned one of the best in the business to earn a starting berth as the tournament entered its business end. A black captain who had overcome all the odds found himself on the verge of achieving the unthinkable. A black wing – Makazole Mapimpi – who himself came from poverty, and just three years earlier had been playing at a second-tier union, was about to score one of his country's most important tries on the biggest stage of them all. All through this squad, there were stories unfolding that had never been told in Springbok rugby before.

'We gave hope to a country and showed them that the past is the past and that we can embrace our differences. This country can be an unbelievable place if we take away how we look and where we're from and just try look at each other as people,' Brits adds.

The controversies involving Langebaan and the Bomb Squad could have ripped the Springboks apart. But that was not going to happen. Not to this group.

The match against Canada was up next, in Kobe on 8 October, and it represented one last hurdle for the Boks to clear before they could look ahead to the knockout rounds.

Chapter 13

Japan's pride

The match against Canada on 8 October, South Africa's last of the group stages, was to take place at the Kobe Misaki Stadium. The severe heat and humidity had been a talking point throughout the tournament, and the stadium's closed roof created a furnace-like environment. It was a match that the Springboks were never likely to lose in any conditions, but the fact that they had arrived in Japan three weeks before the start of the tournament and based themselves in Kagoshima, one of the most humid cities in the country, left them feeling even more confident.

The Boks had beaten Italy just four days earlier in what had been considered their potential banana peel in Pool B, so the depth of the squad would be tested again as Erasmus made wholesale changes for the Canada match. Only captain Siya Kolisi and Damian de Allende, who moved from inside centre to outside centre, would be part of the 'first-string' starting lineup that would contest the World Cup final against England in Yokohama. Kolisi was starting to hit form at the ideal time and, having played all 80 minutes against Italy, Erasmus viewed this as another opportunity to give his captain some high-intensity minutes before the start of the business end of the competition. There was also a start for Damian Willemse at fullback, which interested the South African media. Willie le Roux had come in for some criticism for a perceived lack of form; could Willemse, with an impressive showing, take a step towards displacing Le Roux ahead of the knockouts? Cheslin Kolbe and Duane Vermeulen, who had both picked up niggles against Italy, were left out of the match-day 23.

Canada had lost 48–7 to Italy and 63–0 to the All Blacks and were given no chance against the Boks. This would be their final match in Japan, as their last group game against Namibia was one of the three fixtures called off due to the approach of Typhoon Hagibis. The Boks were predictably dominant from start to finish, and ran in ten tries to claim a comfortable and entertaining 66–7 win.

The day belonged to Bok scrumhalf Cobus Reinach, who scored three tries inside the opening 20 minutes of the match for the fastest ever hat-trick in Rugby World Cup history. Willemse, who played the full 80 minutes, would get his try too, while there were also scores for De Allende, Sbu Nkosi, Warrick Gelant, Frans Steyn, Schalk Brits and Frans Malherbe. It was a special moment for Reinach, a latecomer to the World Cup race, who was below Faf de Klerk and Herschel Jantjies in the pecking order.

There had been suggestions that the Springboks might consider going to Japan with just two specialist number 9's given that Kolbe had operated there in a limited capacity during the 2019 Rugby Championship, but that was never really an option for Erasmus. If the policy on overseas-based players had not changed, the Northampton-based Reinach would probably not have been given a crack at making the World Cup squad. While his game time in Japan was limited, his knowledge of European and, particularly, English rugby would become valuable to the Boks as the tournament progressed into the semi-finals (against Wales) and the final against England. Kolisi, again, got through the full 80 minutes, meaning that he had notched up 160 minutes of World Cup rugby in just five days. With 11 days until South Africa's quarter-final, there was plenty of time for him to rest. What was most important was that he had returned to full fitness, extinguishing any doubts that might have remained over his conditioning with a couple of purposeful performances in which he played with the energy and intensity expected of a Springbok captain.

The Boks had recovered well from their loss to New Zealand. Since then, while they had not met any opposition who had tested them, things had been going their way. Their lineout, in particular, was functioning superbly and they won all 47 of their own throws in the pool stages. They also conceded just three tries, with two of those coming against the All Blacks, while no side scored more than their 27 tries at the end of the group stages.

The approach of Typhoon Hagibis, a large and violent tropical cyclone, threatened several pool matches, with a number of quarter-final places still up for grabs. However, the Boks were able to put their feet up for a couple of days safe in the knowledge that their quarter-final venue and date had been locked in. Even if New Zealand's final pool match, against Italy in Toyota, was called off, as it eventually was, the Boks would finish second in Pool B and play their quarter-final on 20 October at Tokyo Stadium. Erasmus used the opportunity to give his players a couple of days off, while he and the coaching team conducted video analysis of the group stages with the knockouts in mind. The Boks spent two days exploring and enjoying the sights of Kobe. When they were due to return to practice for the weekend, the elements were against them. Despite Kobe being over 500 kilometres away from where Hagibis was at its worst, there was still heavy, persistent rain and devastating wind. The Boks could surely not train in these conditions, yet they did.

'We didn't have much downtime,' scrumhalf Herschel Jantjies says. 'We were so focused on winning the whole time we were there. The guys felt that we had built some momentum and we didn't want to lose that. Our trainings were going so well. We went over with one goal and that was to win the World Cup, not to have fun and be a tourist. We knew that the fun would come if we eventually won the World Cup and I think that's exactly what we did.'

The Boks were in this together.

'Everybody in the management staff had an unbelievable work ethic and you could see it filtering down to the players,' Elton Jantjies remembers. 'The physios were working until eleven, twelve at night some nights. The boys could see the work from the management, and if my coach is working unbelievably hard, I would definitely work hard for him on the field. You could see it. We were all one and the intent wasn't just one guy, it was a collective group having intent together to make a country proud.'

Typhoon Hagibis threatened two key fixtures. The England versus France match in Yokohama on Saturday 12 October would determine who finished top of Pool C, but it was eventually called off and recorded as a 0–0 draw. This meant that England qualified first and France second. France were perhaps hard done by because it meant a quarter-final against Wales instead of the Wallabies, but it was not a disastrous outcome.

The other match in jeopardy, however, had the potential to cause chaos if it was called off. Japan, in the middle of their World Cup fairy tale, were due to meet Scotland in Yokohama on Sunday 13 October – the day after the scrapped England–France clash at the same venue. The tournament organisers were monitoring the weather, and would take the decision to abandon this match too if necessary. That result would have left Japan top of Pool A – good news for them and the Springboks – but it would have meant a group-stage exit for Scotland in the most unfortunate of circumstances. The Scottish Rugby Union reportedly threatened legal action should the game not go ahead, and tournament organisers were criticised for not having allocated more reserve days. The Springboks were fortunate to sidestep the commotion that came with Hagibis, but other nations were not so lucky.

As it turned out, the match went ahead, and Scotland could have no excuses for their group-stage elimination. For Japan, this fixture was do-or-die. The Brave Blossoms had beaten the Springboks at the 2015 World Cup but failed to secure qualification to the quarter-finals that year because of a loss to Scotland in the pool stages, and mathematically they could suffer the same cruel fate in 2019. It was becoming tight enough for the calculators to come out. Before Ireland knocked over Samoa to claim top spot in Pool A, the Boks had three potential opponents for their first knockout encounter – Ireland, Japan or Scotland. For a coach who liked to be prepared, this was a quandary for Erasmus.

Ireland's 47–5 win over Samoa on 12 October meant that Scotland could no longer top the pool, but they could sneak into the playoffs with a win over the hosts. In another incredible display of passion and determination, fuelled by the liveliest of home crowds, Japan scored four tries and withstood a late Scottish charge to claim a famous 28–21 victory in Yokohama. It gave them a clean sweep of four wins from four in Pool A, and secured a first-ever quarter-final appearance at a Rugby World Cup. As Japanese fans danced in the streets of Yokohama and at the many fan parks around the country, they were celebrating one of the great underdog stories in World Cup history.

What Japan had achieved in Brighton in 2015 was the beginning. They proved that day that they were capable of anything, and in 2019 they were doing it all over again. Japanese rugby had reached new heights, and they had done it at home. A nation that was known more for its love of baseball and football had bought into the story of the Brave Blossoms, who were capturing the hearts of the nation and the rugby world. Just how far could this Japanese side go? Their quarter-final against the Springboks in Tokyo was a dream match.

The release of a movie entitled *The Brighton Miracle* told the story of Japan's heroics in 2015. What if they did it again? What if this side found a way to make it all the way to the 2 November final in Yokohama?

There could be absolutely no complacency from the South Africans. They may have been comfortable winners in their pre-tournament warm-up against Japan, and they may have had a stronger team on paper, but they had seen enough from the hosts to know that they would be stretched.

The Boks made the 520-kilometre train journey from Kobe to Tokyo and arrived with their belief stronger than ever. In Japan, though, they would meet opponents who were soaring. The hosts had climbed into the top eight in the world. All Blacks coach Steve Hansen said they were the in-form team at the tournament and now comfortably a tier-one nation. More than that, the quality of the opposition that Japan had knocked over had given them the belief that they could beat anybody on their day. This, combined with the energy from their home support, made the Brave Blossoms a dangerous proposition.

The Japanese had improved their defence significantly and this had been a major factor in their stunning results, but they had also honed an attacking style based on speed and intensity. With pace in their wide channels, they had the ability to hurt their opponents. The Boks, naturally the more physical outfit, prided themselves on set-piece dominance, but there would always be an element of unpredictability about taking on the Japanese. The hosts had proved that anything could happen, and as kick-off approached, the possibility of another upset gathered momentum in the media.

In the top half of the quarter-final draw, England would face Australia in Ōita and the All Blacks would take on Ireland in Tokyo, both on Saturday 19 October. The next day would see the same venues used for Wales versus France, in Ōita, and the weekend's main event, the Springboks against Japan, at Tokyo Stadium.

The Springboks received good news during the build-up: star wing Cheslin Kolbe was declared fit, having struggled with an ankle injury since the win over Italy. When Erasmus arrived in Tokyo, greeted by a large media contingent, he confirmed that all the Boks were fit and available. Herschel Jantjies had been a concern with a slight hamstring strain, but he too was expected to be cleared.

As the Springboks continued their preparations, it became clear that they needed to rely on their traditional strengths. Japan were at their most dangerous when the game was at its quickest, and if the Boks were going to overpower them, then they needed to be smart about it. Territorial dominance would be key again, and that would mean an emphasis on kicking from scrumhalf Faf de Klerk and flyhalf Handre Pollard.

The Bok forwards were incredibly strong, and if they kept the game tight, South Africa would prevail. It would not make for the most entertaining affair, but this was the style that Erasmus, Nienaber and the entire management team had been perfecting for months and this was where it needed to be executed flawlessly. It came as no surprise when Erasmus named the same starting XV that had been so dominant in overpowering Italy, and there were also no changes on the bench. RG Snyman had been impressive and had been pushing for a starting berth, but lock was a position where the Springboks were perhaps most blessed with quality. Lood de Jager and Eben Etzebeth were partners in the starting second row, while Snyman and Franco Mostert provided the firepower off the bench, and in number 7, Pieter-Steph du Toit, the Boks had yet another world-class lock option. Any of those players would have comfortably made the starting lineups of any other side in Japan.

'In each of their own rights, they could have matched Pieter-Steph for player of the year,' Matt Proudfoot says. Du Toit was only one cog in what was a fierce Springbok forwards machine. 'It was the most privileged job to work with a pack of forwards like that,' adds Proudfoot.

Regardless of the opposition, the Springboks would look to their pack to give them the upper hand. This was the blueprint that had brought success against the All Blacks in 2018 and 2019, and against Japan it would again make the difference. Erasmus highlighted the importance of the set piece when he again opted for a forward-dominated, six/two bench split in the knowledge that the frantic Japanese style would be energy-sapping, particularly for the members of the pack.

In the first quarter-final on Saturday, Eddie Jones' England team were far too strong for a game but inferior Australia as they secured a 40–16 win. The English had endured their fair share of ups and downs in the build-up to the World Cup, but they looked to be peaking at precisely the right time. Wallabies coach Michael Cheika, who had been under fire for some time, quit the next day. Then, in Saturday's second kick-off, New Zealand made an emphatic statement by dismantling Ireland on their way to a 46–14 win. It was a timely reminder of just how dangerous the defending champions were when they got things right. Ireland, once fancied as title contenders, limped out of the tournament in disappointing fashion, but the takeaway was that the All Blacks were still very much the favourites. The result set up a blockbuster semi-final between the All Blacks and England that was worthy of being the tournament final. That match would produce one of the great World Cup knockout displays from the English, but a look at the performances of both winning sides in those Saturday quarter-finals suggested that the Springboks were very much on the more favourable side of the draw.

On Sunday, as Japanese fans flooded into Tokyo Stadium to watch the Brave Blossoms embark on another seemingly impossible mission, Wales edged France 20–19 in the third quarter-final in the most bruising of encounters. France, often a dark horse in World Cups past, came close to causing what would have been an upset. A moment of inexplicable madness from French lock Sébastien Vahaamahina in the 49th minute cost his side dearly when he was red-carded for launching an elbow into the face of Welsh flank Aaron Wainwright. Wales coach Warren Gatland acknowledged after the match that 'the better team lost', but the numerical advantage allowed his side to overturn a 19–10 deficit for the win. If the Boks could beat Japan, they would avoid England and New Zealand, but the grit of the Welsh was a daunting prospect.

This was not the time to think ahead, though, and as the Boks walked out at Tokyo Stadium in front of 49 000 roaring fans, they knew immediately that this would be no ordinary Test match. As inspirational as Kolisi had become to South Africa and the Springboks, Japan had their own fearless leader in New Zealand-born Michael Leitch. There was no trepidation on the face of the Japanese, who knew they had the tools to take this one step further by knocking over the mighty Boks. The Japanese crowd, from the very first whistle, was a 16th player for their side.

The Boks had a perfect start when, off the back of an attacking scrum, De Klerk released Makazole Mapimpi down the blindside, and the wing broke through a couple of tame tackles to give his side the lead. It was a crucial score, especially given how tense the rest of the first half was. The Boks endured a scary moment when, on ten minutes, Tendai Mtawarira was shown a yellow card for a tip-tackle on his opposite number, Keita Inagaki. It could very easily have been red. Japan then stunned the powerful Bok pack by shoving them backwards to win a kickable penalty on 19 minutes. The stadium shook as the hosts got back to 5–3 and, remarkably, that would be the score at half-time.

The Boks seemed rattled and, more importantly, very much in a contest. If the Japanese public had not believed before, they did now. De Klerk persisted with his box kicking as South Africans watching at home vented their frustrations on social media. But while the Boks were far from their best in the second period, they did enough to keep Japan out and slowly take the game away through the boot of Handre Pollard. With the Bomb Squad on the field, the Boks then delivered a dominant rolling maul before Malcolm Marx released De Klerk, who scored. The Boks, 21–3 up with just 14 minutes to play, were safe, but it had not been pretty. Mapimpi scored a second after a devastating counterattack, and the Boks emerged 26–3 winners to book their place in the World Cup semi-finals. While they celebrated, it was the end of the road for the Japanese, who left with their heads justifiably held high. After the final whistle, Siya Kolisi dropped to his knees for a spiritual moment of thanks. His Boks had been in a battle, and it would not be any easier against Wales.

As the Japanese spectators filed out of Tokyo Stadium, they did so immensely proud of what their team had achieved. They were disappointed at the result, but nothing could take away from the efforts of their Brave Blossoms. The fans had accompanied this side, brave indeed, on every step of their remarkable journey.

'When the Springboks started running away with the match in the second half, none of the fans left the stadium,' says Gareth Jenkinson, who covered the tournament for Durban's East Coast Radio. 'As they filtered out afterwards, they were still singing, and South African fans were consoling them. The spirits were still high. They bowed out so graciously. What had happened the weekend before with Typhoon Hagibis and the way they stood up to beat Scotland made their people so incredibly proud.'

A nation that had been unsure of what to expect from its own World Cup had punched above its weight. While the Japanese would play no further role on the field, the people of the country had contributed to this being one of the most memorable World Cups. Hagibis had threatened to derail the tournament, but everything else – from logistics to facilities and fan support – was superb as Japan set new hosting standards.

As the Springboks contemplated the way forward and their date with Wales, the feeling was that they needed to be vastly improved if they were going to challenge for the Webb Ellis Cup. England and New Zealand, in particular, had delivered potent quarter-final performances, and there were many who felt that either of these nations would ultimately be crowned world champions. The Boks had battled their way to victory against Japan, and had not been comfortable until late in the game. At half-time, leading by just two points, their future in the competition hung in the balance, and it took some strong words from captain Kolisi to provide perspective. Kolisi was calm but firm, reminding his players to trust in the plans that had been put in place for months and to be patient in their approach. If the Boks stuck to the plan and executed, then the rest would follow. There should be no panic, was the message from the skipper. Duane Vermeulen, too, was vocal at half-time, and Erasmus praised his leaders after the match.

'We're happy to be through to the semi-finals but we were very nervous at half-time,' he said. 'If guys miss tackles and there's a lack of commitment and there are effort errors, harsh words might help. But if it's a bad pass or a missed opportunity or a skill error then it's more a question of trying to get the guys' confidence up, and I guess that was the challenge at half-time. That's where Siya and Duane and those guys did well at half-time. I think Siya did most of the talking and sorted that out.'

There was clearly work to be done, but, crucially, the Springboks had progressed. A semi-final place at the 2019 World Cup had looked a long way away during the dark times of Allister Coetzee, and now that the Boks were there, they could see the finish line.

The heat was on Willie le Roux and Faf de Klerk, though. Le Roux, in particular, was harshly criticised by South Africans who felt that his form had dipped enough to warrant a change at fullback. *Sport24* chief rugby writer Rob Houwing, in his Springbok player ratings, awarded Le Roux just four out of ten after the Japan quarter-final – easily the lowest score of all the Boks. 'Took a couple of nasty head/upper body blows in first quarter … and whole first half was pretty awful from him, in truth. Passing and handling far too scratchy (that was being kind, at times), and just too lotto-like in aerial contestation,' Houwing wrote.

Le Roux had delivered an error-ridden display and, with stiffer opposition ahead, South African critics suggested that maybe the time had come to make the change. Damian Willemse was one option at fullback, while Cheslin Kolbe was another. It would later be revealed that Le Roux, perhaps more than any other player, took the views of the South African public to heart. The constant criticism had an effect right up to the week of the final, but Erasmus would persist with his number 15 until the very end, and he got his reward.

De Klerk, meanwhile, was simply implementing a game plan. Kicking was a major part of the Springbok method, but fans were frustrated by what they perceived as poor execution. Gifting possession to Wales, England or New Zealand the way the Boks had done against Japan would not cut it. Even when they were winning, the Springboks still found themselves under pressure from their expectant supporters back home.

One of the major positives to come out of the Japan game, though, was the dominance of the pack and the heroic performance of skipper Kolisi, who made more tackles than any other player on the field that day. Kolisi, not so long ago, had been in a race against time to get fit for the tournament and had been a major doubt to go to Japan at all. Now, just two wins away from achieving greatness, he had strung together three successive performances for his side. His leadership, too, continued to evolve, and he had come a long way since taking on one of the most challenging roles in South African sport.

A semi-final clash against Wales at International Stadium Yokohama awaited. The Springboks had not beaten the Welsh in four attempts since their epic 2015 World Cup quarter-final at Twickenham. The Boks were about to be pushed to their limits. How badly did they want this?

Chapter 14
The soul of Wales

A Rugby World Cup semi-final is in many ways more daunting than a final. This was certainly the case for several of the Springbok players and coaching staff as they prepared for the clash against Wales at International Stadium Yokohama. By the time a final comes around, the competing sides have done all they can to put themselves in a position to challenge for glory. The rest is down to what happens over the 80 minutes and, perhaps, fate. Falling short at the semi-final stage, though, is potentially more agonising, for it is the final hurdle to the biggest game in all of rugby. In the week leading up to their date with Warren Gatland's men, Rassie Erasmus and his Boks had plenty to think about.

South African referee Jaco Peyper was ruled out of semi-final contention – he would have hoped to land the England versus New Zealand playoff – for mimicking his role in the red-card infringement of Sébastien Vahaamahina by posing for a photograph with Welsh fans after the quarter-finals. It was then announced that Jérôme Garcès would officiate South Africa's semi-final. For Bok supporters, there could not have been a worse appointment given their side's woeful record under the Frenchman. Garcès had refereed the group-stage loss to the All Blacks and had been heavily criticised for poor decisions on both sides.

South Africa's history in matches involving Garcès meant that he was a figure who naturally commanded attention, but the Boks were not biting this time. They had done their homework, analysing Garcès' every decision in that All Blacks match and fine-tuning their strategy. If the Boks lost this semi-final, it was not going to be because of Garcès. They had done all they could to prepare, with captain Siya Kolisi and Vermeulen working together on how they would approach the man in charge. At training and in team meetings, the Boks would role-play, with all of Garcès' personality traits and tendencies in mind. In the week leading up to the match, at a press conference, assistant coach Mzwandile Stick called Garcès one of the best referees in the world. Garcès would not be allowed to be a factor.

Instead, the South Africans focused on exactly what they needed to do on the field. But understanding their opposition proved to be a more difficult assignment. 'We try and identify the soul of every team we play against, and it was difficult to find the soul of Wales,' Erasmus explains. 'On the Tuesday night I said to Jacques: "I'm not sure we have this team's soul," and we sat there and agreed that we didn't.'

Vermeulen, early in the week, told the media that the Boks needed to be more clinical with their opportunities than they had been against Japan, while Bongi Mbonambi, now Erasmus's first-choice hooker, elaborated on the success of the lineout. The Boks, quite remarkably, had now won all 57 of their own lineouts at the tournament following another flawless showing against Japan. Leadership, Mbonambi said, had been a key component of that success, with Lood de Jager, Eben Etzebeth, Franco Mostert and RG Snyman taking ownership of their departments at lineout time.

But what was the soul of the Welsh?

Erasmus sent logistics manager JJ Fredericks to the store across the road, instructing him to buy notebooks for all of the players. Then, in a team meeting, Erasmus, the coaching staff and the players sat in a brainstorming session with the aim of fully embracing exactly what rugby meant to the Welsh and how they went about their business.

'The soul of Wales is not their game plan; it's about their patience. It's their willingness to persist with the same game plan. That's how they win Test matches,' Erasmus says.

Erasmus and Nienaber came to the conclusion that Wales would kick, over and over again, looking to peg the Boks back in their own half until they cracked.

'They were going to persist with their kicking game, strangling us, suffocating us, holding us up in tackles, wanting to play in our half. Because they have been doing it for so long and they are successful, they are going to wait for us to crack and start running in our own half. Understanding that was the challenge,' says Erasmus.

'The moment you think, "Flip, I can't kick this ball back again, I'm going to start running," is when you're in trouble. We had to convince the players to have patience until they [Wales] lost the plot a little bit and they started running from their own half.'

Faf de Klerk, man of the match in the quarter-final, openly discussed his side's kicking tactics. De Klerk was taking the most flak from fans at home over the playing style, but the Boks were comfortable in their decision-making and knew that this was the way to get the job done in Japan. Much of the criticism around the relentless kicking was that it was not accurate enough and that possession was, all too often, being gifted back to the opposition.

It did not always matter, though. The Springbok defence had emerged as one of their major weapons, which meant that even when they did not have the ball, the Boks were putting their opponents under pressure. If a kick from De Klerk or Handre Pollard was not contestable, the territorial gain made by a cohesive, destructive defensive line meant that the Boks made inroads even when they did not have the ball. The Bok plan pointed towards a semi-final that would be hard to watch for the neutral but stressful for those from South Africa or Wales. Nothing in the build-up pointed to it being an open, free-flowing contest, and this was underlined when the Springboks' star of the tournament, Cheslin Kolbe, was ruled out of selection with an ankle injury that he just couldn't shake.

Kolbe had picked up the injury against Italy almost three weeks earlier, and probably should have been rested for the quarter-final against Japan. South Africa's most dangerous weapon on attack had been lost for a game where one moment of magic was likely to be the decider. But Kolbe's absence was about more than just the X factor. Over the tournament, in addition to being a lethal finisher, Kolbe had displayed a refined appreciation and implementation of Jacques Nienaber's defensive structure. Superb in the air on both defence and attack, Kolbe's sense of positioning, aligned to those around him, had been faultless, with his wide right channel nearly impenetrable. He knew exactly when to hold and when to rush, and losing that instinctive trait was as important to the team as losing his pace on attack.

The decision to leave Kolbe out was not a simple one. By the end of the week, he had returned to full fitness, but the Springboks had a policy that if you could not train on the Monday, you would not play at the weekend.

'It was a big thing, deciding if we were going to risk Cheslin or not,' says Erasmus. 'He couldn't train on that Monday, but by Thursday he was flat out, running as hard as he could. He was killing us at training when he was running as the opposition.'

Erasmus stuck to the policy, and so it would be another test of South Africa's world-class depth, as well as an opportunity for Sbu Nkosi, who had been unlucky to miss out on first-team action given how well he played when the chances came his way. There could be no bigger opportunity than this, but the Bok strategy meant that Nkosi's execution of the defensive structure would come into play far more than his finishing ability. It was a change that threw Nkosi straight into the deep end of the tournament. While there would be moments in that semi-final when he committed defensive errors that could have been more costly, he was fiercely competitive in easily the most important game of his life.

It had been a lean four years for the Springboks against Wales since their 2015 World Cup quarter-final. On that day, in front of nearly 80 000 people at Twickenham, the Boks needed a 75th-minute try from captain and scrumhalf Fourie du Preez, with a helping hand from Vermeulen, to secure a narrow 23–19 win and a place in the last four of the competition. At that stage, Wales had only ever beaten the Springboks twice in a staggering 31 attempts. What followed, however, was a run of four straight Test wins for the Welsh against South Africa from 2016 to 2018 – two under Allister Coetzee and two under Rassie Erasmus. None of those matches had been played in South Africa, but recent results had contributed towards Warren Gatland's men being labelled as somewhat of a bogey team for the Boks. Those four Test matches would count for nothing in Japan, in what would prove to be the Springboks' toughest assignment of the playoffs.

The Welsh, with one of the most passionate support bases in world rugby, believed that their time had come, and in Gatland they had one of the game's master tacticians as their primary reason for optimism. Over the years, Wales had evolved into a side as respected and as difficult to beat as any in world rugby. If the Boks were going to book their place in a third World Cup final, they would have to overcome a team that was as passionate as it was capable. It would be a physical encounter, which the Boks were certainly equal to, but where the Welsh were given the edge was in the accuracy of their tactical kicking and in their aerial ability.

Erasmus knew that the Boks would not be able to run the Welsh off the park. He knew that the only way to overcome them was to beat them at their own game, and he knew all too well what the reaction would be at home if the Boks lost while playing that style of rugby.

'Wales played a very similar game plan to us and we knew that if we didn't have the patience against them, we would be in trouble,' he says. 'If that game had been played in South Africa, we would have lost it, because the crowd would have started getting on our backs with the box kicks. We know Wales kick 30 kicks a game, so there were probably going to be about 60 kicks in that game, and I think there were more. If you don't persist with that, you lose against them.

'We knew that it was going to be very close because of the similar styles and, if we were going to lose, we knew that people in South Africa would have been pissed off at our style. But that's the only way you can beat Wales. You can't beat them another way. We've learnt that from playing them a lot and coaching against their coaches in the PRO14. That's why it was a nervous game, because if we were going to lose it, we were going to lose it ugly and people would crucify us in South Africa. If we were going to win it, we were going to win it ugly, but people would be happy because we were in the World Cup final. We had to convince the players that this was really the way.'

Months before the tournament, Erasmus had identified accurate kicking and aerial contesting as key areas to get right if the Boks were going to challenge for the Webb Ellis Cup, and this would be the biggest test of those credentials. It would be a brutal contest of two powerful set pieces, as well as a battle of two watertight defences. The Boks were perhaps the slightest of favourites given their past success at World Cups, but there was nothing in it, and this would prove to be the tensest week for the South African squad since they gathered in Pretoria ahead of the 2019 Rugby Championship. Preparing for this match took everything out of the Bok coaches, who agonised over every decision.

'The Welsh game was the game that scared me and kept me awake at night,' Matt Proudfoot recalls. 'They're a team that wouldn't go away, they were well led, and they play a very difficult style of rugby. They would always be in the contest. It was a game we feared.'

The Boks had been in a knockout frame of mind, knowing that one more defeat would spell the end of their campaign, ever since the loss to the All Blacks in their tournament opener, and while they had overcome a plucky Japanese outfit in the quarters, their mettle would undergo a thorough examination against Wales. Erasmus began to emphasise consistency in performance. The preparation had been done from a tactical perspective; what was as important now was to show concentration for the full 80 minutes of these last two matches. Small margins – a penalty kick or a drop goal, a slipped tackle or a refereeing decision – would almost certainly be the difference between winning and losing, and Erasmus wanted his Boks to be aware of everything going on around them. The mental component was so important.

Predictably, there were no changes to the Bok bench, with Erasmus again going forward-heavy. If Nkosi struggled, there would be limited cover off the bench, where only scrumhalf Herschel Jantjies and the experience of Frans Steyn were backline options. Steyn, the only player in the Bok squad to have won a World Cup before – as part of Jake White's triumphant class of 2007 – was taking on added responsibility. Having recovered from the backlash of the Bomb Squad saga, he was now being asked to step up for his country when it mattered most.

'The only thing I'm surprised about is the fact that he hasn't played 100 Test matches,' Jake White says. 'If he had played in any other country, he would have played 100 Tests. Bringing him back was a masterstroke from Rassie.'

White encountered a similar situation in 2007, having included 1995 World Cup-winning prop Os du Randt when many believed he was too old for international rugby. 'I told the players to listen to him and the youngsters went "yes, yes, yes", as youngsters do,' White recalls. 'I know that in that change room in the 2007 World Cup final just before we went out, it hit home to those young players who were there for the first time. I could see in their eyes that when they looked at Os, they had that sense of security. There is no price for experience. Those players around Frans would have felt a lot better with him there.'

Steyn's inclusion was one of the many decisions Erasmus took that could have backfired. Pulling Schalk Brits out of retirement was another, as was backing the six/two forwards/backs split on the bench. As the knockouts developed, Erasmus also took the decision to back the under-fire Willie le Roux when fans were calling for him to be dropped. Before the tournament, the decision to play a weakened side against Australia in the 2019 Rugby Championship at Ellis Park was another that could have gone the other way. Erasmus's constant commitment to player rotation, sometimes to the detriment of results, was a balancing act he had to master over the 18 months he was in charge.

'It takes its toll, but the coaches that win it are the ones that back their plans 100 per cent,' Jake White adds. 'If he did have doubts, I'm sure he kept those doubts to himself. He would never have shown that in front of the players. You are human and there will be times when you maybe fear that something you've called might not come off, but all credit to Rassie for sticking to his guns.'

By the time the Boks kicked off their semi-final against Wales at

International Stadium Yokohama on Sunday 27 October, they knew that they would face England in the final should they emerge victorious. At the same venue, the day before, Eddie Jones' side had produced one of the great World Cup knockout performances as they outclassed New Zealand from start to finish and in all departments on their way to a 19–7 victory that caught everybody by surprise. The mighty All Blacks, overwhelming favourites to defend their title following their demolition of Ireland in the quarter-finals, were out of the competition and a new benchmark had been set by the English. The Boks would not meet their old foes now, but they could not think about the future until they found a way past a resolute Welsh side.

Welsh fans outnumbered South African fans, but only slightly. The Boks had become crowd favourites among the locals, but they also had a sizeable contingent of support made up of South Africans living in Japan and those who had travelled over specially for the tournament. There were ten Springboks in the squad who had played against Wales in the 2015 quarter-final; even for them, this would be the biggest match of their careers so far. The feeling of tension was palpable throughout the 80 minutes. It was a match that neither side ever controlled, and the feeling that one moment was going to blow the contest wide open never left.

'It was probably the toughest match of the tournament for me,' Springbok centre Lukhanyo Am remembers. 'We knew they were a side that could not be put away, and that is what happened until the very end. They were a very good defensive side, but so were we.'

It will not be a day that many neutrals remember, but for those who were involved, it was a clash that left lasting scars. The look on the faces of the players in the tunnel spoke of intense focus, and the passionate singing of the national anthems confirmed exactly how much it meant to both teams. From the first kick of the game to the very last, this semi-final was on a knife-edge. A strong run from

Nkosi drew a penalty on the ground and Handre Pollard made no mistake to give the Boks a 3–0 lead, but Wales had the metronomic boot of Dan Biggar to keep his side ticking over. At half-time, after an opening 40 minutes that provided little in the way of running excitement but plenty in finding advantages in every metre, the Boks led 9–6 with three Pollard penalties to Biggar's two.

A third Biggar penalty made it 9–9, and as the game approached the hour mark a nervous buzz hovered over the stadium. In South Africa, at pubs and restaurants and at homes all around the country, fans were holding their breath. These were the moments that Erasmus had kept highlighting. The players needed to remain calm, patient and focused. One moment could change everything, and the Boks thought they had found that moment on 57 minutes when Damian de Allende, so good in the quarter-final against Japan too, went powering over from 20 metres to score the game's first try. De Allende, often criticised for not delivering on the hype that had followed him for years at both the Stormers and the Springboks, received a pass from Le Roux and showed incredible strength to brush off a tackle from Biggar and then another from replacement scrumhalf Tomos Williams to bash his way over. The Boks swarmed over De Allende, who looked to have scored the try that would take them to the final. With over 20 minutes to play, though, South Africa's 16–9 lead was far from safe even if their defence had once again been wall-like. It looked all too easy when it happened, but an attacking scrum from Wales on the Bok five-metre line went through the hands down the left for wing Josh Adams to score. The Bok defence had been penetrated, and in simple fashion. Wales had hit back, and when Leigh Halfpenny, who was a late replacement for the injured Liam Williams, slotted the all-important conversion, the scores were locked at 16–16 with just 14 minutes to play.

Every carry, every tackle, every kick, every aerial contest was of vital importance to both sides. Erasmus went to his bench and the entire Bomb Squad took to the Yokohama turf, looking to make the difference when they were needed more than ever. Louw and Steyn – the senior players on the bench – were the last two to join on 69 minutes, with Louw replacing Kolisi, who had emptied the tank in another display that showed exactly why he was the leader of this pack.

With 74 minutes on the clock, Wales were hitting the Boks with persistent waves of attack. Inside Bok territory, Wales could have won the game had they been awarded a kickable penalty at that point. Instead, Louw enforced the most important turnover of his career. He had made countless others for the Boks in his previous 74 Tests but none were as vital as this one. After the match, and upon further scrutiny, the Welsh rugby community felt that referee Garcès had made the wrong call, and that Wales should have been awarded the penalty for Franco Mostert not rolling away. Perhaps it was down to the work the Boks had done in understanding the way their World Cup referees would officiate matches, and perhaps it was not, but the Boks were on the right side of this call. Pollard duly provided the relief and kicked them deep into the Welsh half.

It was from that resulting lineout and rolling maul – two areas Proudfoot had obsessed over – that the Boks won the penalty that kept their tournament alive. It was a victory for the forward-laden Bomb Squad, for Proudfoot, for the Boks and, most importantly, for South Africa. Pollard, who never missed from the tee that day in five attempts, tried an ambitious drop goal and failed, but with the penalty advantage in the bag, he would have a kick to take the lead. With all the composure in the world, South Africa's general knocked over the three points that would secure a famous 19–16 victory. The Springboks, in far from spectacular fashion, were in the 2019 Rugby World Cup final.

It was the pack, once again, that carried the Boks over the line. Vermeulen, Pieter-Steph du Toit, Kolisi, De Jager, Etzebeth ... all were massive in the Springbok engine room while the front row was unflappable in the heated exchanges at scrum time. Le Roux endured another poor outing, De Klerk again failed to win over his critics in a match where he kicked, and kicked, while Nkosi was exposed somewhat in his defensive responsibilities. The Bok midfield of De Allende and Lukhanyo Am was superb, once more, with Am's contributions on defence as noticeable as anything he did with ball in hand. Pollard, meanwhile, was exactly what the Boks needed from their flyhalf. He kicked his points, made his tackles, cleared his lines and was always dependable.

'I think he's always had a very mature head on a young set of shoulders,' 2007 World Cup-winning flyhalf Butch James says of Pollard. 'He has all the attributes of a good flyhalf. Physically, he's big and strong. As a team member on the field, he carries the ball well, passes well and makes good decisions, and of course his kicking was on song at the World Cup as well.'

The Boks would enter the final as underdogs given what England had done to New Zealand, but going the distance in Japan was something few would have thought possible when Erasmus first took charge in early 2018. The cards had fallen their way in terms of the World Cup draw and their path through the knockouts, but the gritty display against Wales fully restored the South Africans to their rightful place as a powerhouse in international rugby.

The semi-final made for some difficult viewing at times. You could almost hear the collective groan from South African supporters every time De Klerk went to the boot to kick away possession, but this was a side clear in its game plan and ability to execute. The supporters who complained about the game plan and the players were also celebrating at the final whistle. As Erasmus had always said, results would inspire South Africans more than anything else, and this proved to be the case. The Boks had given themselves a shot at achieving something unthinkable, a near sporting miracle, and as they celebrated – and dreamed – a nation was coming together.

'To the people back home, we see your messages. Just keep on supporting us and we'll keep doing our best,' were Kolisi's words after the final whistle.

As the dust settled, attention immediately swivelled in the direction of the final, to be played at International Stadium Yokohama on 2 November. It was widely accepted that the difference in quality between the Boks and England was there for all to see in the semi-finals. England played at a much higher intensity and showed a versatility in approach against the world's best, while the Bok game plan appeared one-dimensional. If the Boks were going to knock over Eddie Jones' England, then they would need to find something extra. Would it come in the form of personnel change or a shift in game plan? The answer was neither. From a South African point of view, though, the concern was that their forward-dominated, kicking approach would not fluster an English side that had showed its own imposing defensive capabilities against the All Blacks.

The Springboks would go on to embrace the underdog tag in the week ahead, but Erasmus never once felt like the occasion was too big for him, and his players fed off his confidence.

He did, in a roundabout way, have a long history with Jones.

In 2007, after he left Free State, Erasmus joined the Springboks as a technical advisor under Jake White, the plan being for him to work with the Boks until the end of the World Cup in France. When White controversially took his 'B-team' on the Australasian leg of the 2007 Tri-Nations, where they were beaten 25–17 by Australia and then 33–6 by New Zealand, Erasmus stayed behind and worked with the 'A-team' that would eventually go on to win the World Cup.

When White returned to South Africa, Erasmus informed him that he wanted to focus full-time on his new job as director of rugby at the Stormers and that going to the World Cup would negatively impact on his plans for the 2008 Super Rugby season. Erasmus stepped away from the Boks, and White appointed Eddie Jones as his replacement for the 2007 World Cup.

'It was a bit disappointing because I would have liked him to stay,' White remembers. 'Rassie was very good and he worked hard with those players. I've no doubt that the contributions he made in that time aided us when we eventually did come back and start preparing for the World Cup.'

Now, 12 years on, Erasmus had his own shot at glory. By the time the Boks reached kick-off in the final, they were as composed as they could possibly be. They knew what the plans were, and they took comfort in the fact that they had done all they could. For Erasmus, the job was to keep the players in the right mental space to deliver the goods one more time.

He had his hands full with Le Roux, who was starting to feel the effects of constant sniping by the South African rugby public. The impressionable Le Roux would often take the criticism personally. On the bus ride back to the team hotel after the Wales game, as the Springboks were celebrating, a dejected Le Roux walked over to the coach.

'He came to me in the bus and said: "Don't pick me for the final. I can see you're copping a lot of flak." He could see it was really becoming bad now. People were really getting stuck into him,' Erasmus says.

It took a strong show of leadership from Erasmus and the players around him to remind Le Roux of his value to the Springbok cause and to pull him out of the funk he was in. It would be yet another example of the togetherness that had developed in this group. No one player was better than any other. It was a complete team effort, and they needed to remind Le Roux that he was an integral part of the Bok machine.

Ahead of the semi-final, Erasmus had compiled a video, which was leaked to the media, showing Le Roux's contributions to the Springboks throughout the tournament so far and in previous Test matches. The video was aimed at highlighting Le Roux's involvement, even when he was not on the ball, as well as his role in several Springbok tries. It was Erasmus's way of letting the public, the team and, most importantly, Le Roux himself know how valuable he was to the Bok cause.

The pathway to the final was not without its speed bumps, but the Boks had overcome all of those and were now 80 minutes away from solidifying their place among the greats of the game. Kolisi would command unrelenting attention in the days leading up to the final as the international media latched on to the social significance of a possible Bok win. South Africans, though, had internalised that meaning a long time ago. Still, even the most ardent fan could not have known the magic that was about to unfold. It was the beginning of a week that changed South African rugby, and South Africa, forever.

'It's crazy. To try and explain the roller-coaster of emotions you go through is very difficult,' Francois Louw remembers of World Cup final week. 'When you have the highest levels of exhaustion and you're so emotionally strung, what you fall back on is your preparation. You try and switch off and treat it like another normal week, but the reality is it's not another normal week. It's a flippen World Cup final. You obviously dream about winning it, but you also start thinking about how terrible it will be if you lose.'

Chapter 15
World champions

The Springboks had battled through the most gruelling of assignments against Wales to progress to a World Cup final for the third time, and in the week leading up to rugby's premier match, the excitement coming out of South Africa was deafening. They may have been 14 000 kilometres away from home, but the Boks felt the support of their people and also the weight of expectation. The official Springbok social media hashtag for the tournament was #StrongerTogether. It had been created by the players themselves, and the entire Springbok squad – players, coaches and backroom staff – embraced that mantra in the days leading up to their 2 November date against a high-flying, heavily favoured England.

The Springboks were commanding headlines all over the country. This was a team that, because of its diverse make-up, represented South Africa in a way that the Boks had never done before at a World Cup. They were winning, too, and now that they were just 80 minutes away from glory, their supporters were contemplating the possibility of a remarkable comeback from the lowest point of late 2017. Bok supporters had endured a tough ride since the 2015 World Cup, but they were now one stellar performance away from bragging rights for another four years, and there are not many in world sport who enjoy winning more than South Africans do.

The Springboks did not spend as much time that week on the training field as people might think. It was too late to drastically change tactics or come up with new plans or plays, and coach Rassie Erasmus instead prioritised mental fine-tuning during team meetings. He drove home the message that this was no longer about the players. They were no longer representing themselves but instead a nation of nearly 60 million people. Erasmus told his players to trust in the plans and not dwell on the possibility of making mistakes. Mistakes no longer meant anything, because this was no longer about individual performance. Win or lose, Erasmus wanted the Boks to go out there and play with freedom.

Siya Kolisi was thrust into the international spotlight and comparisons were made to the 1995 World Cup Springboks and the iconic images of Nelson Mandela and Francois Pienaar standing side by side, lifting the Webb Ellis Cup. Kolisi had started as a soft-spoken man who overcame the odds to lead his country. Now he stood on the verge of becoming a beacon of inspiration to the entire country. It takes a special kind of person to remain composed in situations of such grand emotional significance, but Kolisi had surrounded himself with leaders he could depend on. He was not in it alone, and while the world made it all about him, he knew better. Nothing could be achieved without the entire Springbok squad pulling together, and every time he was given an opportunity to answer a question in the media about the significance of his captaincy, he was quick to make it about the team. Kolisi's journey had been emotional enough, but it was ramped up a level in World Cup final week, and the strength he exuded through his calm, level-headed attitude was exactly what the Boks needed. At first there had been doubts about Kolisi's appointment, and then concerns over his fitness heading into the World Cup, but his performances when it mattered most spoke for themselves.

'What Siya has achieved has been remarkable. For a young kid from Zwide township in Port Elizabeth to rise above his circumstances and become Springbok captain, and lead the way he has, it's been inspirational to all South Africans – from all walks of life,' were the words of veteran Tendai Mtawarira in the week of the final. 'We are all proud of him, and we ultimately want to make it very special for him on Saturday.'

Willie le Roux, meanwhile, was struggling.

He felt that if South Africans did not want him to play, then maybe he should not. It was a remarkable revelation, with a World Cup final – every player's dream – just days away. Erasmus, though, was unwavering in his support and never doubted his decision to select Le Roux. Form was temporary, but the pedigree and experience that Le Roux possessed was something that could not be replaced. Le Roux's contributions were about more than simply catching high balls. He was an orchestrator in the Springbok back line and led the back three, marshalling wings Cheslin Kolbe and Makazole Mapimpi into position, particularly on defence. Le Roux's spatial awareness was something that Erasmus and defence coach Jacques Nienaber valued immensely, and that confidence needed to be communicated to Le Roux himself. By the time the final came around, Le Roux knew that he had the full backing of his coaches and the players around him

'We played around Willie,' Mapimpi says. 'He has a lot of experience and he has played wing and fullback for the Springboks. He knows how to communicate with the wings. I learnt a lot from him on how to position myself without the ball.'

Le Roux was also struggling with a stiff shoulder. He had suffered a bump at training a couple of weeks earlier when Pieter-Steph du Toit went sliding into him, and he had tried to brush it off. Now, with days to go until the most important game of his life, Le Roux was starting to feel the pain. It is not public knowledge, but insiders have confirmed that South African billionaire Johan Rupert was in Tokyo at the time and arranged a meeting between Le Roux and his physician that apparently worked wonders. Scans done after the tournament would reveal that Le Roux's shoulder blade was in fact broken – he did not know it at the time – while he also broke his hand during the final itself. Despite these obstacles, Le Roux would go on to deliver his best performance of the World Cup in the final – when the Boks needed him most. Erasmus's decision to keep faith in him was completely justified.

'Sometimes people see the tries, but they don't see Willie creating space or kicking or closing down gaps or making last-gasp tackles. I think that video [that Erasmus had compiled for the team] made a difference to the players. After that, we appreciated Willie a lot more,' Schalk Brits remembers.

There was good news for the Boks when it was confirmed that Kolbe had completely recovered from the ankle injury that had kept him out of the semi-final, and his return for Sbu Nkosi was correctly predicted as the only change to the Bok lineup. Kolbe, in the form of his life, was having a spectacular tournament. Had he not recovered in time for the final, it would been a devastating end for him. While the Boks were expected once more to play a territorial game and rely heavily on their forwards, having Kolbe back in the mix gave them a certain firepower from counterattack and organisation on defence.

Jérôme Garcès, meanwhile, was to referee the World Cup final, which would be his third time in charge of the Springboks during the tournament. The Springboks did not flinch at this decision. They had proved against Wales that the homework they had done on referees, and on Garcès in particular, was paying dividends. The Boks knew what Garcès wanted from the set piece, the breakdown, the offside lines ... it had all been analysed and they were prepared. What they couldn't prepare for, though, was the global attention that came with a World Cup final.

The Springboks started embracing the fact that, through victory, they could achieve something special for South Africa. The obstacles that players such as Kolisi, Mapimpi and Lukhanyo Am had overcome to get to this point were a source of inspiration. For players to escape poverty and make it to a Rugby World Cup final as heroes told South Africans that more was possible. There was hope, and this Springbok team was the vehicle to deliver that hope. In South Africa, racial and social unity came from embracing these diverse Springboks, and this quickly became the core theme of the final. South Africa had a powerful, magical aura, while England took comfort in performance and what they had done to the All Blacks. Nevertheless, England were comfortably the favourites for bookmakers around the world.

On the eve of the final, former British Lions and England World Cup winner and scrumhalf Matt Dawson was quoted as saying that not one Springbok would make a combined England-South African team. Such arrogance did not matter to the Springboks, though. They had overcome numerous challenges over the past 18 months and knew they deserved their place in the final.

Erasmus, by this stage, had announced that this would be his final Test match as head coach. This had always been the plan, and he would be slipping into his full-time role as director of rugby at the end of the tournament. Nienaber would be named as his replacement, maintaining continuity in the coaching setup, but this would only be confirmed months later. Win or lose, what Erasmus had done for the national side and for South African rugby in general was compelling. He had transformed the Boks in every way possible, taking them from a group that was reeling to one on the verge of making history. Every player in this team deserved to be there. There were no political appointments and no question marks hovering over selections. These players – black and white – had been given equal opportunity by Erasmus and they had earned their own tickets to a World Cup final. Erasmus had taken the Boks back to their traditional strengths, and he and the players had received their fair share of criticism for that, but all of Faf de Klerk's box kicking would be forgotten the second that final whistle blew at International Stadium Yokohama.

England ended up backing George Ford at flyhalf over Owen Farrell, but thanks largely to Elton Jantjies' in-depth study and simulation of both at training, the Springboks were prepared for either scenario. Matt Proudfoot, meanwhile, looked at his pack of forwards and knew that there was little more that could be done to prepare them. The Bok engine room would again be responsible for giving them dominance at set piece, and Proudfoot took comfort from what he saw.

'We did our scrumming session on Wednesday and we did six live scrums, and after those, I actually walked away. I said to Rassie: "I can't prepare a pack of forwards better than that." It was the best scrummaging session I've ever seen in my life,' Proudfoot remembers. 'The intensity at which they took each other on, the technical proficiency in working to the plan ... it made me calm. The way we had prepared gave me so much confidence going into the week. The final is about who presents their game the best and we were so confident in our game that we were calm. We lightened the workload on them that week and the players just took control. From Wednesday, they were in control.'

Throughout the week, the Springboks – starters, substitutes and reserves – gave the coaching team a dose of calm. 'We only had two training sessions because we had a six-day turnaround. The players were so mature. It was incredible to see,' Erasmus says. 'They were not "windgat" at all, not overly confident. You'd see guys after a training session looking to fix things and you'd walk past a computer and see two guys sitting there watching and analysing. The reserves were doing profiles on the English players, on the referee. It was just one of those weeks where all of them wanted it so much that if we did lose, I would have felt really bad, but I couldn't have been disappointed in the group.'

The Boks knew they were set from a tactical and physical perspective. The little extra they needed to get over the final hurdle would come from understanding what victory would mean to the people at home. Nobody for a second believed that the Boks could miraculously wipe away the crime, unemployment and political uncertainty or the racial and social divisions that exist in South Africa, but if they could provide some hope and inspiration, then that was a responsibility worth taking on.

'We do have some challenges in our country at different levels and at different avenues, but rugby is one of the things that – for a few minutes and sometimes a few hours, days and months if we win – people seem to forget about their disagreements for a while, and agree,' Erasmus said after naming his team for the final.

Ahead of the 2007 World Cup final in Paris, when these sides last met at the global showpiece, Springbok flyhalf Butch James would lie awake thinking about what could happen. James had been scarred in that year's Super Rugby final when the Sharks had thrown away the match in spectacular fashion in the final stages to go down to the Bulls and Bryan Habana.

'At the World Cup, I'd wake up in the middle of the night and that was the first thing that popped into my head and I wouldn't be able to get back to sleep,' he says.

James and the Boks would go on to beat England 15–6 to win South Africa's second Webb Ellis Cup, and the relief he and his team-mates felt in the moments following the final whistle was something the Springbok class of 2019 were about to experience for themselves. Regardless of how well prepared they were, this was a different level of pressure.

Kolisi, at his captain's press conference the day before the game, was bombarded with questions about being his country's first black captain. For South African journalists, these questions had grown somewhat tiresome over the last 18 months, even if they carried renewed significance now. Kolisi was not a captain who wanted to talk about being black.

After the captain's run on the day before the game, the Boks held what Erasmus calls a 'what if' session, which had become standard procedure throughout the tournament. This was an opportunity for players to voice any concerns or uncertainties ahead of game day. It was a way for Erasmus to ensure that his players all understood the game plan, but it was also a way of avoiding any excuses after the match. 'Everybody must get off their chests what they're still worried about so that you don't have to talk about it after the game,' Erasmus explains.

After that meeting on the Friday, the players had time off and could relax. 'We had all the players' wives and families over there from day one. We had no problem with it, the only rule was that it could not interfere with any rugby stuff,' Erasmus says.

In many corners, as confirmed by Dawson's wild statement, the Springboks were being written off. 'The nice thing about our build-up was that we were the underdogs and everyone was talking about England. We were in a good space and in our own zone. We made sure we prepared very well for the game and on the other side we had a team that was very confident about the final because of the result they had in the semi-final,' Mzwandile Stick recalls. 'We could see that our boys were hurting when it came to the media and everyone talking about them as underdogs. You know that if you make players in South Africa angry, sometimes it means that they will destroy everyone. It was something we enjoyed. We didn't try new things. We just stuck to our normal routine and with the leadership we had in the side, it helped us to stay together. Guys like Siya, Beast, Duane, Handre Pollard ... a lot of guys really stood up in that week and managed to keep everyone together.'

The Springboks were staying in the same hotel as they had ahead of their first match of the tournament, and players recall the intense focus on the morning of the final. Some had battled to sleep, but the enormity of the occasion meant that all were wide awake early and ready for a day that would define their careers. As the players had breakfast and started their day, they were given an unexpected boost when two familiar faces walked through the hotel doors to greet them.

Jesse Kriel and Trevor Nyakane, who had both been sent home with injury at the beginning of the tournament, had been flown over to Japan for the final at SA Rugby's expense. As they reunited with their team-mates. It was the perfect way to lighten the mood before the game. Nyakane, one of the most popular players in the Bok setup, almost infectiously brings laughter with him wherever he goes, and it was exactly the tonic the players needed.

Pollard, meanwhile, was particularly delighted to see Kriel. The pair have travelled a long road together, from being junior team-mates at the Bulls to becoming housemates and best friends. So much would hinge on Pollard's performance for the Boks, and seeing one of his closest mates on the morning of the game was a timely distraction.

There was one more surprise, when South African President Cyril Ramaphosa addressed the group at the team hotel. He did not talk rugby, but rather reminded the players of what they had done for their country and how proud they had made everyone at home. He called the Boks South Africa's 'warriors', wished them luck and shook their hands. This was more than a game of rugby.

In South Africa the braais started early, and pubs, restaurants and taverns throughout the country soon filled up.

There were over 70 000 people packed into International Stadium Yokohama for the final. The overwhelming majority were English. While kick-off was scheduled for 6 pm local time (11 am SA time), spectators started arriving seven hours earlier. The streets surrounding the stadium were overflowing well before kick-off time, and with Japan's relaxed policies on public drinking, vast amounts of beer were being poured down excited throats. Most belonged to English supporters. East Coast Radio rugby journalist Gareth Jenkinson interviewed spectators outside the stadium to get a feel for what they were expecting. 'The English fans were so confident that it was almost arrogant. South Africans were nervous,' he remembers.

How could they not be? Everything about England's performance in their semi-final against the All Blacks suggested they were ready to bag a second World Cup crown. As good as the Boks had been, it was hard to see them dominating the All Blacks the way England had done. Everything was clicking for Eddie Jones' men at precisely the right time, and if they replicated their previous performance in the final, there could surely only be one winner.

England were playing a crisp, fast-paced game under Jones that was most impressive in its accuracy. At the breakdown, on defence, with ball in hand and from the boot, the English had developed into the complete rugby package.

On the morning of the game, Erasmus's first words to his players further examined their preparedness, as the previous day's 'what if' session had done. 'I asked the guys on the morning if anybody had any areas where they felt uncomfortable and nobody said anything. Then I asked if there was anybody who doesn't understand anything, and nobody said anything. If you agree on that and you go and leave everything out on that field, then it cannot be failure. Then you are beaten by a better team,' Erasmus says.

'The chat was that we didn't have to think too much about the plan, because we had drilled it in. We didn't have to think too much about our individual skills, because they were not going to get better from now until the match. All you have to think now is about emptying the tank and getting yourself into battles. There is a Bomb Squad waiting. We talked about physically really dominating these guys. We didn't have to get fancy. We knew we would get our one or two opportunities to score.'

As South Africans settled around their television sets, the Boks arrived at the stadium. They appeared relaxed. Proudfoot walked onto the field for the pre-match training session, looked skywards at the full moon, and, he says, knew in that moment it was going to be a good night. Erasmus and Nienaber were also outwardly calm. Erasmus delivered his pre-match team talk, emphasising that there was no pressure on the players. Pressure, he emphasised, was what ordinary South Africans had to live with, and those were the people the Boks were representing out there on the field.

'That was his message, indirectly, the entire time,' Herschel Jantjies says. 'Coach Rassie has a way of getting you motivated in his own way and it's really effective. I've heard a lot of speeches in my life, but he is so street smart, and he knows exactly how to get you up for a game.'

With the talking over and the speculation complete, Siya Kolisi led out the Springboks in his 50th Test. In the stands were his father, his wife and his family, as well as England's Prince Harry, President Cyril Ramaphosa and the vocal, English-dominated crowd. It was a match that would change Kolisi's life forever. All 23 Springboks on the field, the coaching staff and the reserves passionately sang the national anthem, as did millions of South Africans. After a ten-second countdown from the crowd, referee Garcès blew his whistle as Handre Pollard kicked off a dream evening for the Boks. With 'Swing Low, Sweet Chariot' from countless English throats drowning out the opening 40 seconds of play, the Boks would have quickly realised that the majority of those inside the stadium that day wanted them to lose.

'I've never been to Twickenham, but that day I knew what it would be like,' Jenkinson remembers.

Pollard missed a relatively routine early penalty, perhaps a sign of the enormity of the occasion, but from there things only got better for the Springboks. Looking back, critics have said that it did not matter who the Springboks played on the day; they would have won anyway. It was as if it was meant to be as the Bok forwards dominated the set pieces and the collisions to lay the foundation for what would be the greatest win in South African rugby history.

England were not helped by a game-ending head knock to tighthead prop Kyle Sinckler in just the third minute, exposing replacement Dan Cole to effectively play a full game. The Boks, with plenty of forward firepower on the bench, never looked back and dominated the English scrum. The Boks opened up a 3–0 lead after Duane Vermeulen and Kolisi combined to isolate Farrell and force the penalty, and it was reward for a strong start from a side that quickly shed the underdog tag.

England hit back with a strong attacking spell that the Bok defence kept out before giving away a penalty that Farrell slotted to make it 3–3. It was during this spell that the Boks lost Bongi Mbonambi to a concussion and Lood de Jager to a shoulder injury. It was a devastating end for two men who had played their way into the starting lineup with a superb run of performances in 2019, but the depth of South African quality was on show when Malcolm Marx and Franco Mostert took to the field as replacements.

A scrum penalty for the Boks then allowed Pollard to make it 6–3, but what followed on either side of the 30-minute mark is what many consider to be the turning point of the encounter.

'I really thought that if we played to our best, we would have a good chance of winning the game. Where I was very nervous was when they were on our touchline just before half-time. I wasn't nervous before the game or at half-time, but I was nervous then,' Erasmus recalls.

England, camped on the South African line, were bashing away in search of the opening try of the match and more than once looked certain to get over. The green wall of the South African defence, however, could not be knocked over as every player on the field made tackles and cleanouts. England went left, went right, kept it with the forwards and went to the backline, but despite being so close they just could not get over the line. The South African defence was almost unbelievable, with Vermeulen displaying superhuman strength to keep his opposite number, Billy Vunipola, out on one of countless England surges towards the line. No matter what England came up with or who they gave the ball to, the Boks hammered them backwards. England left that frantic period with a penalty, to level the score at 6–6, but how they didn't score was remarkable and testament to the work done by Jacques Nienaber in turning this Bok defence into the best in the world.

'The defence just got better and better through the competition and I think the crux of the whole game was that little period of play. When we defended that well, it just gave the team so much confidence. Big players stepped up in that part of the game,' Proudfoot says.

Vermeulen, who was having a magnificent game, then enforced another turnover penalty as Pollard kicked the Boks into a 9–6 lead before another scrum penalty – Mtawarira and Frans Malherbe were proving far too strong for Cole and Mako Vunipola – after the hooter made it 12–6 at half-time. It was every bit as brutal as had been expected from a World Cup final. England were playing with intensity at times, but the Boks were doing the basics better, while their defence and forward dominance was astounding.

The chat at the break from Erasmus and Kolisi was to keep the pressure on and remain patient. There were a few tactical instructions on where to tighten up, but the Boks were in the driving seat. Erasmus had told his players before the game that, unlike the Welsh, England would eventually buckle under enough pressure. Whereas sides like Wales and France would never go away, Erasmus believed that the English had a point where they would cave. The key was to get to that point. The scoreboard may have been tight, but the Springboks had started to exert clear dominance at the set piece, in contact and on the ground. England's breaking point would eventually come in a second half that saw the Boks enjoy some of their finest moments ever on a rugby field.

Yet another scrum penalty, with Steven Kitshoff on for Mtawarira, allowed Pollard to make it 15–6 from 50 metres shortly after half-time. At that point, South Africa were overwhelming favourites. England, against the run of set-piece play, were then rewarded at a scrum to narrow the score to 15–9. Pollard kicked his sixth penalty of the day to take it back out to 18–9, but the Boks were penalised directly off the resulting restart for Farrell to narrow it down to 18–12.

With the game heading into its final quarter, all three results after 80 minutes were still a possibility. Then, almost out of nowhere, the Boks sent South Africa into uncontrolled, unparalleled elation. It was a moment that would be replayed countless times in the weeks and months to come. Having received a kick just inside

English territory, Le Roux went to ground to set up play for the Boks just about 50 metres out. De Klerk then opted to go left, where there was less space, as the ball went through Am and Marx before finding its way to Mapimpi, who made the break before kicking ahead. The bounce of the ball saw it sit up perfectly for Am, who gathered and then executed the most audacious 'no look' pass to his left, where Mapimpi was on hand, making no mistake in rounding off the move. It was South Africa's first-ever try in a Rugby World Cup final, but, far more importantly, it had almost certainly taken them out of England's reach.

'I don't think it comes from anywhere. I think I've just always been cool and composed in those situations,' Am says, on reflection. It was a moment of incredible skill, enterprise and faultless execution, and perfectly illustrated what can be achieved when opportunities are given. South African rugby was stunning the world.

'Even after we invited him to his first Springbok camp, a lot of people doubted his ability and potential. Even during the World Cup, there were a lot of people doubting him,' Stick says of Mapimpi. 'For him to score the first try in a World Cup final by a South African was very special. I look at his background and I have been through that and where he comes from … it's very tough out there. It was such a special moment, not only for our black community, but for all the young kids out there in the rural areas.'

Pollard added the extras, the Boks led 25–12, the English were rocked, and the Yokohama crowd knew that the contest was over. The Boks, however, were not done.

England continued to bash away without any reward as the brilliance of the South African defence shone. Then, in the 74th minute, the Boks pounced on a dropped ball that had come from a huge hit from Marx, showing the counterattacking power they always knew they had. In another moment of sublime composure, Am was quickest to react, gathering the ball and offloading to Pieter-Steph du Toit, who then moved it to Kolbe. Having hit the ball at pace but still 40 metres out, Kolbe dazzled his way through an English defence that had already thrown in the towel to score his side's second try in spectacular fashion. South Africans were hysterical, in the stadium and at home, as English skipper Farrell fell victim to Kolbe's devastating feet. England had reached breaking point and South Africa's relentless physicality and clinical execution had prevailed. The Springbok wings, wearing 11 and 14, had scored tries in a Rugby World Cup final. It was the perfect tribute to fallen 1995 heroes Chester Williams and James Small.

'Four seasons back, everyone said that he doesn't have what it takes when it comes to his physique. They said he was too small. He is currently probably one of the best players in rugby,' Stick says of Kolbe.

With the bench all on the field, and the Boks dominant, there was no way back for England. As the clock hit 80 minutes and with the scoreboard reading 32–12, the Boks were in possession. Herschel Jantjies whipped the ball to Pollard, who kicked it deep into the stands, where the English supporters had fallen silent. Garcès blew the full-time whistle and all over the Yokohama turf there were Springboks on their knees in disbelief, digesting what had just happened. The Boks, the underdogs, had just beaten the favourites by 20 points in a World Cup final. They had been labelled 'boring' all tournament long, but this performance in the final showed that their recipe for success was close to perfect: the forwards created the platform with a world-class set piece; the tacklers were ferocious and aligned; the carriers created go-forward ball; the breakdown specialists secured possession; the kicking was accurate and precise; and, when given the opportunity, the pace and skill of the Springbok backs buried their opponents.

Siya Kolisi, who had been substituted at 63 minutes, leapt from the bench, ran straight to his former Stormers team-mate Kolbe, and embraced him. Eben Etzebeth, who had endured weeks of off-field pressure, picked up Herschel Jantjies and squeezed the life out of him. Others, like Mtawarira and Francois Louw, soaked it all in, in the knowledge that this was the perfect way to bring the curtain down on their glittering international careers. Every Springbok had his own unique story that had led to this moment, but what they had achieved, they had achieved together. Back home, South Africa erupted. Few nations celebrate sporting successes like South Africa. The townships, the city centres, the suburbs and the farms ... all were heard in those minutes following the final whistle. The South Africans at International Stadium Yokohama, journalists included, wept tears of joy. This was about so much more than a World Cup.

Somewhere out there on the Yokohama turf, Duane Vermeulen broke down. He had just delivered a man-of-the-match performance in a World Cup final and was instrumental in the Boks' winning a third World Cup, but as he hugged Proudfoot and sobbed, his mind was elsewhere. Vermeulen was thinking about his father, Andre, who had passed away when he was eight years old.

'The moment that got me was looking at Duane. I knew what it was about for him and what he had gone through to make this moment happen,' Proudfoot says. 'That whole moment tied things together for Duane and he now had a legacy to pass on to his boys. That's what gives Duane purpose in life, and that was what was so special about being on this journey with these players.'

The Boks, while caught up in their own story, were classy enough to console the devastated English players. For Kolisi, this was the beginning of a media storm that would last for months. It started with the post-match television interview. The 28-year-old Kolisi delivered a powerful, eloquent, inspirational message.

'We can achieve anything if we work together as one,' he said in the final words of the interview.

In a later interview with ITV, Kolisi summed up why this moment was so significant from a social point of view and why it was so inspiring. 'This gives hope. I never thought I would be living this experience. When I was a kid all I was thinking about was getting my next meal,' he said.

At the medal presentation, Kolisi begged Erasmus to lift the trophy with him. The coach was not having any of it. This was a moment for his players, and their leader would do the honours. 'I think he was a bit nervous or shy to do it alone,' Erasmus says. 'He wanted me to go with him and I said, "No man, don't be stupid! You guys did all the work ... we'll get our chance later." The players started chanting, "Siya, Siya, Siya!" He was just humble.'

With his players behind him and the world in front of him, Kolisi lifted the Webb Ellis Cup skywards, letting out a roar that was heard by millions back in South Africa. A moment that had once seemed impossible was unfolding, and the whole world was watching. The Boks were the best on the planet. Erasmus was the conductor, but this moment was for the players. Their celebrations expressed relief as much as joy. The Boks had been on an incredible journey together and, dramatically, had achieved their goal.

'I don't know where this has come from,' Matt Dawson said afterwards. 'It's come from the gods. South Africa's defensive line, their line speed, their discipline, their energy, has been simply fantastic. An amazing performance from a Springbok team who everybody wrote off. A lot of their supporters probably didn't believe this was possible.'

The change-room celebrations that followed would reach the world, thanks to social media. Prince Harry, welcomed to the dressing room by De Klerk in his South-African-flag underpants, politely refused a 'down-down' but shared a beer with the Boks and warmly praised the players in an impromptu speech. There were images shot there of memories that will last a lifetime. There were casualties – Mbonambi, De Jager, Pollard and Le Roux had all picked up injuries – but the satisfaction and feeling of triumph were greater than any of those knocks. Le Roux, after a nightmarish few weeks of abuse, had demonstrated his worth and repaid Erasmus's faith with a mature, high-quality showing. Nothing could have been sweeter for him than the feeling in the Bok change room afterwards.

After at least two hours of media responsibilities, the players were free to leave the stadium and head back to the team hotel. There, a fines session – or a Kontiki, as the Boks call it – of epic proportions unfolded. Mtawarira, Louw and Brits were retiring, and they were sent off in style. All the preparation and sacrifice had led to this moment. Back home, a country was partying, and the Boks would do the same. After the fines meeting, family members joined in the celebrations, which went on into the early hours of the morning. Some, like Mbonambi, did not want it to end. He wore his Springbok match jersey throughout.

'We didn't leave the hotel. Our floor was a bit like a university res dormitory,' Louw recalls. 'Every door was open, and you'd just pop in and out for a wine with that guy and then a brandy with the other guy and there was music playing from different rooms. The next morning was the same thing ... it just didn't stop.'

The Springboks, and South Africa, were champions of the world, and their coach would enjoy his slice of the celebrations too. 'We drank a lot. I was already tired from the previous night and the whole day,' Erasmus remembers. 'We had a Kontiki and when I thought it was over, I went to my room. When I got there, there were 20-odd people sitting there waiting for me.

'My family, a few of Jaco Peyper's mates, Marius [Jonker], my cousins ... it was about 1 am and we all sat there watching the highlights of the match on TV. Then I got a WhatsApp saying the Kontiki was continuing, so I put on my shoes and socks and headed back downstairs.

'My wife eventually came and fetched me at around 4.15, saying that the people in my room were still there.'

Chapter 16
Legacy

The dust took weeks to settle after the Springboks' victory in Yokohama. In being crowned world champions for the third time, South Africa joined New Zealand, until then the most decorated side in the tournament's history. Comparisons to the 1995 Springboks were quickly made, given the symbolism of Siya Kolisi's captaincy and what the win meant for the country – the class of 2007 could understandably feel somewhat neglected – but what happened in Japan smashed down barriers in the sport. This will be the legacy of the World Cup-winning Boks of 2019.

'It's about the belief,' Makazole Mapimpi says. 'We stayed strong together as a team. We fought for this country. We saw a lot of things going on in South Africa at that time. Xenophobia, people burning things, strikes, kids getting raped … we did well for the country by giving them hope.'

Few in the World Cup squad typified that legacy better than Mapimpi. He had travelled a seemingly hopeless road. A product of Jim Mvabaza High School in King William's Town, having grown up in the township of Mdantsane, Mapimpi had defied the odds to get to the top. He was playing club rugby with Swallows and Winter Rose as recently as 2014 before a move to Border and, even then, a Springbok future looked a long way away. Yet, in 2019, Mapimpi returned home a World Cup hero. He, too, had shattered the stereotype that black kids from the township could not go on to do great things in Springbok colours. He had done so, first and foremost, because he had the talent and ability and worked his socks off. But he had also achieved the unthinkable because, in Rassie Erasmus, he had a coach who was prepared to provide equal opportunity.

'For me, the thing that people miss is that Mapimpi's story is actually as big, if not bigger than Siya's story,' Erasmus says. 'Myself and Jacques saw Mapimpi and Lukhanyo Am way back in 2011 or 2012 when Border was under administration and SA Rugby had to take over the union. We were flying down to Border every Wednesday and Thursday and we would coach their club players there. We saw Mapimpi and he was this amazing freak of a guy, but he couldn't catch, pass or kick a ball. He was just exceptionally fast.

'How he, at the age of 29, taught himself high-ball skills, contesting at the breakdown, chip kicking ... for me, that is the biggest story. He became a leader.'

Siya Kolisi's story would reach the world in the months before, during and after the World Cup. He too overcame the odds and reached the very pinnacle of sport. Along the way, he gained the affection of the fans and the respect of his team-mates and opponents.

The legacy of 2019 is the changing of a sport that had been dominated by whites for decades. There were brilliant players of colour who came through the system between 1995 and 2019, and many of them enjoyed impressive international careers with the Boks, but there was something fundamentally different about the class of 2019. Mapimpi, Kolisi, Am, Mbonambi, Mtawarira ... these were black Africans who were pivotal to the World Cup success of the champion side. Different backgrounds, different races. Kolisi would repeatedly use these terms in the weeks to come, and while they described the Springboks, they also described South Africa. If the Boks, in all their diversity, could find a way to pull together towards a common goal, then so could South Africa. That was Kolisi's message. Springboks were not supposed to come from places like Zwide and Mdantsane, yet here they were, back home in front of thousands who were looking up to them as examples of exactly how challenges can be overcome.

Mzwandile Stick, once labelled a 'quota coach', was now a World Cup winner who had earned the respect and appreciation of his peers and the entire rugby community. If you speak to those who worked under Stick, they will tell you of a passion for the game that presented itself in an indisputable work ethic and a willingness to spend time with his players in the pursuit of improvement. The work he did with the outside backs on their aerial game was crucial to the Springbok cause, while his Sevens experience had also given him a cultured understanding of spatial awareness that Erasmus employed for the work the Boks were doing off the ball. Once called inexperienced and incompetent, Stick's story of redemption was one of the unsung South African triumphs of Rugby World Cup 2019.

The lessons learnt from these Springboks and their fearless head coach were vast. Erasmus showed what could be achieved through preparation and a clear plan. He showed the value of attention to detail, of transparency in decision-making, of inclusion, of trusting your instincts, of making bold calls and of backing people when they need it most. Eben Etzebeth and Willie le Roux received that backing from Erasmus when they found themselves in challenging situations, but every member of the Bok squad – players and management – had Erasmus's unwavering support throughout. That accountability stemmed from a trust he had in his staff, and the result was a group that was prepared to go the extra mile for him.

'He is the most calculating coach I've ever worked with,' Francois Louw says.

Every squad member, the bit players and the world-class stars, from Damian Willemse to Pieter-Steph du Toit, all helped the Boks to their finest hour. Egos were dumped and they were all involved in the process. It will surely be the blueprint for every Bok side in the future.

Tendai 'Beast' Mtawarira, a soldier of South African rugby who had experienced xenophobia while representing this side all those years ago, emerged as a great of the game. His 11 years, three World Cups and 117 Tests make him a behemoth in world rugby history, but the professionalism he displayed throughout tells its own story of the quality of the individual.

Duane Vermeulen, South Africa's very own 'Thor', put his body on the line and provided a superhuman performance in the World Cup final. He will go down as one of the most impactful players South Africa has ever seen.

Pieter-Steph du Toit was named 2019 World Rugby Player of the Year. Soft-spoken and humble, his tears in Wellington in 2018 and his contribution to the Springboks, even in the dark times under Coetzee, cannot be measured. He remains one of South African rugby's most prized assets. He would go on to turn down lucrative European moves to commit his future to the Stormers and South Africa. Being as prepared as possible for the 2021 British & Irish Lions tour, Du Toit said, was a major factor in his decision.

Frans Malherbe, a man who quietly went about his business in Japan, had his fair share of doubters in the build-up to the tournament. But he let his performances do the talking and emerged as one of the finest tightheads in world rugby.

Le Roux and Faf de Klerk, two pedigreed professionals whom Erasmus trusted implicitly, suffered the slings and arrows but came out with smiles on their faces and World Cup winners' medals around their necks. The abuse had been tough, especially for Le Roux, but he persevered in the face of adversity and was rewarded.

Handre Pollard, rated so highly since his youth, overcame the disappointments of the 2015 World Cup and the career-threatening injuries that followed and produced the polished display that the kick-heavy Springboks desperately needed in Japan. He was class throughout, on and off the field.

Schalk Brits proved that age was merely a number by coming out of retirement and playing a key leadership role for the Boks, while a new megastar was born in Cheslin Kolbe.

All through the squad, from the starters to the Bomb Squad to the reserves who only had game time against the minnows, these Boks had their own journeys to the World Cup, their own obstacles to overcome.

Louw, Mtawarira and Brits retired after the World Cup, but this was the crowning moment of their careers and they left an important legacy. For others, like young scrumhalf Herschel Jantjies and Willemse, it was the most glittering start to what should be long and successful careers.

'What's better than winning a World Cup? Probably winning a World Cup twice,' Jantjies says. 'I'm not the best scrumhalf in the world yet, but my dream is to get there. I'm working towards that. I try not to get ahead of myself, but I hope I get to play as many games as Beast and Bryan Habana did.'

Jantjies, who has achieved so much in such a short space of time, has those aspirations now, but he has already become a player whom young South Africans will want to emulate.

As the Bok bus travelled to all parts on the trophy tour, it was so abundantly clear how far-reaching this achievement was. Everywhere they went, there were young children looking up at these players with stars in their eyes. Kolisi, Vermeulen, Mapimpi, De Klerk ... they were all heroes to the next generation. That is the legacy these Boks leave behind. They will not cure HIV/Aids or bring a screeching halt to poverty. They will not stop corruption, crime or xenophobia. They cannot do any of those things. What they have done, though, is to show South Africa what is possible.

'I went places on the bus tour where I had never been before without an ounce of fear, giving hugs to people that I didn't know,' Brits remembers. 'They didn't see Schalk Brits, a white boy from Mossel Bay. They saw a Springbok rugby player that represented the country. That will always stay with me.'

Kolisi became the poster boy for the Bok success. It was inevitable given the circumstances, but his leadership would face another stern test with this newfound global superstardom. He had become a rock star overnight and was in demand all over the world. He spread himself far and wide, but there were concerns that it would all become too much for him. Entitlement, as Erasmus had always said, was an unavoidable phase of being a Springbok. Travelling to Anfield to meet Jürgen Klopp, signing a deal with American megastar Jay-Z's sports agency, being inundated with potential endorsements … through it all, he kept his feet on the ground. The 'main thing' needed to stay the 'main thing'.

Keen to take the message of hope and unity to as many as possible, Kolisi set up charities in Port Elizabeth and Paarl to impact young lives through rugby. As the Stormers began their pre-season training ahead of the 2020 Super Rugby season, Kolisi returned as the familiar, friendly guy that coach John Dobson remembered before he set out on that magical ride to the World Cup, which changed everything. Success, even worldwide fame, would not change the kid from Zwide who had seen it all on his way to becoming a World Cup-winning captain.

The Springboks, after a couple of months, eventually announced in January 2020 that Jacques Nienaber would replace Erasmus as head coach. It came as no surprise. Erasmus would slip into his role as director of rugby on a full-time basis, looking to grow the South African game in all aspects, and Nienaber was a natural fit to replace him as head coach. The pair had come a long way together, and this was the start of the next chapter. For Erasmus, the legacy of what was achieved in 2019 does not end there.

'We as a team actually asked for the hashtag #StrongerTogether because it means that we are playing and training as hard as we can on the field and the fans support as hard as they can too. Negative or positive, they must never stop supporting us,' he says. 'How do you get 60 million people to buy into it? It's a representative team that is transformed, it is a team that works together, it is a team that believes in the same things and it is a team that everybody can associate with.

'Players are not always role models. They mess up sometimes, just like a mechanic or a surgeon messes up. But the idea that we are this third-world African country that doesn't have the money and intelligence and that we don't work together is just not true. We can be stronger together and I feel that is what gives hope, not the fact that we win a match. The fact that we could do it together, with all of these different things going on, is what I'm most proud of. It's what I want to try and continue so desperately.

'Let us make sure that the Under-20s do it, that the next team that comes in does it. Let us continue, otherwise it will be the same as 1995 and 2007 when it was just happiness for a while. At this stage, I'm very proud that we are stronger together with 60 million people. I think every South African felt that this team represented them.'

A host of players left South Africa to join clubs in Europe and Japan after the World Cup, but the new contracting model that Erasmus unveiled in mid-2019 meant they were not lost to the Springboks. It was another Erasmus decision that many critics believe was a masterstroke in the long-term context of keeping the game in South Africa lucrative.

With the wave of raw emotion finally subsiding, the Springboks returned to the spotlight when they won the coveted Team of the Year Award at the 2020 Laureus World Sports Awards in Berlin. Nienaber, Kolisi, Kolbe, Louw, De Klerk and Brits accepted the award on behalf of the Boks as Kolisi again stood up on a global platform and delivered his message. It had been over three months since the 2019 final, but the world was still listening.

'With this group of players, we have Afrikaans guys, Xhosa guys, guys from the farms, and we've all lived different challenges,' Kolisi said after accepting the award. 'We came together because of the game that we love. We came together with one goal and we fought so hard for each other because our country at the time was going through quite a difficult period.

'We inspired a lot of kids. Now, a kid from the township who can't afford school shoes and who walks to school and who doesn't eat every day can stand here and be a Rugby World Cup-winning captain.'

The Boks had already cleaned up at the 2019 World Rugby Awards, held in Tokyo after the final, where they won Team of the Year, Erasmus won Coach of the Year, and Du Toit won Player of the Year. This was not about those accolades, though. The only goal had been winning the World Cup. Everything that came afterwards was a direct result of that. If you perform and deliver winning rugby, then everything else will follow. You cannot inspire if you are not winning. What was seen in the streets of South Africa in the weeks following the Springboks' return happened because they won the World Cup. Such welcomes are not reserved for sides that finish second. Was this win more significant than 1995? It depends whom you ask. The man who was the central figure 24 years earlier believes it was.

'This is bigger. This is bigger because it is a transformed team, 58 million people watching in South Africa yesterday morning, and all races would have woken up wearing green, which wouldn't have happened in my time,' Francois Pienaar told *The Guardian*.

What happened on the field in Japan was the stuff of dreams, and the astonishing turnaround that Erasmus facilitated equally so, but Kolisi was the essence of what made the Springboks of 2019 different from their predecessors. Would there have been the same intensity of national reaction if the Springbok captain in Japan had been white? Probably not.

'A lot of black people, especially from the lowers LSMs, resonate with Siya's story,' rugby analyst and commentator Kaunda Ntunja explains. 'They understand Siya's story and they know how important it is for him to be successful to inspire kids that come from poverty. Duane has also got his own story, but I don't know that he would be able to pull at the heartstrings of those people in that way.'

Naturally, it took time for Kolisi to understand the significance of his role. Now, looking back, he sees it all clearly. All of the Springboks do. What started out as a journey to become a rugby champion ended as a social obligation to be a champion of South Africa. And, along the way, relationships were formed that will last a lifetime.

'Winning the World Cup moment was massive for me, but what means more is Eben contacting me the other day or Pieter-Steph asking me for something or being in contact with Beast in America or wishing Frans Malherbe a happy birthday,' Matt Proudfoot says. 'That's what means the most. I was so fortunate to share that with these guys and it will stay with me for the rest of my life.'

The 1995 World Cup-winning Springboks, to this day, have a WhatsApp group that keeps them in touch. They have lost a few soldiers along the way, but the bonds that were formed around achieving one of the most celebrated and important moments in South Africa's sporting history are strong. It is early days yet, but what is certain is that the 33 Springboks of the 2019 World Cup squad will never forget their journey or each other. Together, they went away to fight for a common cause and came back champions. From losing to the All Blacks in their tournament opener, the Boks bounced back to win their next six matches in Japan and they grew stronger along the way. By the time they were done, this side was as slick as any ever seen, in complete control of everything they were doing on the field. Some actions were second nature. They knew their game so well. They knew each other so well. They knew the country they were representing so well. It was down to preparedness, a collective buy-in and a decision to do whatever it takes in the pursuit of victory. These players did it together.

Francois Louw probably sums it up best.

'We share emotions with each other that nobody else can and will ever share. It might be someone who I may not speak to for ten years because of geography and where we are in the world, but when you see that man again, you'll look him in the eye and remember what you achieved.'

Appendix

South Africa 2019 Rugby World Cup squad*

Forwards (17)

Schalk Brits (Bulls), Lood de Jager (Bulls), Pieter-Steph du Toit (Stormers), Eben Etzebeth (Stormers), Steven Kitshoff (Stormers), Vincent Koch (Saracens, England), Siya Kolisi (captain, Stormers), Francois Louw (Bath, England), Frans Malherbe (Stormers), Malcolm Marx (Lions), Bongi Mbonambi (Stormers), Tendai Mtawarira (Sharks), Franco Mostert (Gloucester, England), Trevor Nyakane (Bulls), Kwagga Smith (Lions), RG Snyman (Bulls), Duane Vermeulen (Bulls)

Backs (14)

Lukhanyo Am (Sharks), Damian de Allende (Stormers), Faf de Klerk (Sale Sharks, England), Warrick Gelant (Bulls), Elton Jantjies (Lions), Herschel Jantjies (Stormers), Cheslin Kolbe (Toulouse, France), Jesse Kriel (Bulls), Makazole Mapimpi (Sharks), Sbu Nkosi (Sharks), Willie le Roux (Toyota Verblitz), Handre Pollard (Bulls), Cobus Reinach (Northampton Saints, England), Frans Steyn (Montpellier, France)

* Thomas du Toit (Sharks) and Damian Willemse (Stormers) were not in the original 31-man squad, but they replaced the injured Jesse Kriel and Trevor Nyakane, respectively, during the tournament.

South Africa 2019 Rugby World Cup match summaries

21 September (Pool B) South Africa v New Zealand (Yokohama)

South Africa 13 (3)
Try: Pieter-Steph du Toit
Conversion: Handre Pollard
Penalty: Pollard
Drop goal: Pollard

New Zealand 23 (17)
Tries: George Bridge, Scott Barrett
Conversions: Richie Mo'unga (2)
Penalties: Mo'unga (2), Beauden Barrett

Teams

South Africa

15 Willie le Roux, 14 Cheslin Kolbe, 13 Lukhanyo Am, 12 Damian de Allende, 11 Makazole Mapimpi, 10 Handre Pollard, 9 Faf de Klerk, 8 Duane Vermeulen, 7 Pieter-Steph du Toit, 6 Siya Kolisi (captain), 5 Franco Mostert, 4 Eben Etzebeth, 3 Frans Malherbe, 2 Malcolm Marx, 1 Steven Kitshoff

Substitutes: 16 Bongi Mbonambi, 17 Tendai Mtawarira, 18 Trevor Nyakane, 19 RG Snyman, 20 Francois Louw, 21 Herschel Jantjies, 22 Frans Steyn, 23 Jesse Kriel

New Zealand

15 Beauden Barrett, 14 Sevu Reece, 13 Anton Lienert-Brown, 12 Ryan Crotty, 11 George Bridge, 10 Richie Mo'unga, 9 Aaron Smith, 8 Kieran Read (captain), 7 Sam Cane, 6 Ardie Savea, 5 Scott Barrett, 4 Sam Whitelock, 3 Nepo Laulala, 2 Dane Coles, 1 Joe Moody

Substitutes: 16 Codie Taylor, 17 Ofa Tuungafasi, 18 Angus Ta'avao,

19 Patrick Tuipulotu, 20 Shannon Frizell, 21 TJ Perenara, 22 Sonny Bill Williams, 23 Ben Smith

28 September (Pool B) South Africa v Namibia (Toyota)

South Africa 57 (31)

Tries: Bongi Mbonambi (2), Francois Louw, Makazole Mapimpi (2), Lukhanyo Am, Warrick Gelant, Siya Kolisi, Schalk Brits
Conversions: Elton Jantjies (6)

Namibia 3 (3)

Penalty: Cliven Loubser

Teams

South Africa

15 Warrick Gelant, 14 Sbu Nkosi, 13 Lukhanyo Am, 12 Frans Steyn, 11 Makazole Mapimpi, 10 Elton Jantjies, 9 Herschel Jantjies, 8 Schalk Brits (captain), 7 Kwagga Smith, 6 Francois Louw, 5 Lood de Jager, 4 RG Snyman, 3 Vincent Koch, 2 Bongi Mbonambi, 1 Tendai Mtawarira
Substitutes: 16 Steven Kitshoff, 17 Thomas du Toit, 18 Eben Etzebeth, 19 Siya Kolisi, 20 Franco Mostert, 21 Cobus Reinach, 22 Damian de Allende, 23 Cheslin Kolbe

Namibia

15 Johan Tromp, 14 Chad Plato, 13 JC Greyling, 12 Peter John Walters, 11 Lesley Klim, 10 Cliven Loubser, 9 Eugene Jantjies, 8 Adriaan Booysen, 7 Muharua Katjijeko, 6 Thomasau Forbes, 5 Tjiuee Uanivi (captain), 4 Johan Retief, 3 AJ de Klerk, 2 Louis van der Westhuizen, 1 Desiderius Sethie
Substitutes: 16 Obert Nortje, 17 Andre Rademeyer, 18 Johannes Coetzee, 19 Prince Gaoseb, 20 Janco Venter, 21 Wian Conradie, 22 Helarius Axasman Kisting, 23 Johan Deysel

4 October (Pool B) South Africa v Italy (Shizuoka)

South Africa 49 (17)
Tries: Cheslin Kolbe (2), Makazole Mapimpi, Bongi Mbonambi, Lukhanyo Am, RG Snyman, Malcolm Marx
Conversions: Handre Pollard (4)
Penalties: Pollard (2)

Italy 3 (3)
Penalty: Tommaso Allan

Teams

South Africa

15 Willie le Roux, 14 Cheslin Kolbe, 13 Lukhanyo Am, 12 Damian de Allende, 11 Makazole Mapimpi, 10 Handre Pollard, 9 Faf de Klerk, 8 Duane Vermeulen, 7 Pieter-Steph du Toit, 6 Siya Kolisi (captain), 5 Lood de Jager, 4 Eben Etzebeth, 3 Frans Malherbe, 2 Bongi Mbonambi, 1 Tendai Mtawarira

Substitutes: 16 Malcolm Marx, 17 Steven Kitshoff, 18 Vincent Koch, 19 RG Snyman, 20 Franco Mostert, 21 Francois Louw, 22 Herschel Jantjies, 23 Frans Steyn

Italy

15 Matteo Minozzi, 14 Tommaso Benvenuti, 13 Luca Morisi, 12 Jayden Hayward, 11 Michele Campagnaro, 10 Tommaso Allan, 9 Tito Tebaldi, 8 Sergio Parisse (captain), 7 Jake Polledri, 6 Braam Steyn, 5 Dean Budd, 4 David Sisi, 3 Simone Ferrari, 2 Luca Bigi, 1 Andrea Lovotti

Substitutes: 16 Federico Zani, 17 Nicola Quaglio, 18 Marco Riccioni, 19 Alessandro Zanni, 20 Federico Ruzza, 21 Sebastian Negri, 22 Callum Braley, 23 Carlo Canna

APPENDIX

8 October (Pool B) South Africa v Canada (Kobe)

South Africa 66 (47)

Tries: Damian de Allende, Sbu Nkosi, Cobus Reinach (3), Warrick Gelant, Frans Steyn, Schalk Brits, Damian Willemse, Frans Malherbe
Conversions: Elton Jantjies (8)

Canada 7 (0)

Try: Matt Heaton
Conversion: Peter Nelson

Teams

South Africa

15 Damian Willemse, 14 Warrick Gelant, 13 Damian de Allende, 12 Frans Steyn, 11 Sbu Nkosi, 10 Elton Jantjies, 9 Cobus Reinach, 8 Francois Louw, 7 Kwagga Smith, 6 Siya Kolisi, 5 Franco Mostert, 4 RG Snyman, 3 Vincent Koch, 2 Schalk Brits, 1 Thomas du Toit

Substitutes: 16 Malcolm Marx, 17 Steven Kitshoff, 18 Frans Malherbe, 19 Eben Etzebeth, 20 Pieter-Steph du Toit, 21 Herschel Jantjies, 22 Handre Pollard, 23 Willie le Roux

Canada

15 Andrew Coe, 14 Jeff Hassler, 13 Conor Trainor, 12 Ciaran Hearn, 11 DTH van der Merwe, 10 Peter Nelson, 9 Phil Mack, 8 Tyler Ardron (captain), 7 Matt Heaton, 6 Lucas Rumball, 5 Kyle Baillie, 4 Evan Olmstead, 3 Jake Ilnicki, 2 Andrew Quattrin, 1 Hubert Buydens

Substitutes: 16 Benoit Piffero, 17 Djustice Sears-Duru, 18 Matt Tierney, 19 Josh Larsen, 20 Michael Sheppard, 21 Jamie Mackenzie, 22 Shane O'Leary, 23 Guiseppe du Toit

20 October (quarter-final) South Africa v Japan (Tokyo)

South Africa 26 (5)
Tries: Makazole Mapimpi (2), Faf de Klerk
Conversion: Handre Pollard
Penalties: Pollard (3)

Japan 3 (3)
Penalty: Yu Tamura

Teams

South Africa

15 Willie le Roux, 14 Cheslin Kolbe, 13 Lukhanyo Am, 12 Damian de Allende, 11 Makazole Mapimpi, 10 Handre Pollard, 9 Faf de Klerk, 8 Duane Vermeulen, 7 Pieter-Steph du Toit, 6 Siya Kolisi (captain), 5 Lood de Jager, 4 Eben Etzebeth, 3 Frans Malherbe, 2 Bongi Mbonambi, 1 Tendai Mtawarira

Substitutes: 16 Malcolm Marx, 17 Steven Kitshoff, 18 Vincent Koch, 19 RG Snyman, 20 Franco Mostert, 21 Francois Louw, 22 Herschel Jantjies, 23 Frans Steyn

Japan

15 Ryohei Yamanaka, 14 Kotaro Matsushima, 13 Timothy Lafaele, 12 Ryoto Nakamura, 11 Kenki Fukuoka, 10 Yu Tamura, 9 Yutaka Nagare, 8 Kazuki Himeno, 7 Lappies Labuschagne, 6 Michael Leitch (captain), 5 James Moore, 4 Luke Thompson, 3 Koo Ji-won, 2 Shota Horie, 1 Keita Inagaki

Substitutes: 16 Atsushi Sakate, 17 Isileli Nakajima, 18 Asaeli Ai Valu, 19 Wimpie van der Walt, 20 Amanaki Lelei Mafi, 21 Fumiaki Tanaka, 22 Rikiya Matsuda, 23 Lomano Lava Lemeki

27 October (semi-final) South Africa v Wales (Yokohama)

South Africa 19 (9)
Try: Damian de Allende
Conversion: Handre Pollard
Penalties: Pollard (4)
Wales 16 (6)
Try: Josh Adams
Conversion: Leigh Halfpenny
Penalties: Dan Biggar (3)

Teams

South Africa

15 Willie le Roux, 14 Sbu Nkosi, 13 Lukhanyo Am, 12 Damian de Allende, 11 Makazole Mapimpi, 10 Handre Pollard, 9 Faf de Klerk, 8 Duane Vermeulen, 7 Pieter-Steph du Toit, 6 Siya Kolisi (captain), 5 Lood de Jager, 4 Eben Etzebeth, 3 Frans Malherbe, 2 Bongi Mbonambi, 1 Tendai Mtawarira

Substitutes: 16 Malcolm Marx, 17 Steven Kitshoff, 18 Vincent Koch, 19 RG Snyman, 20 Franco Mostert, 21 Francois Louw, 22 Herschel Jantjies, 23 Frans Steyn

Wales

15 Leigh Halfpenny, 14 George North, 13 Jonathan Davies, 12 Hadleigh Parkes, 11 Josh Adams, 10 Dan Biggar, 9 Gareth Davies, 8 Ross Moriarty, 7 Justin Tipuric, 6 Aaron Wainwright, 5 Alun Wyn Jones, 4 Jake Ball, 3 Tomas Francis, 2 Ken Owens, 1 Wyn Jones

Substitutes: 16 Elliot Dee, 17 Rhys Carre, 18 Dillon Lewis, 19 Adam Beard, 20 Aaron Shingler, 21 Tomos Williams, 22 Rhys Patchell, 23 Owen Watkin

2 November (final) South Africa v England (Yokohama)

South Africa 32 (12)
Tries: Makazole Mapimpi, Cheslin Kolbe
Conversions: Handre Pollard (2)
Penalties: Pollard (6)

England 12 (6)
Penalties: Owen Farrell (4)

Teams

South Africa

15 Willie le Roux, 14 Cheslin Kolbe, 13 Lukhanyo Am, 12 Damian de Allende, 11 Makazole Mapimpi, 10 Handre Pollard, 9 Faf de Klerk, 8 Duane Vermeulen, 7 Pieter-Steph du Toit, 6 Siya Kolisi (captain), 5 Lood de Jager, 4 Eben Etzebeth, 3 Frans Malherbe, 2 Bongi Mbonambi, 1 Tendai Mtawarira

Substitutes: 16 Malcolm Marx, 17 Steven Kitshoff, 18 Vincent Koch, 19 RG Snyman, 20 Franco Mostert, 21 Francois Louw, 22 Herschel Jantjies, 23 Frans Steyn

England

15 Elliot Daly, 14 Anthony Watson, 13 Manu Tuilagi, 12 Owen Farrell (captain), 11 Jonny May, 10 George Ford, 9 Ben Youngs, 8 Billy Vunipola, 7 Sam Underhill, 6 Tom Curry, 5 Courtney Lawes, 4 Maro Itoje, 3 Kyle Sinckler, 2 Jamie George, 1 Mako Vunipola

Substitutes: 16 Luke Cowan-Dickie, 17 Joe Marler, 18 Dan Cole, 19 George Kruis, 20 Mark Wilson, 21 Ben Spencer, 22 Henry Slade, 23 Jonathan Joseph

Acknowledgements

To everybody who has taken the time to help me tell this special story, thank you. To the amazing team at Jonathan Ball, the patience and understanding you have given me throughout this project is appreciated. To Adriaan Basson, thank you for believing in me enough to push me into unfamiliar, uncomfortable territory. To John Bishop and Lungani Zama, my former *Witness* colleagues and dear friends, thank you both for your honesty. There have been so many people in my life whom I have leant on over the last six months, in some way, and I will always be grateful to you. Lastly, to my mother, Lynda, and the rest of the Burnard family in Pietermaritzburg, thank you for your boundless, unconditional love and support.

About the author

Lloyd Burnard has worked as a journalist for more than a decade. He is a former sports editor of *The Witness* newspaper in KwaZulu-Natal and currently an award-winning senior journalist at *Sport24*. He has been covering the Springboks extensively since 2015, culminating in their 2019 Rugby World Cup triumph, and has reported on numerous other major sporting events including the 2010 FIFA World Cup, the 2016 Olympic Games in Rio de Janeiro and the 2019 Cricket World Cup in England. This is his first book.